THE GRAVEYARD SHIFT

A Family Historian's Guide To

New York City CEMETERIES

THE GRAVEYARD SHIFT

A Family Historian's Guide To

New York City CEMETERIES

Carolee Inskeep

Library of Congress Cataloging-in-Publication Data

Inskeep, Carolee R.
    The graveyard shift : a family historian's guide to New York City cemeteries /
Carolee Inskeep.
        p.cm.
    Includes bibliographical references and index.
    ISBN 0-916489-89-2
        1. Cemeteries—New York (State)—New York—Directories. 2. Cemeteries—
New York (State)—New York—History. 3. New York (N.Y.)—History, Local. 4. New
York (N.Y.)—Genealogy—Directories. I. Title.

F128.61.A1 I57 1999
974.7'1—dc21

                                                                    99-055059

Dedication

———— ✿ ————

This volume is dedicated to the following

children

whose search for family inspired this book.

Stephen Franz

Giovanni Gauna

Josephine Hefferman

Sophia Kaminsky

Contents

Acknowledgments

———— ❦ ————

I am grateful to everyone who assisted in the preparation of this book. In particular, I would like to thank the innumerable cemetery, church, government, and library employees who patiently answered my countless questions. This book would have been an impossible task without their assistance.

There are certain individuals who went out of their way to be helpful, or whose hospitality, generosity, and support deserve special thanks. Among them are Marianne Anderson, special projects coordinator of Van Cortlandt and Pelham Bay Parks; Anne W. Brown, trustee of the New York Marble Cemetery; Stanley "The Head Stone" Cogan, president of the Queens Historical Society; Fred Crane, vice president of Friends of Abandoned Cemeteries of Staten Island; Steve Inskeep, for championing this project; Adele A. Lerner, archivist at New York Hospital-Cornell Medical Center; Cate Ludlam, president of the Prospect Cemetery Association; Elayne "Copy Chick" Schneiderman, for her creative genius; Stephanie Schoeller, for keeping her door open; and Loretto Szucs, my editor at Ancestry, for her patience and confidence in this book.

Many thanks to Philip Brown, Mary F. Clauss, Constance P. Harmon, Stephen B. Nathan, Patty Smith, and Debra Osborne Spindle who generously shared their research.

I also wish to thank the librarians in the Geography and Map Reading Room of the Library of Congress, who were unruffled when I asked to look at *all* of their pre-1860 New York City maps.

Finally, my greatest debt of gratitude goes to Harry Macy, Jr. of the New York Genealogical and Biographical Society, who graciously critiqued this manuscript and shared his expertise.

—Carolee Inskeep

Introduction

———— ❦ ————

Trying to find some peace in the "City that Never Sleeps" has always been difficult for New Yorkers, including dead New Yorkers. Rapid development, rising property values, a lack of space, health concerns, and government regulation have all conspired to move the dead from one graveyard to the next, much like homeless men who are told to move along by the local police officer making his rounds at night.

When New York City was first laid out on Manhattan Island in the seventeenth century, it was little more than a small town, with single family homes, small shops, and outlying farms. New Yorkers were buried a short distance away from their homes. As the years went by, as the city population increased, and as cemeteries became more crowded, objections to burials in a crowded urban area began to grow.

Complaints about "pestilential vapors" emerged during the Revolutionary War. Soldiers who died during the winter were buried in shallow graves in the frozen ground of Trinity Churchyard. The ensuing odor ripened as the ground began to thaw. Complaints about the stench persisted for the next fifty years. One report, written in 1822, claimed that nearly 125,000 people were buried in Trinity Churchyard, making it so crowded that some bodies were interred just eighteen inches below ground. Fifty-two casks of lime were spread over Trinity Churchyard that fall, just to combat the odor.

That same report ultimately blamed the yellow fever epidemic of 1822 on the impure air emanating from graveyards, particularly those of the Presbyterian and Reformed Dutch churches.

In response to the report, New York City began to regulate burials. An ordinance passed in 1823 forbade all burials in a grave or vault south of Canal, Sullivan, and Grand Streets in Manhattan. The City's concern culminated in 1851, when it forbade interments south of 86th Street and prohibited the creation of new cemeteries. These ordinances, coupled with the rising value of

real estate in lower Manhattan, encouraged most churches to sell their cemetery property to developers.

The dead left Manhattan in a mass exodus.

Thousands of bodies were transferred to the new, park-like cemeteries, such
as Calvary, Cedar Grove, Evergreens, Green-Wood and Woodlawn, which were
formed in adjacent communities. Thousands more were removed to Bayside,
Lutheran, Moravian, Prospect Park, and Saint Michael's cemeteries. Cypress
Hills Cemetery received more than 35,000 bodies from Manhattan graveyards
after it opened in 1849. In fact, Manhattan graves were reinterred in cemeteries throughout the metropolitan area. So many were removed that of the
one hundred or so burial grounds originally located in Manhattan, less than
one dozen remain.

In some cases, graveyards were redeveloped without removing the bodies.
The African Burial Ground and the Reformed Dutch Churchyard, in lower
Manhattan, were simply graded and sold for real estate development. The
graveyards of Seneca Village are beneath Central Park, while the bodies and
gravestones of the 10,000 people buried in Saint John's Cemetery are now at
rest beneath James J. Walker Park. Madison Square Park and Washington
Square Park were created on the grounds of city-owned cemeteries. Saint
Mark's-in-the-Bowery paved over its churchyard for use as a playground.

Cemeteries were redeveloped in the outer boroughs, too. The Colored
Cemetery of Flushing, Queens, became Everett P. Martins Field, a playground.
Morrisania Cemetery, in the Bronx, became Saint Mary's Park. Shell Oil built
a gas station above the African Methodist Episcopal Church Cemetery of
Staten Island, and the Methodist Cemetery in Brooklyn was simply sold off as
building lots.

Abandoned family burial grounds and churchyards suffered similar fates.
Most were just neglected and forgotten over time. A few were removed to
larger cemeteries, converted to playgrounds, or victimized by real estate developers. In some cases, the old graveyards became garbage dumps and hang-
outs. In other cases, neighborhood children broke into burial vaults and dug
up the graves. Area residents stole headstones for use as flagstones, benches,
and steps. Local farmers allowed their livestock to roam freely in unfenced
cemeteries. Time eroded the remaining stones.

Fortunately for the genealogist, several historians copied gravestone inscriptions between 1880 and 1935. Their work is particularly important because,
in many cases, their manuscripts are the only evidence that a graveyard existed at all. William T. Davis, Charles W. Leng, and Royden W. Vosburgh copied
the gravestone inscriptions in Staten Island's churchyards and family burial
grounds. Charles Powell and Alice Meigs recorded the gravestone inscriptions
in the private and abandoned cemeteries of Queens. William Eardeley and
Josephine Frost copied thousands of gravestone inscriptions in Brooklyn and
Queens. The Daughters of the American Revolution recorded gravestone
inscriptions in the Bronx.

If you are researching ancestors who died after 1851, you will probably find them buried in one of the large cemeteries in Brooklyn or in Queens. In most cases, these cemeteries will not answer your request for information unless you provide a specific name and date of death. Their records are usually arranged by date of death, and since most of these cemeteries have thousands, even millions, of graves, a request for the burial record of everyone with a particular surname is impossible to answer. With a little creativity, you can still find the information you seek.

Jan Arman, who is researching her New York City roots from Minnesota, wanted to learn more about her aunt, Ida Arnold. Jan wrote to Saint Raymond's Cemetery and asked for Ida's burial record, as well as the name of the person who purchased the plot and the names of everyone buried in that plot. From them, Jan learned that Ida is buried next to her husband, Joseph Arnold, in a plot paid for by their son. Saint Raymond's Cemetery voluntarily included the gravestone inscriptions.

Walter Davis, of Florida, had similar results when he asked Cypress Hills Cemetery for the burial record of Charlotte Lequesne, the name of the person who purchased her plot, and the names of everyone buried with her. Walter received the name, age, date of death, cause of death, and place of death for fourteen of Charlotte's descendants.

Alexis Kinney Carrington, coordinator of the New York City GenWeb Page, on the Internet, advises researchers to ask if their ancestors' plot is in perpetual care and who pays for it. Carrington also notes that many cemetery clerks do not realize that African Americans were sometimes buried in segregated sections of the cemetery and that a second set of records might exist for such burials.

Whenever possible, visit the grave of the person you are researching. You may be delighted with the results and rewarded with information that you cannot obtain in any other way. Life-like portraits are engraved on the polished black granite gravestones of Asian Jews in Mount Carmel Cemetery, giving one the eerie sensation of standing among living persons. Marijuana leaves and dice are engraved on one tombstone at Cypress Hills Cemetery. Offerings of food and incense are found at Chinese and Greek graves in Cypress Hills Cemetery, while the elaborate monuments at Green-Wood Cemetery testify to the great wealth of the Victorian-era families buried there. The bland information obtained from death certificates and burial records may never match the rich information found on a gravestone. One has to wonder what was listed under the official cause of death in the case of poor George Spenser, who died at the age of fifteen in 1909. His epitaph tells the "real" story: *Lost life by stab in falling on ink eraser, evading six young women trying to give him birthday kisses in office of Metropolitan Life Building.*

On the other hand, gravestone inscriptions are engraved by humans, and humans make mistakes. A piece of information is not necessarily correct, or even true, just because it is written in stone. Recently, a researcher at the Daughters of the American Revolution Library in Washington, D.C. was presented with two conflicting dates of death for her ancestor. One date was writ-ten in a Bible, the other in a transcription of gravestone inscriptions. After some deliberation with a friend, she decided that the date on the gravestone must be the correct one because people don't make mistakes on stone! It never occurred to this woman that the engraver may have been given the wrong date, that the engraver accidentally engraved the wrong date, or that the transcriber copied it incorrectly.

Please keep an open mind about where your ancestors are buried. New Yorkers turn up in the least expected places. Some wealthy New Yorkers are buried in the "potter's field" because they died of contagious disease. African American slaves were sometimes buried alongside their owners. Jews are buried in Linden Hill Methodist Episcopal Cemetery, and Methodists are buried in Lutheran Cemetery. Many New Yorkers are buried great distances from the city limits in cemeteries in Connecticut, New Jersey, New York State, and on Long Island. Others were buried within the city limits, only to be rein-terred near their children years later—in southern and western states.

For a thorough treatment of the usefulness and pitfalls of cemetery records, consult *The Source: A Guidebook of American Genealogy*, edited by Loretto Dennis Szucs and Sandra Hargeaves Luebking (Ancestry, revised 1997), and the *Researcher's Guide to American Genealogy*, by Val D. Greenwood (GPC, 1990).

CEMETERY ENTRIES

Acacia Cemetery

CATEGORY: Jewish
YEARS OF USE: 1891 to date
LOCATION: 83-84 Liberty Avenue, between Bayside Cemetery and 84th Street, Ozone Park, Queens.
HISTORY: The Pike Street Synagogue of Manhattan established Acacia Cemetery in 1891. The congregation has expired, but the cemetery survives and is managed by the United Hebrew Congregation.
MAILING ADDRESS: Acacia Cemetery
83-84 Liberty Avenue
Ozone Park, New York 11417-1297
PHONE NUMBER: (718) 845-9240
RECORDS: The Mokom Sholom Cemetery Recording Project is working to record the name of everyone buried in Acacia Cemetery through the use of cemetery records, death certificates, obituaries, wills, family histories, and gravestones.
RESOURCES: The Mokom Sholom Cemetery Recording Project's list of names is distributed as MOKOMCEM.EXE and is available on the Internet at
<ftp://ftp.cac.psu.edu/pub/genealogy/text/jewish/mokomcem.exe>.

African Burial Ground

CATEGORY: African, Public
YEARS OF USE: circa 1690 to 1794
LOCATION: The cemetery includes the area enclosed by Duane Street, Chambers Street, Centre Street, and Broadway, Manhattan.
HISTORY: No one knows when the African Burial Ground was set aside for

use as a cemetery. Some date its creation to 1697 when Trinity Church prohibited the burial of Africans in its Churchyard, which also served as the public cemetery. Some historians suggest that the grounds were in use as early as
1690. It does not appear on a map until 1754.

The African Burial Ground did not have an organized cemetery association, nor did it maintain sexton records. However, in May 1768 a man by
the name of J. Teller settled into a recently built house near the cemetery. He
claimed the burial ground as his land, maintained a fence around it, and took
payment for its use. The Teller family controlled the African Burial Ground
until the British Army occupied its home during the Revolutionary War.

The British used the cemetery to bury their dead prisoners-of-war. By the
time they left New York in 1781, the fence around the burial ground, as well
as the Tellers' house, had been destroyed.

Of all the indignities the cemetery suffered, the loss of its fence was cer-
tainly the least. For many years, the burial ground was surrounded by compa-
nies like the Remmey and Crolius Pottery Works who dumped their kiln
refuse into the yard. In 1788, the African community filed a petition with the
New York City Common Council, protesting the desecration of their dead by
local medical students who were digging up bodies for use in classroom dissec-
tions. The extension of Chambers Street cut through the cemetery in 1792.
Ultimately, in 1795, the grounds were laid out in lots and developed.

During its one-hundred-year history, an estimated ten- to twenty-thousand
people were buried in the cemetery. Paupers, soldiers, and victims of epidemic
disease were buried there, but the dead were primarily enslaved Africans.

In the fall of 1991, the United States government hired a team of archae-
ologists to analyze the site before it began construction of a thirty-four-story
federal office building. The team uncovered hundreds of artifacts including
shroud pins, beads, coins, jewelry, and British Navy buttons. They also
exhumed four hundred bodies. The remains were sent to Howard University
in Washington, D.C. for further study. Anthropologists who examined the
remains estimated that ninety-two percent were of African origin, three to
five percent were of European descent, and the remaining of Native
American ancestry. Half of the bodies were children under the age of twelve.
When analysis is complete, the remains will be returned to New York for
reinterment beneath a memorial pavilion that has been erected over the original site. The cemetery has been designated a national historic landmark. It is
called "The African Burial Ground and Historic Commons District."

This cemetery is historically referred to as "The Negroes' Burial
Ground."

MAILING ADDRESS: Office of Public Education and Interpretation
                 African Burial Ground and the Commons Historic District
                 290 Broadway
                 New York, New York 10007-1823
PHONE NUMBER: (212) 432-5707

RECORDS: N/A

RESOURCES: Garnett, Carla. "The Dead do Tell Tales: Colonial-Era Burial Project Provides Current Research Cohort." *The National Institute of Health Record* 49, no. 8 (April 22, 1997): 1. (describes the lifestyles and funerals of the deceased)

Hansen, Joyce, and Gary McGowan. *Breaking Ground, Breaking Silence: The Story of New York's African Burial Ground.* New York: Henry Holt and Company, 1998. (detailed history, maps, and photos)

Kutz, David, dir., and Christopher Moore, assoc. dir. *The African Burial Ground: An American Discovery.* United States General Services Administration. Four, 30-min. segments, 1994. Videocassette.

African Methodist Episcopal Zion Church Cemetery, Seneca Village

CATEGORY: African, Methodist Episcopal

YEARS OF USE: 1827 to 1851

LOCATION: 85th Street between 7th and 8th Avenues, Manhattan.

HISTORY: When New York City closed the potter's field at Washington Square in 1827, it eliminated the burial ground used by the African Methodist Episcopal Zion Church. The congregation then turned a portion of its property at 85th Street and Eighth Avenue into a cemetery. Two decades later, the city declared eminent domain over that burial ground, using it as Central Park.

In 1871, laborers digging up trees at 85th Street and Eighth Avenue uncovered a coffin. In the 1920s, a park gardener discovered an entire graveyard. The cemetery was nicknamed "Gilhooley's Burial Plot" after the man who discovered it. Gilhooley's Burial Plot may have been the African Methodist Episcopal Zion Church Cemetery or its neighbor, All Angels' Church Cemetery.

MAILING ADDRESS: AME Zion Church
475 Riverside Drive, Suite 1935
New York, New York 10115-0025

PHONE NUMBER: (212) 870-2952

RECORDS: Records of early burials were lost in an 1839 fire. Some burials may be found with those of All Angels' Church, available at the New York Historical Society and at All Angels' Church (see entry for All Angels' Church Cemetery).

RESOURCES: Rozenzweig, Roy and Elizabeth Blackmar. *The Park and the People: A History of Central Park.* New York: Henry Holt and Company, 1992, 65–73. (description of neighborhood; limited genealogies)

Schwartzman, Paul. "Central Park's Vanished Black Settlement." *The New York Times.* January 19, 1997, page 18. (history of cemetery, names some burials)

African Methodist Episcopal
Zion Church Cemetery, Staten Island

See Cherry Lane Second Asbury African Methodist Episcopal Cemetery.

African Methodist Episcopal
Zion Church Cemetery, Washington Square

CATEGORY: African, Methodist Episcopal
YEARS OF USE: 1807 to 1827
LOCATION: Washington Square, Manhattan.
HISTORY: Complaints about the "offensive odor" emanating from the burial
vault beneath the African Methodist Episcopal Zion Church caused the New
York City Council to prohibit further burials at the property in August 1807.
Later that month, the City Council granted the congregation a fifty-foot-
square burial plot in the city cemetery at Washington Square. The congrega-
tion used that plot until Washington Square Cemetery was closed in 1827.
MAILING ADDRESS: AME Zion Church
                475 Riverside Drive, Suite 1935
                New York, New York 10115-0025
PHONE NUMBER: (212) 870-2952
RECORDS: Records of early burials were lost in an 1839 fire.
RESOURCES: N/A

African Methodist Episcopal
Zion Churchyard and Vault

CATEGORY: African, Methodist Episcopal
YEARS OF USE: 1773 to 1807
LOCATION: 158 Church Street, between Duane and Worth Streets, Manhattan.
HISTORY: In August 1807, the New York City Council heard testimony that
the African Methodist Episcopal Zion Church had buried approximately 750
people in a vault beneath its church edifice during the previous five years.
This resulted in an "offensive odor." The Council passed an ordinance pro-
hibiting further burials in the vault. The congregation then used a plot at
Washington Square.
    Although the churchyard predates the inception of the African Methodist
Episcopal Zion Church, it became the burial ground of that congregation
when it broke away from the John Street Church.
MAILING ADDRESS: AME Zion Church
                475 Riverside Drive, Suite 1935
                New York, New York 10115-0025
PHONE NUMBER: (212) 870-2952
RECORDS: Records of early burials were lost in an 1839 fire.
RESOURCES: N/A

Ahavath (Ahawath) Chesed-Shaar Hashomayim Cemetery
See Linden Hill Cemetery of Central Synagogue.

All Angels' Church Cemetery

CATEGORY: African, Protestant Episcopal
YEARS OF USE: circa 1848 to 1852
LOCATION: 85th Street between 7th and 8th Avenues, Manhattan.
HISTORY: All Angels' Church opened for worship in 1848 at 85th Street and 8th Avenue. Its racially mixed congregation was two-thirds black and one-third white. Black parishioners lived in the surrounding area known as Seneca Village, while whites came from the Irish and German settlements within one mile of the church. Burials in the churchyard probably came to an end in 1851, when New York City passed laws prohibiting burials below 86th Street. In 1857, the city declared eminent domain over the church's property and took it for use as Central Park. The congregation moved to a new building at 80th Street and 11th Avenue.

There is no indication that the remains in the cemetery were removed. In 1871, laborers digging up trees in Central Park, near 85th Street and 8th Avenue, uncovered the coffin of Margaret McIntay, a sixteen-year-old member of All Angels' church who died in 1852. During the 1920s, a park gardener named Gilhooley discovered an entire graveyard. The cemetery was subsequently dubbed "Gilhooley's Burial Plot." Gilhooley's Burial Plot may have been All Angels' Church Cemetery or that of its neighbor, the African Methodist Episcopal Zion Church.
MAILING ADDRESS: All Angels' Church
                 251 West 80th Street
                 New York, New York 10024-5798
PHONE NUMBER: (212) 362-9300
RECORDS: The New York Historical Society compiled a list of known burials based on All Angels' *Parish Record Book, 1847 to 1874*. The Historical Society gave a copy of the list to All Angels' Church.
RESOURCES: Rozenzweig, Roy and Elizabeth Blackmar. *The Park and the People: A History of Central Park*. New York: Henry Holt and Company, 1992, 65–73. (description of neighborhood; limited genealogies)

Schwartzman, Paul. "Central Park's Vanished Black Settlement." *The New York Times*. January 19, 1997, page 18. (history of cemetery, names some burials)

Allen Street Methodist Episcopal Churchyard

CATEGORY: Methodist Episcopal
YEARS OF USE: circa 1810 to 1851
LOCATION: 128 Allen Street, east side of the street between Delancey Street and Rivington Street, Manhattan.

HISTORY: After a ban on burials below 86th Street in Manhattan, the trustees of the Allen Street Methodist Episcopal Church removed the dead in their churchyard to a plot in Cypress Hills Cemetery. The removals began in 1854 and lasted for two years. The *Brooklyn Daily Eagle* quoted a watchman who stated that the bones and coffins were buried in trenches, while the best headstones were "put up to look good."

The Allen Street congregation disbanded in 1902.

MAILING ADDRESS: c/o Cypress Hills Cemetery
                              833 Jamaica Avenue
                              Brooklyn, New York 11208-1593

PHONE NUMBER: (718) 277-2900

RECORDS: Cypress Hills Cemetery prefers written requests for searches.

RESOURCES: *Cypress Hills Cemetery*. Brooklyn, N.Y.: Cypress Hills Cemetery, 1880. (Extensive list of plot owners and location of plot, maps, rules, and history of cemetery)

"The Forgotten Dead: Many Neglected Graves in Cypress Hills Cemetery." *The Brooklyn Daily Eagle*, 13 August 1893, p.8, col. 7. (description of the Methodist plot)

Almshouse Cemetery and Burial Vaults

CATEGORY: Public

YEARS OF USE: circa 1757 to circa 1794

LOCATION: 31 Chambers Street, between Elk Street and Broadway, Manhattan. Current site of the Municipal Archives, formerly the Tweed Courthouse.

HISTORY: On 24 October 1998, workers from the Department of Environmental Protection were digging up Chambers Street to reach a broken water main when they discovered skull fragments and a clay pipe. Charles Sturkin, a spokesman for the agency, told *The New York Times* "there is an indication that there is a Colonial-era cemetery near the Tweed Court House." Indeed, it is the former site of the Almshouse Cemetery and Burial Vaults.

The cemetery was created on 19 March 1757 when the New York City Common Council met at the Almshouse to "cause a small piece of ground to the eastward of and adjoining to the fence of the said workhouse of the length of two boards to be enclosed and fenced in for a burial place for the poor belonging to the said workhouse." It is part of, or next to, the African Burial Ground.

On 1 August 1785, the City Council suggested that the ground behind "the barracks" be used as a burial ground for the dead from the Almshouse and Bridewell Prison. Four months later, a committee charged with finding a "proper" place for the burial ground reported that it would be more economical to build "two large vaults in the back of the Almshouse garden."

When the Madison Square Cemetery opened in 1794, the Almshouse began burying its dead there.

MAILING ADDRESS: c/o The Municipal Archives
                 31 Chambers Street, Room 103
                 New York, New York 10007-1210
PHONE NUMBER: (212) 788-8582
RECORDS: The Municipal Archives maintains the admission, discharge, and
census records for the Almshouse. Records begin in 1758.
RESOURCES: N/A

Alsop Family Burial Ground

CATEGORY: Private
YEARS OF USE: Gravestones dated 1718 to 1881
LOCATION: The Alsop's burial ground is within the first section of Calvary
Cemetery, north of the intersection of Review Avenue and Laurel Hill
Boulevard, Woodside, Queens.
HISTORY: On 29 October 1845, the Archdiocese of New York purchased one
hundred and fifteen acres from Ann Alsop, widow of John Alsop, who agreed
to sell her property for use as Calvary Cemetery on the condition that her
family's burial ground be preserved. There are about forty known burials in
the yard.
      The Alsop Family Burial Ground is the only known Protestant burial
ground within a Catholic cemetery.
MAILING ADDRESS: c/o Calvary Cemetery
                 49-01 Laurel Hill Boulevard
                 Woodside, New York 11377-7396
PHONE NUMBER: (718) 786-8000
RECORDS: Calvary Cemetery does not have any record of the persons buried
in the Alsop Family Burial Ground. The inscriptions on the gravestones are
nearly illegible today.
RESOURCES: Frost, Josephine C. *Underhill Genealogy: Descendants of Captain
John Underhill*. vol. 2. New York: Myron C. Taylor for The Underhill Society
of America, 1932, 68, 70–74. (photo of cemetery, gravestone inscriptions)
      Powell, Charles U., comp., and Alice H. Meigs, ed. *Description of Private
and Family Cemeteries in the Borough of Queens*. City of New York,
Borough of Queens, Topographical Bureau. Jamaica, N.Y.: Queens Borough
Public Library, 1932. (gravestone inscriptions and maps)

Amiable Child Monument

CATEGORY: Private
DATE OF USE: 15 July 1797
LOCATION: Riverside Park, west of LaSalle Street, near the north end of the
oval formed by Riverside Drive West and Riverside Drive East, Manhattan.
HISTORY: A stone urn "Erected to the Memory of an Amiable Child" marks

the grave of Saint Claire Pollock, a five-year-old boy who was killed by a fall from the cliffs in the park onto rocks beside the Hudson River.

George Pollock, Saint Claire's uncle and owner of the estate on which the child was buried, sold the property soon after Saint Claire's death. On 18 January 1800, George wrote to the new owner:

"There is a small enclosure near your boundary fence within which lie the remains of a favorite child, covered by a marble monument. You will confer a peculiar and interesting favor upon me by allowing me to convey the enclosure to you so that you will consider it a part of your own estate, keeping it, however, always enclosed and sacred."

MAILING ADDRESS: N/A
PHONE NUMBER: N/A
RECORDS: N/A

Amity Street Churchyard

CATEGORY: Baptist
YEARS OF USE: Pre-1833 to 1851
LOCATION: On the north side of West Third Street, between Greene Street and Mercer Street, Manhattan.
HISTORY: Interments in the Amity Street Churchyard probably came to an end with the 1851 ban on interments south of 86th Street in Manhattan. The remains were eventually reinterred in the plot of the Madison Avenue Baptist Church in Cypress Hills Cemetery.

Amity Street Church was also known as Third Baptist Church.
MAILING ADDRESS: c/o Cypress Hills Cemetery
                833 Jamaica Avenue
                Brooklyn, New York 11208-1593
PHONE NUMBER: (718) 277-2900
RECORDS: Cypress Hills Cemetery prefers written requests for searches.
RESOURCES: *Cypress Hills Cemetery*. Brooklyn, N.Y.: Cyprus Hills Cemetery, 1880. (Extensive list of plot owners and location of plot, maps, rules, and history of cemetery)

Androvert Family Burial Ground

CATEGORY: Private
YEARS OF USE: Gravestones dated 1734 to 1821
LOCATION: Cornelia Avenue, Prince's Bay, Staten Island.
HISTORY: The Androvert Family Burial Ground is the oldest known family burial ground on Staten Island. At the turn of the century, it contained several gravestones with the names of early Staten Island families: Androvert, Cole, DuBois, Fay, Grun, Gunton, Johnson, Lakerman, Parlee, and Taylor. While the oldest extant gravestone was dated 1734, there were several unmarked

stones which may have been older. The cemetery was destroyed in 1930 with the construction of Cornelia Street, the entrance to Wolfe's Pond Park. Loring McMillen, then Richmond Borough Historian, visited the site in 1932 and found two gravestones that had been pushed aside. McMillen took them for safekeeping. He suspected that the other gravestones had been appropriated by neighbors for use as flagstones.

MAILING ADDRESS: N/A

PHONE NUMBER: N/A

RECORDS: N/A

RESOURCES: Davis, William T. "Homestead Graves." *Proceedings of the Natural Science Association of Staten Island.* Staten Island, N.Y. (December 1889), special no. 09 (gravestone inscriptions)

Androvette Family Burial Ground

CATEGORY: Private

YEARS OF USE: Gravestones dated 1773 to 1844

LOCATION: "Southern slope of Androvette's Hill" overlooking the Arthur Kill in Charleston, Staten Island.

HISTORY: Members of the Androvette, Butler, DuBois, Ellis, Johnson, and Tappen families are buried here. Over a dozen gravestones were standing in 1934, but by 1948, they had been severely vandalized by neighborhood boys.

MAILING ADDRESS: N/A

PHONE NUMBER: N/A

RECORDS: N/A

RESOURCES: Davis, William T. "Homestead Graves." *Proceedings of the Natural Science Association of Staten Island.* Staten Island, N.Y. (December 1889), special no. 9 (gravestone inscriptions)

Anshe-Chesed Cemetery

CATEGORY: Jewish

YEARS OF USE: 1839 to 1855

LOCATION: 89th Street, near Madison Avenue, Manhattan.

HISTORY: Congregation Anshe-Chesed, which became Temple Beth-El in 1852, used this burial ground for about fifteen years. In February of 1880, its trustees announced that the cemetery was going to be removed. Any remains that were not claimed by family, and interred privately, were taken to Beth-El Cemetery about 8 March 1880. At that time, there were only fifty-three gravestones.

MAILING ADDRESS: Beth-El Cemetery
80-12 Cypress Avenue
Flushing, New York 11385-6715

PHONE NUMBER: (718) 366-3558

RECORDS: Records are housed at the cemetery.
RESOURCES: "Reinterring the Jewish Dead." *The New York Times.*
(February 28, 1880): 3.   (Description of the cemetery)

Aqueduct Cemetery
See Southside Cemetery.

Asbury African Methodist Episcopal Cemetery
See Cherry Lane Second Asbury African Methodist Episcopal Cemetery.

Asbury Methodist Episcopal Churchyard and Cemetery

CATEGORY: Methodist Episcopal
YEARS OF USE: circa 1803 to date
LOCATION: South side of Amsterdam Place, between Richmond Avenue and
Freedom Avenue, Bull's Head, Staten Island.
HISTORY: The Asbury Methodist Episcopal Church was organized in 1803.
Its graveyard has two sections. The first occupies the land on the north side
of the church. It was known as "The Churchyard." The second is on the
south side of the church and was known as "New Springville Cemetery."
The entire cemetery was renamed "The Asbury Methodist Cemetery" in
1955. It was abandoned in 1971.

Friends of Abandoned Cemeteries of Staten Island reports that the cemetery is "reinstated with plans to offer unused burial plots for sale." It is now
called Asbury Cemetery.

This graveyard is also known as "Northfield Methodist Episcopal
Churchyard," "Old Neck Cemetery," and "Springville Cemetery."
MAILING ADDRESS: Asbury Cemetery Association
                              Post Office Box 621
                              Staten Island, New York 10302-0621
PHONE NUMBER: N/A
RECORDS: An interment list has been posted on the Richmond County
RootsWeb project Web site. The address is:
                    <http://www.rootsweb.com/~nyrichmo>
RESOURCES: McKimm, James A. *Gravestone Inscriptions in the Asbury
Methodist Cemetery* First Transcribed in 1922 by Davis, William T., Revised
and Map Added. New Springville, Staten Island, N. Y. August 1971.

Vosburgh, Royden Woodward, trans. *Records of the Asbury Methodist
Episcopal Churchyard.* Staten Island, N. Y. November 1922. (churchyard
gravestone inscriptions, 1839–1870; Springville Cemetery gravestone inscriptions, 1871–1890; deaths, 1858–1881)

Associate Presbyterian Church Cemetery
See University Place Cemetery.

Associate Presbyterian Churchyard
See Scotch Presbyterian Church burial grounds.

Associate Reformed Presbyterian Church Cemetery
See University Place Cemetery.

Astoria Reformed Dutch Church Vaults

CATEGORY: Reformed Dutch
YEARS OF USE: mid-1800s
LOCATION: 12th Street, near 26th Avenue, Astoria, Queens.
HISTORY: The Astoria Reformed Dutch Church was organized in 1839. The family vaults in the rear of the church include those of the Ayers, Halsey, Thorburn, and Whitney families.
MAILING ADDRESS: First Reformed Dutch Church of Astoria
            2735 12th Street
            Long Island City, New York 11102-3741
PHONE NUMBER: (718) 721-4047
RECORDS: N/A
RESOURCES: N/A

Astoria Village Cemetery, First

CATEGORY: Public
YEARS OF USE: 1842 to 1849
LOCATION: Bounded by 14th Place, 26th Avenue, 18th Street, and 25th Road, Astoria, Queens.
HISTORY: Astoria was incorporated as a village in 1835. The remains in its public cemetery were removed to the new Astoria Village Cemetery in 1849.
MAILING ADDRESS: N/A
PHONE NUMBER: N/A
RECORDS: N/A
RESOURCES: N/A

Astoria Village Cemetery, Second

CATEGORY: Public
YEARS OF USE: 1850 to 1869
LOCATION: Broadway, between Crescent Street and 29th Street, Astoria, Queens.
HISTORY: When this cemetery closed, the bodies were removed to a plot in

Saint Michael's Cemetery. In 1885, and again in 1888, construction workers unearthed skulls and bones that were missed during the removal. The *Newtown Register* reported that on both occasions, local children began playing with the bones after workmen dug them up.

MAILING ADDRESS: c/o Saint Michael's Cemetery and Mausoleums
                72-02 Astoria Boulevard
                Flushing, New York 11370-1094
PHONE NUMBER: (718) 278-3240
RECORDS: Saint Michael's records are housed on-site.
RESOURCES: N/A

Attorney Street Methodist Protestant Churchyard and Vaults

CATEGORY: Methodist Protestant
YEARS OF USE: Pre-1837 to 1851
LOCATION: 61 Attorney Street, Manhattan.
HISTORY: Burials probably came to an end with the 1851 ban on interments south of 86th in Manhattan.
MAILING ADDRESS: N/A
PHONE NUMBER: N/A
RECORDS: N/A
RESOURCES: N/A

Barkelou-Cortelyou Burial Ground

CATEGORY: Military, Private

YEARS OF USE: Gravestones date 1788 to 1841

LOCATION: Southwest corner of Narrows Avenue and Mackey Place, between 70th and 71st Streets, Bay Ridge, Brooklyn.

HISTORY: The Battle of Brooklyn was fought on this site during the Revolutionary War. The Cortelyou family, who owned the land, allowed the ground to be used as a graveyard for some sixty soldiers who died during the battle. Simon Cortelyou and Lieutenant Harmanus Barkelou were among those soldiers interred in the cemetery. Members of the Stillwell, Suydam, and Wardell families may have been buried there as well.

Only a few of those interred have been identified. There is some speculation that the headstones were carried off for use as doorsteps, or that the bodies were removed to other cemeteries after the Revolution. In 1976, the Veterans of Foreign Wars, Robert I. Porter Post 986, unveiled a monument dedicated to the Revolutionary War heroes buried here.

MAILING ADDRESS: N/A

PHONE NUMBER: N/A

RECORDS: N/A

RESOURCES: *Cemetery, Church, and Town Records of New York State*. vol. 70. Washington, D. C.: Daughters of the American Revolution, 1935, 220–221. (gravestone inscriptions)

Eardeley, William A., trans. *Cemeteries in Kings and Queens Counties, Long Island, New York: 1753 to 1913*. vol. 1. Brooklyn, NY: published by the author, 1914. (gravestone inscriptions)

Baron Hirsch Cemetery

CATEGORY: Jewish
YEARS OF USE: circa 1901 to date
LOCATION: 1126 Richmond Avenue, on the west side of the street adjacent to Hillside Cemetery, Port Richmond, Staten Island.
HISTORY: Baron Hirsch Cemetery was established in the late 1800s by Jewish immigrants from Eastern Europe and Germany. It is jointly owned by 435 congregations and Jewish groups.
MAILING ADDRESS: Baron Hirsch Cemetery
                       1126 Richmond Avenue
                       Staten Island, New York 10314-1589
PHONE NUMBER: (718) 698-0162
RECORDS: The earliest recorded burials date back to 1901.
RESOURCES: N/A

Bartow-Pell Family Burial Ground
See Pell Family Burial Ground.

Bay Ridge Cemetery
See Barkelou Burial Ground.

Bayside Cemetery
Sometimes refers to Acacia and Mokom Sholom Cemeteries.

Bayside Cemetery

CATEGORY: Jewish
YEARS OF USE: 1860 to date
LOCATION: 80-35 Pitkin Avenue, north side of the avenue between Mokom Sholom Cemetery and Acacia Cemetery, Ozone Park, Queens.
HISTORY: More than 30,000 people are buried in Bayside Cemetery. It is often the target of vandalism, and the grounds are overgrown and neglected. Caretakers complain that they lack enough funds to maintain and protect the grounds.

The cemetery's precarious financial situation was brought about, in part, by the large number of burial societies that purchased plots in the cemetery and have since disbanded, leaving no money to pay for maintenance of their grounds.

Few families paid for perpetual care, and there are no graves for sale.

Bayside Cemetery is owned by Congregation Shaare Zedek of Manhattan. The congregation recently hired extra workers to cut the grass, clear the paths, and pick up the garbage. The cleanup, and heightened watches by the 106th Police Precinct, are expected to reduce vandalism. The congregation is working on a long-term solution to the cemetery's problems.

MAILING ADDRESS: Bayside Cemetery
      80-35 Pitkin Avenue
      Jamaica, New York 11417-1228

PHONE NUMBER: (718) 843-4840

RECORDS: The Mokom Sholom Cemetery Recording Project is working to record the name of everyone buried in Bayside Cemetery through the use of cemetery records, death certificates, obituaries, wills, family histories, and gravestones.

RESOURCES: The Mokom Sholom Cemetery Recording Project's list of names is distributed as MOKOMCEM.EXE and is available on the Internet at <ftp://ftp.cac.psu.edu/pub/genealogy/text/jewish/mokomcem.exe>.

Bedell-Decker Family Burial Ground

CATEGORY: Private

YEARS OF USE: Gravestones date 1781 to 1848

LOCATION: On a hill near Richmond Creek, current site of Latourette Public Golf Course, Richmond Hill Road, Richmondtown, Staten Island.

HISTORY: This is the burial ground of pre-Revolutionary War families, British soldiers, and "embattled farmers." Members of the Bedell, Cole, Decker, Doty, Little, Rezeau, and Winant families are interred here. In 1901, the twenty-three gravestones still standing had been damaged by grazing cattle. Friends of Abandoned Cemeteries of Staten Island reports that the graveyard is now obliterated.

  The burial ground is also known as Burial Hill, Cemetery Hill, and Ketchum's Hill.

MAILING ADDRESS: N/A

PHONE NUMBER: N/A

RECORDS: N/A

RESOURCES: Davis, William T. "Homestead Graves." *Proceedings of the Natural Science Association of Staten Island, New York.* Staten Island, N.Y., (December 1889), special no. 9. (gravestone inscriptions)

  Wade, Stuart C. "Sepulchral Stones of Staten Island." *The New York Genealogical and Biographical Record* 32, no. 1 (1901): 40–41. (gravestone inscriptions) (Note: The article says the listing was to be continued in a future issue of the *Record*, but it could not be found.)

Bedford Street Methodist Episcopal Church Cemetery and Vaults

CATEGORY: Methodist Episcopal

YEARS OF USE: circa 1810 to 1851

LOCATION: Southeast corner of Bedford Street and Morton Street, Manhattan.

HISTORY: The Bedford Street Methodist Episcopal Church was organized in 1805. Its church was erected in 1810 and remained at Bedford Street until 1913. That year, New York City condemned the church building and extended Seventh Avenue directly through the property.

On 3 October 1913, the *New York Times* reported that "several hundred dead are interred in the old vaults beneath the church edifice . . . no records have been preserved of the names of those buried there, but it is known they include many well-known residents of early Greenwich... the church organization now is making arrangements to buy a plot, probably in Mount Olivet Cemetery... a large memorial monument will be erected."

The congregation celebrated its last sermon on 23 November 1913 and was subsequently absorbed by the Metropolitan-Duane United Methodist Church.

This church was also known as the Greenwich Village Methodist Episcopal Church.

MAILING ADDRESS: c/o Metropolitan-Duane United Methodist Church
201 West 13th Street
New York, New York 10011-7795
PHONE NUMBER: (212) 243-5740
RECORDS: N/A
RESOURCES: N/A

Bensonia Cemetery
See Morrisania Cemetery.

Bergen Family Burial Ground

CATEGORY: Private
YEARS OF USE: Pre-1864
LOCATION: In the middle of the block bounded by 39th Street, 40th Street, 3rd Avenue, and 4th Avenue, Brooklyn.
HISTORY: This burial ground appears on a map of the Simon Bergen farm. After Simon's death, the property was surveyed and laid out in lots, apparently at the direction of his executors, Peter Bergen and John Morris. The Bergen family house was situated approximately one block west of the graveyard. The property was formerly owned by the Delaplaine family.
MAILING ADDRESS: N/A
PHONE NUMBER: N/A
RECORDS: N/A
RESOURCES: Robinson, Elisha. *Certified Copies of Important Maps of the City of Brooklyn.* New York: the author, 1889. Reference map no. 706.

Berrian-Bashford Burial Ground
See Kingsbridge Burial Ground.

Berrian Family Burial Ground

CATEGORY: Private

YEARS OF USE: Gravestones date 1810 to 1863

LOCATION: Southeast corner of Sedgwick Avenue and West Fordham Road, University Heights, Bronx.

HISTORY: Dating back to the days when the Fordham Manor Reformed Dutch Church stood across the street, this cemetery was used as a place for its interments. The congregation was organized in 1696 and erected its first church ten years later. The church building was torn down in 1849, and the congregation moved to a new building at 71 West Kingsbridge Road, not far away.

In 1891, Sedgwick Avenue was cut through the cemetery. At that time, the burial ground was unfenced, neglected, and vandalized. Some of the gravestones had been stolen, while others had fallen over and were used as stepping stones.

Shortly thereafter, the Berrian family heirs claimed that the Reformed Dutch Church had only been allowed to use the cemetery as a favor by their family. They reclaimed the property and put it up for sale. The remains in the cemetery were placed in a packing box, taken to an undertaker, and rein-terred in Kensico Cemetery, Valhalla, Westchester County. Among those buried in the Berrian Family Burial Ground were members of the Baker, Berrian, Cromwell, DeVoe, Hart, Lawrence, and Valentine families.

Virginia Poe, the wife of Edgar Allan Poe, was temporarily buried here following her death in 1846. In 1885, her remains were transferred to her husband's plot in Westminster Hall Burial Ground, Baltimore.

MAILING ADDRESS: Fordham Manor Reformed Church
2705 Reservoir Road
Bronx, New York 10468-3458

PHONE NUMBER: (718) 796-4980

RECORDS: N/A

RESOURCES: Haacker, Fred C., compiler. *Burials in the Dyckman-Nagle Burial Ground, and the Berrian Graveyards, Near Kingsbridge, New York City.* Manuscript. U.S. History, Local History and Genealogy Division, New York Public Library, Fifth Avenue and 42nd Street, New York, 1954, 13–14. (gravestone inscriptions)

K., W.E. "Notes and Queries." *The New York Genealogical and Biographical Record* 22, no. 4 (1891): 208. (gravestone inscriptions; condition of cemetery)

Berrien-Remsen Family Burial Ground

CATEGORY: Private

YEARS OF USE: Gravestones dated from the eighteenth century to 1810

LOCATION: Near 20th Avenue and 21st Street, Astoria, Queens.
HISTORY: This burial ground was at the north end of Berrien's Lane, facing Berrien's Creek and Berrien's Island. It was obliterated in 1902 for construction of a gas manufacturing plant. Con-Edison now occupies the site.
MAILING ADDRESS: N/A
PHONE NUMBER: N/A
RECORDS: N/A
RESOURCES: N/A

Bethel Baptist Churchyard and Burial Vaults

CATEGORY: Baptist, Congregational
YEARS OF USE: circa 1818 to circa 1842
LOCATION: Delancey Street, between Chrystie Street and the Bowery, Manhattan.
HISTORY: Land for the Bethel Baptist Church was conveyed to the congregation by William and Mary Rhinelander in 1818. About 1840, the Bethel Baptist Church dissolved, and the building was then occupied by the Second Congregational Church. The First Free Congregational Church took over the grounds in 1845, and, in 1849, it was occupied by the Bethesda Baptist Church.

New York City purchased the property in 1856 and erected a school on the site. The school was torn down during the 1930s for construction of Sara Delano Roosevelt Park. In 1964, construction of a senior citizens' recreation center came to a halt when workers unearthed the coffins of nearly two hundred men and women. Many were marked with silver-plated name plates. Elizabeth Morell and Emma Buchler, who died in 1821, and Martha Darby, who died in 1823, were among them. Workers noted that the foundations of the school had been sunk down into the burial vaults.

Earlier removals may have taken place. *Gotham, A History of New York City to 1898* by Edwin G. Burrows notes that about 1842, Walt Whitman, then editor of the *New York Aurora,* "recounted the efforts of a large crowd of women to block workmen from digging up a Baptist cemetery at Chrystie and Delancey."
MAILING ADDRESS: N/A
PHONE NUMBER: N/A
RECORDS: N/A
RESOURCES: N/A

Beth-El Cemetery, Manhattan
See Anshe-Chesed Cemetery.

Beth-El Cemetery, Queens

CATEGORY: Jewish
YEARS OF USE: circa 1864 to Date
LOCATION: Cypress Hills Street, between Machpelah Cemetery and 80th Avenue, Glendale, Queens.
HISTORY: In 1895, the *Brooklyn Daily Eagle* wrote that Congregation Beth-El, of Manhattan, "is one of the wealthiest in New York City... They have a magnificent new temple erected on Fifth Avenue, New York, something grand." Of Congregation Beth-El's cemetery in Queens, the *Eagle* went on to say that it "is nicely laid out... There are also costly monuments on which work has just begun, " including the Straus Family Vault, of Abraham and Straus fame. Actor Edward G. Robinson is interred here as well.

A spokeswoman for the cemetery was unable to confirm its date of creation, but did say that burials began "in the mid- to late-1800s." Beth-El Cemetery is also known as "New Union Fields Cemetery."
MAILING ADDRESS: Beth-El Cemetery
        80-12 Cypress Avenue
        Flushing, New York 11385-6715
PHONE NUMBER: (718) 366-3558
RECORDS: Records are housed at the cemetery.
RESOURCES: N/A

Bethel United Methodist Episcopal Church Cemetery

CATEGORY: Methodist Episcopal, Non-sectarian
YEARS OF USE: 1842 to date
LOCATION: North side of Amboy Road, between Bethel Avenue and Page Avenue, Tottenville, Staten Island.
HISTORY: The Bethel United Methodist Church was erected in 1842. It was destroyed by fire in 1886, but was immediately rebuilt.
MAILING ADDRESS: Bethel United M.E. Church
        7033 Amboy Road
        Staten Island, New York 10307
PHONE NUMBER: (718) 984-1277
RECORDS: Researchers should check the Staten Island RootsWeb page on the Internet to see if this cemetery has been added to their cemetery database. The address is <http://www.rootsweb.com/~nyrichmo>.
RESOURCES: Vosburgh, Royden W., editor and transcriber, *Staten Island Gravestone Inscriptions*, vol. 2, New York City, April 1925 (typed manuscript). An interment list has been posted on the Web site of the Richmond County RootsWeb Project. The address is <http://www.rootsweb.com/~nyrichmo>

Bethesda Baptist Churchyard
See Bethel Baptist Churchyard and Burial Vaults.

Beth-Olom Fields Cemetery

CATEGORY: Jewish
YEARS OF USE: 1851 to date
LOCATION: West side of Cypress Hills Street, between the Interboro Parkway (Jackie Robinson Parkway) and Salem Fields Cemetery, on the Brooklyn-Queens border near East New York, Brooklyn.
HISTORY: Beth-Olom is jointly owned by three Manhattan synagogues: Congregation Shearith Israel, Congregation B'nai Jeshurun, and Temple Shaaray Tefilah.
    Supreme Court Justice Benjamin Cardozo (1870-1938), poet Emma Lazarus (1849-1887), and Admiral Uriah Phelps Levy (1792-1862) are among those buried here.
MAILING ADDRESS: Beth-Olom Cemetery
                    2 Cypress Hills Street
                    Brooklyn, New York 11208-1408
PHONE NUMBER: (718) 277-6255
RECORDS: Obtain records at the cemetery office and with each congregation.
RESOURCES: N/A

Betts Family Burial Ground

CATEGORY: Private
YEARS OF USE: Gravestones date 1762 to 1896
LOCATION: In the eastern section of Mount Zion Cemetery, near the north side of 54th Avenue, Maspeth, Queens.
HISTORY: Legend holds that the family patriarch, Captain Richard Betts, dug his own grave a few days before he died at the age of one hundred in 1713. The location of his grave, however, is unmarked, presumably because his sons were Quaker and, therefore, did not believe in the use of headstones. Descendants named Betts, Crommelin, Gillzean, Hanson, and Hervey are buried here.
MAILING ADDRESS: c/o Mount Zion Cemetery
                    5963 54th Avenue
                    Flushing, New York 11378-1298
PHONE NUMBER: (718) 335-2500
RECORDS: N/A
RESOURCES: Frost, Josephine C. trans. *Long Island Cemetery Inscriptions*. vol. 1. Brooklyn, N.Y. March 1912. (gravestone inscriptions)
    Klein, H.L. *Captain Richard Betts, Patriarch of Maspeth*. Long Island, N.Y.: Long Island Press, 20 February 1976. (description of cemetery and family history)

Powell, Charles U., comp., and Alice H. Meigs, ed. *Description of Private and Family Cemeteries in the Borough of Queens*. City of New York, Borough of Queens, Topographical Bureau. Jamaica, N. Y.: Queens Borough Public Library, 1975 supplement. (gravestone inscriptions and map)

"Walks through Old Cemeteries." *The Newtown Register*, 15 March 1877, p. 4, col. 2. (gravestone inscriptions)

Billop Family Burial Ground

CATEGORY: Private
YEARS OF USE: Gravestones date 1735 and 1750
LOCATION: 7445 Hylan Boulevard, three hundred yards east of the Manor House, Tottenville, Staten Island.
HISTORY: The Billop Family Burial Ground was located east of the Manor House built by the British sea captain, Christopher Billop, circa 1680. According to one story, Billop won Staten Island for the colony of New York in a 1664 boat race. The proprietors of New Jersey claimed Staten Island as part of their territory, not New York's. To settle the dispute, the Duke of York agreed to award the island to that colony whose citizen could circumnavigate the Island in twenty-four hours. Billop won.

The Billops held onto the estate until shortly after the Revolutionary War. In a deed of 1781, they reserved the right to be buried in their sixty-square-foot cemetery, but apparently never exercised that option. The estate changed hands several times before General Lloyd Aspinwall purchased the property about 1850. According to one historian, Aspinwall ordered the removal of "two generations of Billops and their slaves" and reinterred them in a garden near Saint Paul's Methodist Episcopal Church.

Two headstones were left on the estate, that of Thomas Billop and his wife, Eugenia. They have been preserved by the Conference House Association.
MAILING ADDRESS: The Conference House Association
                 7445 Hylan Boulevard
                 Staten Island, New York 10307-2119
PHONE NUMBER: (718) 984-2086
RECORDS: N/A
RESOURCES: Davis, William T. *The Conference or Billop House*. New York: Staten Island Historical Society, 1926, 176–177, 179. (two gravestone inscriptions)

Blackwell Family Burial Ground

CATEGORY: Private
YEARS OF USE: Known burials 1780 to 1857
LOCATION: West side of Vernon Boulevard, between 36th Avenue and 37th Avenue, Astoria, Queens.

HISTORY: More than sixty people were interred in the Blackwell Family
Burial Ground. The remains were taken to Saint George's Churchyard,
Astoria, in October of 1900. Among those buried there were Colonel Jacob
Blackwell (died 1780), Major Robert Moore (died 1843), and another whose
coffin-plate bore the date of 1857.

A bottle factory was eventually constructed on the site.

MAILING ADDRESS: N/A
PHONE NUMBER: N/A
RECORDS: N/A
RESOURCES: *The Long Island Star*, 6 June 1884. (history of the cemetery;
limited genealogical data)

The Long Island Star, 5 October 1900. (history of the cemetery; limited
genealogical data)

Powell, Charles U., comp., and Alice H. Meigs, ed. *Description of Private
and Family Cemeteries in the Borough of Queens.* City of New York,
Borough of Queens, Topographical Bureau. Jamaica, N.Y.: Queens Borough
Public Library, 1975 supplement. (gravestone inscriptions in Saint George's
Churchyard; Blackwell family)

Blazing Star Burial Ground

CATEGORY: Public
YEARS OF USE: Gravestones date 1751 to 1865
LOCATION: North side of Arthur Kill Road, at the water's edge, between
Huguenot Avenue and Rossville Avenue, Rossville, Staten Island.
HISTORY: Before Rossville was named in 1837, the community was known as
Old Blazing Star, after a local tavern run by John and Joshua Mersereau.
The burial ground was one of the first public cemeteries on Staten Island and
the names of some of the earliest Staten Island settlers are found here.
Among them are Burbank, Cole, Lockerman, Marshall, Oakley, Parlee,
Simonson, Sleight, Van Clief, and Winant. About half of the stones are dedi-
cated to members of the Seguine family.

The gravestones are arranged in fifteen rows, one to six headstones in
each row. The earliest is that of Jacob Slaght who died 20 June 1751. The
most recent is that of John G. Shea who died on 8 October 1865. A descendant removed the gravestone of Peter Winant, who died on 8 August 1758.

Although the cemetery was abandoned, Friends of Abandoned Cemeteries
of Staten Island (FACSI) has taken an interest in the grounds. FACSI reports
that "The Burial Ground Environmental & Historic Documentation and
Education Project, of the Urban Resources Partnership-National Parks
Service, has awarded a grant to the Staten Island Institute of Arts and
Sciences to document the historic Blazing Start Cemetery in all its aspects."
FACSI will assist with the project.

This cemetery is also known as the Oakley Burying Ground, the Rossville

Burial Ground, the Seguine Burial Ground, and the Sleight-Winant Family
Burial Ground.
MAILING ADDRESS: c/o Staten Island Institute of Arts and Sciences
            75 Stuyvesant Place
            Staten Island, New York 10301-1998
PHONE NUMBER: (718) 727-1135
RECORDS: The records of Saint Andrew's Church, Saint Luke's Church, and
the Reformed Dutch Churches supplemented a study of the social status of
women interred in the Blazing Star Burial Ground, conducted by Vince
Lenza, History Intern, Wagner College, Staten Island, 1997.
RESOURCES: Davis, William T. "Homestead Graves." *Proceedings of the
Natural Science Association of Staten Island.* Staten Island, N.Y. Special
Number 9, December 1889. (gravestone inscriptions)

Bloomingdale Churchyard and Vaults

CATEGORY: Reformed Dutch
YEARS OF USE: circa 1809 to 1851
LOCATION: Broadway, between 68th Street and 69th Street, Manhattan.
HISTORY: Burials in the churchyard of the Bloomingdale Church probably
came to an end with the 1851 ban on interments south of 86th Street in
Manhattan. The congregation dissolved in 1913.
MAILING ADDRESS: c/o Gardner Sage Library
            New Brunswick Theological Seminary
            21 Seminary Place
            New Brunswick, New Jersey 08901-1187
PHONE NUMBER: (908) 247-5243
RECORDS: Original records are now at the Gardner Sage Library in New
Brunswick.
RESOURCES: N/A

B'nai Jeshurun Cemetery

CATEGORY: Jewish
YEARS OF USE: circa 1827 to 1851
LOCATION: North side of West 32nd Street, between 6th and 7th Avenues,
Manhattan.
HISTORY: The bodies in this burial ground were removed to an unspecified
cemetery in Queens, circa 1857. Congregation B'nai Jeshurun is part owner of
Beth-Olom Fields Cemetery, located in Queens, and the bodies may be there.
MAILING ADDRESS: Congregation B'nai Jeshurun
            100 West 89th Street
            New York, New York 10024
PHONE NUMBER: (212) 787-7600

RECORDS: N/A
RESOURCES: N/A

B'nai Jeshurun-Shearith Israel Cemetery
See Beth-Olom Fields Cemetery.

Bowne-Parsons Family Burial Ground

CATEGORY: Private
YEARS OF USE: Gravestones date 1804 to 1906
LOCATION: Roosevelt Avenue and Bowne Street, Flushing, Queens.
HISTORY: This burial ground was probably set aside by a provision in the will
of Anne Bowne, who died circa 1800. It contained all of the gravestones
that were removed from the nearby Old Bowne Family Burial Ground at 10
Bowne Street, southeast corner of Northern Boulevard, where interments
began as early at 1665. The Parsons family later inherited the new burial
ground.

   The remains in the Bowne-Parsons Family Burial Ground were reinterred in
Flushing Cemetery about 1934, along with family remains from the Friends'
Meeting House Cemetery. In total, less than two dozen graves were moved.
MAILING ADDRESS: Flushing Cemetery
                  163-06 46th Avenue
                  Flushing, New York 11358-3241
PHONE NUMBER: (718) 359-0100
RECORDS: N/A
RESOURCES: Frost, Josephine C. trans. *Long Island Cemetery Inscriptions*.
       vol. 9. Brooklyn, N. Y. 1914. (gravestone inscriptions)

Brainard Presbyterian Churchyard

CATEGORY: Presbyterian
YEARS OF USE: circa 1836 to 1851
LOCATION: 91 Rivington Street, between Ludlow Street and Orchard Street,
Manhattan.
HISTORY: The Brainard Presbyterian Church was organized in 1834 and
erected its church two years later. The property was sold to the Allen Street
Methodist Episcopal Church, circa 1854.
MAILING ADDRESS: N/A
PHONE NUMBER: N/A
RECORDS: N/A
RESOURCES: N/A

Braisted Family Burial Ground
See Merrell Family Burial Ground.

Brick Presbyterian Churchyard and Vaults

CATEGORY: Presbyterian

YEARS OF USE: circa 1768 to 1823

LOCATION: Beekman Street, between Park Row and Nassau Street, Manhattan.

HISTORY: Claiming that their church was "altogether incapable of containing the congregation" and the "cemetery too small for the decent interment" of their dead, the First Presbyterian Church asked the City of New York to grant them a new piece of property.

The "New Church" opened on 1 January 1768. With the creation of a third Presbyterian Church in 1798, the New Church became "The Brick Church."

Interments in the churchyard began to decrease about 1800. On 18 January 1804, trustees of the First Presbyterian Church banned the creation of new graves in the Brick Churchyard. On 27 October 1823, the City of New York passed an ordinance prohibiting burials in all vaults and graves south of Grand Street. The penalty for any violation was $250, but some families from The Brick Church paid that fine.

The Brick Church decided to sell its property in 1853.

James S. Hall, church sexton, announced in the 27 May 1856 *New York Times* that, "The Brick Presbyterian Church... having been sold, the trustees have procured a beautiful location in the Cemetery of the Evergreens to which place all the remains of the dead found in the graveyard will be removed, unless otherwise indicated by surviving friends." The bodies in the vaults were taken to several other cemeteries, including Green-Wood Cemetery.

MAILING ADDRESS: Brick Presbyterian Church
                         62 East 92nd Street
                         New York, New York 10128-4108

PHONE NUMBER: (212) 289-4400

RECORDS: The records of the Brick Presbyterian Church may be found with those of the First Presbyterian Church prior to 1809 (see entry for First Presbyterian Churchyard and Vaults).

RESOURCES: Knapp, Shepherd. *Personal Records of the Brick Presbyterian Church in the City of New York, 1809 to 1908.* New York: the church, 1909. (list of deaths)

Roney, Lila James. "Gravestone Inscriptions from the Burial Grounds of the Brick Presbyterian Church." *The New York Genealogical and Biographical Record* 60, no. 1 (January 1929): 8–14. (also contains vault inscriptions and genealogical data)

Bridewell Cemetery

See Almshouse Burial Vaults.

Brighton Heights Reformed Dutch Churchyard
See Tompkinsville Reformed Dutch Churchyard.

Brinkerhoff-Adriance Cemetery

CATEGORY: Private
YEARS OF USE: Gravestones date 1730 to 1872
LOCATION: East side of 182nd Street, north corner of 73rd Avenue, Fresh
Meadows, Queens.
HISTORY: "Occupying a commanding position, on the bluff overhanging
Flushing Bay, is the Brinkerhoff Cemetery," wrote William Munsell in 1882.
"It is beautiful in the summer and wild in the winter... as the tempest sweeps
over the resting place of an extinct family."

The Brinkerhoffs were among the early settlers of Long Island. By 1920,
most of their property had been sold, and the family was dispersed.
Forgotten, neglected, and ultimately abandoned, the burial ground was illicit-
ly seized by the City of New York for non-payment of taxes. It was put up
for auction in 1953. Joseph Dedomenico, who lived next door to the cemetery, purchased the land with the intent to develop it. As word of his plan
became public, the Queens Borough President, the court system, and other
interested parties intervened to halt construction.

The cemetery has been neglected ever since. The Queens Historical
Society hopes to reach a settlement with Dedomenico, obtain title to the
ground, form the Brinkerhoff-Adriance Cemetery Association, and restore the
grounds.

Seventy-six gravestones were standing in 1932; most were from the
Adriance, Brinkerhoff, and Snedecker families. Although no gravestones are
standing today, it is thought that they are buried beneath the cemetery's topsoil.
MAILING ADDRESS: Brinkerhoff-Adriance Cemetery
                 c/o Queens Historical Society
                 Kingsland Homestead
                 143-35 37th Avenue
                 Flushing, New York 11354-5729
PHONE NUMBER: (718) 939-0647
RECORDS: N/A
RESOURCES: Frost, Josephine C. trans. *Long Island Cemetery Inscriptions*.
vol. 1 Brooklyn, N. Y. March 1912.

Meigs, Alice H., ed., and The Topographical Bureau, comps.
Description of Private and Family Cemeteries in the Borough of Queens.
Jamaica, N.Y.: The Queens Borough Public Library, 1932. (gravestone
inscriptions and maps)

Munsell, W.W. *History of Queens County, New York*. New York:
W.W. Munsell & Company, 1882, 343–344. (genealogical data; description
of cemetery)

Wilford, Sarah. "Gravestones Crumble on Hellfire Lane." *Long Island Daily Press*, 5 August 1935. (vignette and photograph)

Bronxville Cemetery
See Covenantor Cemetery.

Brooklyn Navy Yard
See United States Naval Hospital Cemetery and Wallabout Bay.

Brooklyn Village Cemetery

CATEGORY: Public
YEARS OF USE: circa 1830s
LOCATION: Boerum Place, between Schermerhorn Street and Livingston Street, Brooklyn.
HISTORY: This community cemetery was situated on land purchased from the Schenck family. During construction in 1862, workers unearthed a gravestone marked "Peter Tyler 183–." The site is now covered by a department store.
MAILING ADDRESS: N/A
PHONE NUMBER: N/A
RECORDS: N/A
RESOURCES: The Brooklyn Historical Society has a transcript of gravestone inscriptions from this burial ground.

Bryant Park Cemetery

CATEGORY: Public
YEARS OF USE: 1823 to 1847
LOCATION: 5th to 6th Avenues, between 40th and 42nd Streets, Manhattan. (Current site of Bryant Park and the New York Public Library.)
HISTORY: This burial ground served as New York City's public cemetery through epidemics of cholera, pneumonia, smallpox, tuberculosis, and typhoid fever.

The remains in this cemetery may have been removed to another burial ground in 1852 to make way for The Crystal Palace, an entertainment venue, which opened on this site the following year.
MAILING ADDRESS: N/A
PHONE NUMBER: N/A
RECORDS: N/A
RESOURCES: N/A

Bunn Cemetery
See Colored Cemetery of Flushing.

Burbanck Family Burial Ground

CATEGORY: Private
YEARS OF USE: Gravestones date 1822 to 1865
LOCATION: Northeast corner of Todt Hill Road and Four Corners Road, Todt Hill, Staten Island
HISTORY: Abraham Burbanck's will, recorded 5 June 1823, directed his "executors... pay to my son, Isaac Burbanck, $30 for the lot of land I purchased for him for a burying ground... It is for my heirs and the Baptist Church of Staten Island." There is no record that the Baptist Church ever used the cemetery. In 1898, the gravestones were removed to Moravian Cemetery. They include the surnames Burbanck, Barton, Sharrot, and Wait.

The Burbanck Family Burial Ground was also known as the Iron Hill Cemetery.
MAILING ADDRESS: c/o Moravian Cemetery
2205 Richmond Road
Staten Island, New York 10306-2557
PHONE NUMBER: (718) 351-0136
RECORDS: The Moravian Cemetery records, which date back to 1763, are housed at the cemetery. They are also available on microfilm at the Staten Island Institute of Arts and Sciences.
RESOURCES: Davis, William T. "Homestead Graves." *Proceedings of the Natural Science Association of Staten Island.* Staten Island, N. Y. Special Number 9, December 1889. (gravestone inscriptions)

Burroughs Family Burial Ground

CATEGORY: Private
YEARS OF USE: Gravestones date 1793 to 1871
LOCATION: Alstyne Avenue, between Corona and Junction Boulevard, Elmhurst, Queens.
HISTORY: The Burroughs Family Burial Ground was on the rear portion of a lot facing the commons of Newtown. The family eventually abandoned their private cemetery in favor of Saint James' Churchyard.

About 1930, the burial ground was cut in half by Alstyne Avenue. New York City attempted to sell the lot in 1960, but failed to do so because it could not get clear title to the property while there were still bodies in the ground.

Burroughs, Jones, Vandervoort, and Waters were among the family surnames found on sixteen gravestones in 1932.
MAILING ADDRESS: N/A
PHONE NUMBER: N/A
RECORDS: N/A
RESOURCES: Meigs, Alice H., ed., and The Topographical Bureau, comps.

Description of Private and Family Cemeteries in the Borough of Queens.
Jamaica, N.Y.: The Queens Borough Public Library, 1932. (gravestone
inscriptions and maps)

Bushwick Reformed Dutch Churchyard

CATEGORY: Reformed Dutch
YEARS OF USE: Gravestones date 1655 to 1852
LOCATION: Opposite 451 Humboldt Street, between Withers Street and Frost
Street, Williamsburg, Brooklyn.
HISTORY: The Bushwick Reformed Church dates back to 1654. Its graveyard
was in the rear of the church, about 10 feet above the sidewalk. Members of
the Clark, Conselyea, Debevoise, Marshall, and Thursby families were buried
there.
    The Bushwick Reformed Dutch Church disbanded in 1919.
    In 1940, a man who grew up on Humboldt Street recalled that burials
took place in the graveyard until 1870. The cemetery was enclosed by a tall,
iron fence and was taken care of by a neighbor, William Language and his
sons, Bill and Jack. In 1872, the graves were removed to Cypress Hills
Cemetery. The following year, the cemetery land was divided into lots and
sold at auction.
    Despite this man's recollections, there were five stones standing in 1935.
Two were illegible. The surnames on the three remaining stones were
Ferrington, Meserole, and Robbins. By that time, the lot was completely
abandoned and used by the neighborhood children as a playground.
MAILING ADDRESS: c/o Gardner Sage Library
                 New Brunswick Theological Seminary
                 21 Seminary Place
                 New Brunswick, New Jersey 08901-1187
PHONE NUMBER: (908) 247-5243
RECORDS: Records of interments were packed into a trunk in the mid-1850s
and stored in a loft. When they were taken out years later, the papers fell
apart, having been eaten by mice. The surviving death registers date back to
1845 and were sent to the Gardner Sage Library when the congregation dis-
banded.
RESOURCES: Armbruster, Eugene L. "In Bushwick Churchyard." *The
Eastern District of Brooklyn*. New York. 1912, 157–58. (*See* the reprint of
Sparrow's Inscriptions below.)
    Cemetery, Church, and Town Records of New York State. vol. 70.
Washington, D.C.: Daughters of the American Revolution, 1935, 222.
(gravestone inscriptions)
    Eardeley, William A., trans. *Cemeteries in Kings and Queens Counties,
Long Island, New York: 1753 to 1913*.   vol. 1. Brooklyn, N.Y. June
13, 1914. (gravestone inscriptions)

Sparrow, George. "Tombstone Inscriptions in the Burial Ground of the Old Bushwick Church, Brooklyn, New York, Copied August 1880." *Kings County Genealogical Club Collections*, vol. 1, no. 4 (1888).

Bushwick Village Cemetery

CATEGORY: Public
YEARS OF USE: Gravestones date 1655 to 1845
LOCATION: Kingsland Avenue, between Woodpoint Road and Withers Street, Greenpoint, Brooklyn.
HISTORY: This cemetery was the burial ground of the early settlers of Bushwick. With the extension of Kingsland Avenue through the cemetery in 1879, the remains were removed to a vault beneath the Bushwick Reformed Dutch Church. At the time of removal, there were less than a dozen gravestones, one dated 1655.
MAILING ADDRESS: N/A
PHONE NUMBER: N/A
RECORDS: N/A
RESOURCES: Armbruster, Eugene L. "Inscriptions on Tombstones in Ancient Bushwick Graveyard Still Visible in 1861." *The Eastern District of Brooklyn*. New York. 1912, 155.

Calvary Cemetery

CATEGORY: Roman Catholic
YEARS OF USE: 1848 to date
LOCATION: Bisected by the Long Island Expressway and the Brooklyn-Queens Expressway, Woodside, Queens.
HISTORY: Owned and managed by the Archdiocese of New York, Calvary Cemetery has had more interments than any other cemetery in the United States. In the early 1990s, there were nearly three million graves, a number greater than the living population of Queens. For many years, there were more burials at Calvary Cemetery than in any other cemetery in the city.

In the mid-1800s, Calvary was the only cemetery where the "deserving poor" could be buried for free (excepting New York City's public cemeteries). These graves were obtained only upon the recommendation of a clergyman.

During the Civil War, Calvary set aside four plots for the interment of Catholic soldiers whose remains were not otherwise provided for. New York City erected a soldiers' monument on the site in 1866.

The first section of the cemetery is known as First Calvary Cemetery, Calvary Cemetery, and Old Calvary Cemetery. It includes the Alsop Family Burial Ground, the only known Protestant burial ground within a Roman Catholic cemetery. Poor Irish immigrants from the tenements of lower Manhattan were among the first to be buried in First Calvary. It is located on the west side of Laurel Hill Boulevard, between the Long Island Expressway and Review Avenue.

By 1867, First Calvary Cemetery was full, and the trustees began to purchase nearby farms for the creation of Second Calvary Cemetery. Second Calvary is on the west side of 58th Street, between Queens Boulevard and the

Brooklyn-Queens Expressway. Land acquisition for this section ended in 1888.

Third Calvary Cemetery was established in 1879, on the west side of 58th Street, between the Brooklyn-Queens Expressway and the Long Island Expressway. Fourth Calvary Cemetery was established in 1900, on the west side of 58th Street, between the Long Island Expressway and 55th Avenue.

Individually, and together, Second, Third, and Fourth Calvary Cemeteries have all been referred to as New Calvary Cemetery.

MAILING ADDRESS: Calvary Cemetery
                        49-02 Laurel Hill Boulevard
                        Flushing, New York 11377-7396

PHONE NUMBER: (718) 786-8000

RECORDS: Burial records are available for a fee. You must know the date of death or burial, since Calvary's records are arranged by date. There are no records for the years 1848 to 1852.

RESOURCES: Ardolina, Rosemary Muscarella. *Old Calvary Cemetery: New Yorkers Carved in Stone.* Bowie, Md: Heritage Books, 1996. (limited number of gravestone inscriptions)

Canarsie Cemetery

CATEGORY: Non-sectarian

YEARS OF USE: circa 1888 to date

LOCATION: 1370 Remsen Avenue, on the west side of the street, between Church Lane and Avenue K, Canarsie, Brooklyn.

HISTORY: This property has been a municipal cemetery since its purchase in 1888 by the Town of Flatlands, which later became part of New York City. New York City has been trying to sell the burial ground for the last thirty years. An estimated 6,400 people are buried here.

MAILING ADDRESS: NYC Department of General Services
                        2 Lafayette Street
                        New York, New York 10007-1378

PHONE NUMBER: (718) 251-6934

RECORDS: Burial records are housed at the New York City Department of General Services. Requests for information must be made in writing.

RESOURCES: N/A

Cannon Street Baptist Church Cemetery

CATEGORY: Baptist

YEARS OF USE: circa 1835 to circa 1855

LOCATION: Woodpoint Road, between Withers Street and Frost Street, Bushwick, Brooklyn.

HISTORY: This burial ground was used by the Cannon Street Baptist Church of Manhattan. Although the remains in the burial ground were probably removed to Cypress Hills Cemetery in 1864, the cemetery remained on maps until 1869.

MAILING ADDRESS: Cypress Hills Cemetery
                        833 Jamaica Avenue
                        Brooklyn, New York 11208-1593

PHONE NUMBER: (718) 277-2900

RECORDS: Records are housed on site. Write for searches.

RESOURCES: *Cypress Hills Cemetery*. Brooklyn, N. Y.: Cyprus Hills Cemetery, 1880. (extensive list of plot owners and location of plot, maps, rules, and history of cemetery)

Carmel Cemetery
See Mount Carmel Cemetery or Our Lady of Mount Carmel Churchyard.

Carmine Street Presbyterian Churchyard and Vaults
See West Presbyterian Churchyard and Vaults.

Cedar Grove Cemetery

CATEGORY: Non-sectarian

YEARS OF USE: August 1893 to date

LOCATION: 13004 Horace Harding Expressway, Flushing, Queens. The cemetery borders Mount Hebron Cemetery and 61st through 64th Roads.

HISTORY: N/A

MAILING ADDRESS: Cedar Grove Cemetery
                        13416 Horace Harding Expressway
                        Flushing, New York 11367-1099

PHONE NUMBER: (718) 939-2041

RECORDS: Inquire by mail, including name of deceased, date of death, and location of grave (if known). A 1902 pamphlet for the cemetery indicated that its registers contain the name of owner of plot, name of deceased, place of birth, age, married or single, place of death, time of death, cause of death, name of undertaker, size of coffin, date of interment, and time of departure for the cemetery.

RESOURCES: N/A

Cedar Street Presbyterian Churchyard
See Scotch Presbyterian Churchyard.

Cemetery of the Ascension Burying Ground
See Trinity Chapel Burial Ground.

Cemetery Hill
See Bedell-Decker Family Burial Ground.

Cemetery of Congregation Shaare Zedek

CATEGORY: Jewish
YEARS OF USE: circa 1848 to 1851
LOCATION: Madison Avenue, at an undetermined location between 70th and 79th Streets, Manhattan.
HISTORY: The Cemetery of Congregation Shaare Zedek closed in 1851, following a ban on burials below 86th Street in Manhattan. The dead were removed to Bayside Cemetery.
MAILING ADDRESS: c/o Bayside Cemetery
      80-35 Pitkin Avenue
      Jamaica, New York 11417-1228
PHONE NUMBER: (718) 843-4840
RECORDS: The Mokom Sholom Cemetery Recording Project has attempted to mark down the names of everyone in Bayside Cemetery through the use of cemetery records, death certificates, obituaries, wills, family histories, and gravestones.
RESOURCES: The Mokom Sholom Cemetery Recording Project's list of names is distributed as MOKOMCEM.EXE and is available on the Internet at
  <ftp://ftp.cac.psu.edu/pub/genealogy/text/jewish/mokomcem.exe>.

Cemetery of the Evergreens

CATEGORY: Non-sectarian
YEARS OF USE: 1851 to date
LOCATION: 1629 Bushwick Avenue, at Interborough Parkway (Jackie Robinson Parkway), East New York, Brooklyn.
HISTORY: In an 1895 review of cemeteries, the *Brooklyn Daily Eagle* extolled the virtues of this burial ground. "It abounds in beauties, and its great natural advantages have been aided by the skill of the landscape gardener... Inviting footpaths wind their pleasant ways over and around the hills and explore each shady nook and dell." The *Eagle* added optimistically, "Evergreens, though easily accessible from all parts... is so far removed from Brooklyn that the city will not surround it for many years to come."

Cemetery of the Evergreens received over 100,000 bodies in its first forty years; many of those were removed from graveyards in Manhattan. Among the many thousands buried here are victims of the Triangle Shirtwaist Fire of 1911.
MAILING ADDRESS: Cemetery of the Evergreens
      1629 Bushwick Avenue
      Brooklyn, New York 11207-1849
PHONE NUMBER: (718) 455-5300
RECORDS: The cemetery will verify interment over the phone, but you must

make requests for copies of the burial record in writing. The records contain the decedent's name, age, date of death, place of death, and date of burial.
RESOURCES: N/A

Cemetery of the Holy Cross
See Holy Cross Cemetery.

Cemetery of the Resurrection

CATEGORY: Roman Catholic
YEARS OF USE: 1979 to date
LOCATION: 361 Sharrott Avenue, between Amboy Road and Hylan Boulevard, Mount Loretto, Staten Island.
HISTORY: Cemetery of the Resurrection is owned by the Archdiocese of New York.
MAILING ADDRESS: Cemetery of the Resurrection
                  361 Sharrott Avenue
                  Staten Island, New York 10309-3321
PHONE NUMBER: (718) 356-7738
RECORDS: Records are housed at the cemetery.
RESOURCES: N/A

Cemetery of Saints Patrick and Peter

CATEGORY: Roman Catholic
YEARS OF USE: 1828 to 1842
LOCATION: 49th to 50th Streets, between Park Avenue and 5th Avenue, Manhattan.
HISTORY: In 1828, Saint Patrick's Cathedral and Saint Peter's Church jointly purchased this property for use as a cemetery. The land turned out to be too rocky for its intended purpose. In 1842, the Church of Saint John the Evangelist was erected on the site, but it was torn down in 1852 to make way for Saint Patrick's Cathedral. There were no known burials at this site.
MAILING ADDRESS: N/A
PHONE NUMBER: N/A
RECORDS: N/A
RESOURCES: N/A

Cemetery of Temple Shaaray Tefilah

CATEGORY: Jewish
YEARS OF USE: Circa 1845 to 1853

LOCATION: South side of West 105th Street, between 9th and 10th Avenues, Manhattan.

HISTORY: The remains in this cemetery were removed to an unspecified location, possibly to Beth-Olom Fields Cemetery of which Shaaray Tefilah is part-owner.

The congregation was formed in 1845 by members of the Elm Street Synagogue.

MAILING ADDRESS: Temple Shaaray Tefilah
                  250 East 79th Street
                  New York, New York 10021-1294
PHONE NUMBER: (212) 535-8008
RECORDS: N/A
RESOURCES: N/A

Chaari-Zedek Cemetery
See Bayside Cemetery.

Chatham Square Cemetery

CATEGORY: Jewish
YEARS OF USE: circa 1656 to 1831
LOCATION: Chatham Square, Manhattan.
HISTORY: Congregation Shearith Israel began in 1654 with the arrival in New York of twenty-three Sephardic Jewish refugees from Brazil. The congregation was granted land for use as a burial ground on 12 February 1656. The cemetery expanded in 1681, and again in 1729. It eventually covered all of Chatham Square. The oldest burials were in the section nearest to Madison Street.

During the Revolutionary War, the burial ground was fortified by Patriot Soldiers to defend New York City from the British.

The Chatham Square Cemetery was actively used for over a century, but new laws and encroaching development overtook the grounds. Around 1800, the opening of Madison Street destroyed a portion of the cemetery. Part of the property was sold for the extension of Oliver Street in 1822. The following year, the cemetery virtually shut down when burials in the southern portion of Manhattan were prohibited.

The cemetery suffered its final indignity when the Bowery was extended to Franklin Square in 1856. That year, Congregation Shearith Israel was forced to moved 253 graves to its cemetery on 21st Street, in Manhattan, and three graves to Beth-Olom Fields Cemetery, in Queens. Only seventy bodies were identified. The remains were deposited in separate coffins and placed in separate graves. Where possible, the new graves were marked by gravestones from the old burial ground and the inscriptions were copied. The earliest date of death was 1669, the most recent was 1831.

A small portion of the cemetery remains today. Gershom Mendex Seixas, a prominent rabbi and Patriot of the Revolution, is among those buried at Chatham Square.

This cemetery is sometimes referred to as The Jews' Burial Ground, 13 and 1/2 Oliver Street, and 55 Saint James Place.

MAILING ADDRESS: c/o Congregation Shearith Israel
  8 West 70th Street
  New York, New York 10023-4601

PHONE NUMBER: (212) 873-0300

RECORDS: N/A

RESOURCES: *Cemetery, Church, and Town Records of New York State.*
  vol. 116. Washington, D.C.: Daughters of the American Revolution, 1938-1939, 193–264. (gravestone inscriptions)

  de Sola Pool, Rev. Dr. David. *Portraits Etched in Stone: Early Jewish Settlers 1682 to 1831.* New York: Columbia University Press, 1952, 491–504. (burials and removals)

  Phillips, Rosalie S. "A Burial Place for the Jewish Nation Forever." *Publications of the American Jewish Historical Society* vol. no. 17. (1909): 93–122. (gravestone inscriptions and list of removals)

Cherry Lane Second Asbury African Methodist Episcopal Cemetery

CATEGORY: African, Methodist Episcopal

YEARS OF USE: circa 1850 to circa 1951

LOCATION: Forest Avenue and Livermoore Avenue, Port Richmond, Staten Island.

HISTORY: John W. Blake deeded this property to the Second Asbury African Methodist Episcopal Church on 25 March 1850. Historian William T. Davis visited the site in 1889 and noted that the church building had been pulled down and used for fencing. He also observed that the majority of the graves in the yard had been marked with wooden stakes and mounds of dirt. There were two gravestones. The first was a broken marble slab dedicated to the memory of Augustin Jones who died 18 February 1873 at the age of thirty-three. The second was a white wooden board, neatly lettered in black, to the memory of Aaron Bush, born "April 5, 1842, King and Queen County, Virginia," and died "August 2, 1889, aged 46 years, 4 months, and 2 days."

The cemetery remained in limbo until a few surviving members of the congregation formed the African Methodist Church Cemetery of Staten Island in 1927. The Second African Methodist Episcopal Church deeded the property to the new group in 1929, and the cemetery remained on Richmond County maps until 1951.

The City of New York illegally seized the cemetery for non-payment of taxes in 1950. In a settlement with the City, the trustees of the African

Methodist Episcopal Church Cemetery agreed to sell the property. It was purchased by the Shell Oil Company for use as a gas station.

The remains in the burial ground may have been removed to the Moravian Cemetery, but human bones are still found on the property.

The gas station was subsequently torn down, and the site is now home to a shopping center. At the request of The Friends of Abandoned Cemeteries of Staten Island, a plaque was placed inside the shopping center, denoting the property's significance as an African-American cemetery.

Benjamin Prine (Perine), the last person to live under slavery on Staten Island, was buried in this cemetery. He died on 3 October 1900 at the age of 104.

This cemetery is also known as the Old Slave Burying Ground.

MAILING ADDRESS: N/A

PHONE NUMBER: N/A

RECORDS: N/A

RESOURCES: Davis, William T. "Homestead Graves." *Proceedings of the Natural Science Association of Staten Island*. Staten Island, N. Y. Special Number 9, December 1889. (gravestone inscriptions)

Dickenson, Richard, and Julie Moody Ojelade, comps. *Afro-American Vital Records and 20th Century Abstracts: Richmond County, Staten Island, 1915 and 1925 New York State Census Records*. Staten Island, N.Y.: Sandy Ground Historical Society, 1986, 189–192. ("The Old Slaves Burying Ground and Benjamin Perine")

Chevra B'nai Sholau Cemetery
See Mount Zion Cemetery.

Christ Lutheran Churchyard

CATEGORY: Lutheran

YEARS OF USE: 1750 to circa 1823

LOCATION: Northeast corner of Frankfort Street and William Street, Manhattan.

HISTORY: Christ Church was established in 1750 by German-speaking members of Trinity Lutheran Church. Trinity's Church was destroyed by fire during the Revolutionary War and, in 1784, the two churches merged. The new congregation was known as The United German Lutheran Churches in the City of New York. Services were held in the building of the former Christ Church. The congregation joined Saint Matthew's Church when The United Church closed its doors in 1831.

The churchyard probably closed when interments south of Canal Street were banned in 1823.

Christ Church was nicknamed "The Swamp Church," after the swampy land that once surrounded its property.

MAILING ADDRESS: c/o Saint Matthew's Lutheran Church
                         200 Sherman Avenue
                         New York, New York 10034-3301
PHONE NUMBER: (212) 567-2172
RECORDS: Original records are held at St. Matthew's Church.
RESOURCES: "Christ Church Burials." *Church Records*. vol. 86. New York: Holland Society of New York. (burials, 1784–1804)
    Register of Christ Church. (New York Genealogical and Biographical Society, New York. Microfilm, no. 32.1, reel no. 2. (burials, 1752–1808)
    Register of Christ Church. New York Genealogical and Biographical Society, New York. Microfilm, no. 32.1, reel no. 3. (burials, 1767–1773; funerals, 1808–1838)

Christ Mission Methodist Church Cemetery
See Lake Cemetery.

Christ Mission Rehoboth Pentecostal Church Cemetery
See Lake Cemetery.

Christ Protestant Episcopal Churchyard

CATEGORY: Protestant Episcopal
YEARS OF USE: circa 1794 to 1823
LOCATION: Ann Street, between Nassau Street and William Street, Manhattan.
HISTORY: Christ Episcopal Church was established on Ann Street in 1794, where it remained until 1823. The bodies in the churchyard were removed to an unspecified location about ten years later.
MAILING ADDRESS: Christ and Saint Stephen's Episcopal Church
                        122 West 69th Street
                        New York, New York 10023
PHONE NUMBER: (212) 787-2755
RECORDS: N/A
RESOURCES: N/A

Chrystie Street Cemetery
May refer to Saint Philip's Cemetery, among others.

Church of Ascension Churchyard
See Trinity Chapel Burial Ground.

Citizens' Union-Mount Pleasant Cemetery

CATEGORY: African, Non-sectarian
YEARS OF USE: circa 1851 to 1869

LOCATION: The cemetery was generally in the area bounded by Lincoln Place, Ralph Avenue, Rochester Avenue, and Sterling Place, Bedford-Stuyvesant, Brooklyn.

HISTORY: Citizens' Union Cemetery was established in September 1851 on nearly thirty acres. Its founders advertised that the cemetery did not have any "rule which excludes any person from sepulture within its borders, on account of complexion," although the grounds were "designed more particularly as a burial place for the colored."

Fees were minimal and sometimes waived in cases of extreme poverty. Citizens' Union suffered immediate financial losses, causing it to reorganize as the Mount Pleasant Cemetery Association in June of 1853. Even so, the cemetery was still advertised as the Citizens' Union Cemetery.

Financial problems continued to plague the trustees. By 1866, more than half the cemetery property had been sold to raise money. Infighting and neighborhood opposition to the cemetery contributed to its demise. The trustees stopped advertising in 1869, selling part of the remaining grounds to the City of Brooklyn that year. A condition of the sale required that the bodies be removed from the property. The remainder of the cemetery was sold in 1872.

The trustees purchased a one-acre plot at Cypress Hills Cemetery and hired two men to remove all the bodies from Citizens' Union. Construction workers later discovered several bodies that were surreptitiously buried by one of the cemetery founders, and thus missed in the removal. These were allegedly removed by steam shovel and dumped alongside the road.

MAILING ADDRESS: c/o Cypress Hills Cemetery
833 Jamaica Avenue
Brooklyn, New York 11208-1593

PHONE NUMBER: (718) 277-2900

RECORDS: Cypress Hills' records are housed on site. Write for searches.

RESOURCES: *Cypress Hills Cemetery.* Brooklyn, N.Y.: Cyprus Hills Cemetery, 1880. (extensive list of plot owners and location of plot, maps, rules, and history of cemetery)

City Cemetery of Flushing
See Colored Cemetery of Flushing.

Clove Meeting House Cemetery

CATEGORY: Baptist
YEARS OF USE: Gravestones date 1821 to 1868
LOCATION: Richmond Road, on the west side, between Clove Road and Douglas Road, Emerson Hill, Staten Island.
HISTORY: Erected in October 1809, the Clove Meeting House was the first Baptist church on Staten Island. Its congregation diminished in size during

the ensuing years, and the church building was finally lost in an 1868 lawsuit. The German Mission of Saint John's Episcopal Church leased the property in 1865, followed by the Edgewater School in 1869. The church building was torn down in 1877.

The cemetery was neglected and ultimately abandoned. Its gravestones are mostly gone, although some are now stored at the Richmondtown Restoration on Staten Island. In 1998, Friends of Abandoned Cemeteries of Staten Island reported that the headstones of Hendrick Kruser (died 1831) and Charles Ford Martin (died 1825) were the only two remaining in the graveyard.

This cemetery is sometimes called Fountain Cemetery because there are more members of the Fountain family buried in the yard than any other family.

MAILING ADDRESS: N/A

PHONE NUMBER: N/A

RECORDS: N/A

RESOURCES: Bricks, Morris. "The Old Clove Baptist Church and Cemetery: 1809 to Present." *Staten Island Historian*. vol. 4, no. 3–4 (Winter/Spring 1987): 25–28. (history of cemetery; limited genealogical data; gravestone inscriptions; photo)

Davis, William T. "Homestead Graves." *Proceedings of the Natural Science Association of Staten Island*. Staten Island, N.Y. Special Number 9, December 1889. (gravestone inscriptions)

Lane, Doris. "God's Quarter Acre: Old Clove Cemetery." *The FACSI Newsletter*, vol. 15, issue 1/2 (Spring/Summer 1998). (some gravestone inscriptions)

Clover Hill Burial Ground

CATEGORY: Military

YEARS OF USE: American Revolution

LOCATION: Clover Hill, intersection of Hicks Street and Orange Street, Brooklyn Heights, Brooklyn.

HISTORY: This burial ground was used by the British Army during the American Revolution. When the Hicks family took possession at the end of the war, they leveled the cemetery.

MAILING ADDRESS: N/A

PHONE NUMBER: N/A

RECORDS: N/A

RESOURCES: N/A

Cole Family Burial Ground and Vault

CATEGORY: Private
YEARS OF USE: circa 1820 to 1845
LOCATION: Intersection of Bailey Avenue and Albany Crescent, Kingsbridge, Bronx.
HISTORY: This burial ground was established by Jacob Cole in 1820. When he sold his property in 1845, Cole reserved his family's right to use the cemetery.

During the 1890s, the burial vault was severely vandalized by neighborhood boys who were known to roll skulls down the street or carry them about on sticks. Members of nearby Saint Stephen's Methodist Church were so incensed by the boys' behavior that they published a protest in an 1892 church bulletin. The burial ground was ultimately condemned in 1895 for a construction project. When the contractor attempted to remove the bodies in August of that year, Charles Schuyler claimed to be a descendant of Jacob Cole and had the remains transferred to his plot in Woodlawn Cemetery. Some jewelry was recovered during the transfer.

Although there were a few individual graves, most burials were in the family vault. Gravestones, if any, were few in number.
MAILING ADDRESS: c/o Woodlawn Cemetery
                  233rd Street and Webster Avenue
                  Bronx, New York 10471
PHONE NUMBER: (718) 920-0500
RECORDS: Woodlawn Cemetery records are housed on-site.
RESOURCES: N/A

Colored Cemetery of Flushing

CATEGORY: African, Public
YEARS OF USE: circa 1838 to 1898
LOCATION: North side of 46th Avenue, between 164th Street and 165th Street, Flushing, Queens.
HISTORY: The Town of Flushing purchased land from the Bowne family for use as a public cemetery in the late 1830s. Many of those buried here died during the cholera epidemics of 1838 and 1857, and during the small pox epidemics of 1844 and 1867. In total, there were an estimated 500 to 1,000 burials during the cemetery's sixty-year history. A recent study of town death registers suggests that over sixty percent of those buried here were of African heritage. More than half of the dead were under of the age of five.

The burial ground became Everett P. Martin Field, a playground, during the 1930s. Workers digging the park's wading pool unearthed "bones galore" and rare, valuable pennies that had once covered the eyes of the dead. Construction is said to have continued, "because there was no way to identify the dead." Indeed, only four gravestones were standing when the inscriptions were copied down in 1932.

The cemetery was recently "rediscovered." In February of 1997, city councilwoman Julia Harrison introduced a plan to end use of Everett P. Martin Field as a playground. The New York State Office of Parks, Recreation and Historic Preservation announced that the cemetery is eligible to be on the State and National Registers of Historic Places.

This burial ground is also known as the Old Flushing Cemetery and as the Bunn Cemetery.

MAILING ADDRESS: N/A
PHONE NUMBER: N/A
RECORDS: N/A
RESOURCES: Powell, Charles U., comp., and Alice H. Meigs, ed. *Description of Private and Family Cemeteries in the Borough of Queens.* City of New York, Borough of Queens, Topographical Bureau. Jamaica, N.Y.: Queens Borough Public Library, 1932. (gravestone inscriptions and maps)

Cooper's Cemetery
See Silver Mount Cemetery.

Cornell Family Burial Ground

CATEGORY: Private
YEARS OF USE: Gravestones date 1841 to 1850
LOCATION: 225th Street and the Long Island Expressway, Little Neck, Queens.
HISTORY: All efforts to preserve this cemetery at its original site failed in 1952 when construction work at a nearby shopping center opened some of the graves. The entire burial ground was removed to the Douglaston Zion Churchyard the following year.

Only four gravestones were standing in 1919. They were dedicated to the memory of members of the Cornell, Herrick, and Penny families.

MAILING ADDRESS: c/o Douglaston Zion Church
                243-01 Northern Boulevard
                Flushing, New York 11362-1161
PHONE NUMBER: (718) 225-0466
RECORDS: N/A
RESOURCES: Meigs, Alice H., ed., and The Topographical Bureau, comps. *Description of Private and Family Cemeteries in the Borough of Queens.* Jamaica, N.Y.: The Queens Borough Public Library, 1932. (gravestone inscriptions and maps)

Richard Cornell Family Burial Ground

CATEGORY: Private

YEARS OF USE: 1694 to 1821

LOCATION: Caffery Avenue, between Mott Avenue and New Haven Avenue, Far Rockaway, Queens.

HISTORY: Richard Cornell, the first European settler in the Rockaways, acquired Far Rockaway in 1687. He owned one of the first foundries on Long Island, held political office, and helped draft the Flushing Remonstrance, a plea for religious freedom in Queens. When he died on 11 August 1694, his family chose to bury him at a site where he enjoyed taking his evening walks. This site became the Richard Cornell Family Burial Ground. Cornell is buried with over two dozen relatives. Among them are Revolutionary War and War of 1812 veterans, colonial legislators, and a Native-American.

The estate remained in the Cornell family until it was sold for development in the nineteenth century. The cemetery was forgotten, and it fell into disrepair. By 1991, all of the gravestones were missing. Some believe that the city took the stones for safekeeping when the cemetery was landmarked in 1970, but the New York City Landmarks Commission says that the stones were not taken under its auspices. With the formation of the Cornell Cemetery Corporation in 1991, two stones were recovered: both taken by men who used to play in the cemetery as children. These stones are now at the Rockaway Museum.

The Cornell Cemetery Corporation has spent most of its resources cleaning the grounds, overseeing a non-invasive archaeological dig, and searching for additional gravestones. The Corporation hopes to recover land that has been encroached upon by the cemetery's neighbors, begin landscaping, and erect a single memorial shaft with the names of everyone buried in the cemetery. Restoration is scheduled to be finished by the year 2000.

MAILING ADDRESS: Cornell Cemetery Corporation
      c/o The Wave of Long Island
      Post Office Box 97
      Rockaway Beach, New York 11693-0097

PHONE NUMBER: (718) 634-4000

RECORDS: N/A

RESOURCES: Frost, Josephine C. trans. *Long Island Cemetery Inscriptions*. vol. 4. Brooklyn, N.Y.: PUBLISHER, March 1912. (gravestone inscriptions)

Powell, Charles U., comp., and Alice H. Meigs, ed. *Description of Private and Family Cemeteries in the Borough of Queens*. City of New York, Borough of Queens, Topographical Bureau. Jamaica, N.Y.: The Queens Borough Public Library, 1975 supplement. (gravestone inscriptions and maps)

Corpus Christi Monastery and Convent Cemetery

CATEGORY: Private
YEARS OF USE: 1889 to date
LOCATION: 1230 Lafayette Avenue, between Tiffany Street and Manida Street, Hunt's Point, Bronx.
HISTORY: This is the burial ground of sixty Nuns of Perpetual Adoration.
MAILING ADDRESS: Corpus Christi Monastery and Convent
      1230 Lafayette Avenue
      Bronx, New York 10474-5399
PHONE NUMBER: (718) 328-6996
RECORDS: N/A
RESOURCES: N/A

Corsa Family Burial Ground

CATEGORY: Private
YEARS OF USE: Pre-1840
LOCATION: The circular garden behind Saint John's Hall, Rose Hill Campus, Fordham University, Bronx.
HISTORY: The Corsa family once owned the land that Fordham University now occupies. Their burial ground was discovered in the 1840s during construction of Saint John's Hall.
MAILING ADDRESS: c/o Fordham University Archivist
      Fordham University-Rose Hill Campus
      441 East Fordham Road
      Bronx, New York 10458-9993
PHONE NUMBER: (718) 817-1000
RECORDS: N/A
RESOURCES: N/A

Cortelyou-Barkelou Burial Ground
See Barkelou-Cortelyou Burial Ground.

Covenantor Cemetery

CATEGORY: Reformed Presbyterian
YEARS OF USE: circa 1851 to 1938
LOCATION: Poplar Street, Westchester, Bronx.
HISTORY: The oldest grave in this cemetery was that of infant Eliza Acheson who died on 13 April 1805. She was moved to this cemetery with her mother, and others, from the Scotch Presbyterian Church Cemetery on West 28th Street, probably after the 1851 ban on burials below 86th Street in Manhattan.

Gravestone inscriptions indicate that most of the burials were of Scotch-Irish immigrants. Scotch Presbyterian Church conducted a mission in Manhattan's Chinatown, and there is anecdotal evidence to suggest that some deceased Chinese immigrants were temporarily buried here until their families could afford to send the remains back to China.

Scotch Presbyterian Church is known as "Second Presbyterian Church" today. Second Presbyterian was unable to give further details about this cemetery, as it was not aware of its existence.

Covenantor Cemetery is also known as Bronxville Cemetery.

MAILING ADDRESS: Second Presbyterian Church
            6 West 96th Street
            New York, New York 10025-6506

PHONE NUMBER: (212) 749-1700

RECORDS: The Second Presbyterian Church does not have records dating back to the nineteenth century. A spokesperson for the church stated that if anyone kept burial or death registers, Second Presbyterian Church does not know where they are located today.

RESOURCES: *Cemetery, Church, and Town Records of New York State.* vol. 118. Washington, D.C.: Daughters of the American Revolution, 1939, 50–54. (gravestone inscriptions)

Cruser Family Burial Ground and Vault

See Cornelius Kreuzer Family Burial Ground and Vault.

Cumberson Family Burial Ground

CATEGORY: Private

YEARS OF USE: Gravestones date 1829 to 1849

LOCATION: West side of 58th Street between 47th Avenue and Queens Boulevard, Woodside, Queens.

HISTORY: The Cumberson Family Burial Ground is now part of Calvary Cemetery. Among those buried here are members of the Cornish, Cumberson, Ford, and Gnezer families.

MAILING ADDRESS: c/o Calvary Cemetery
            49-02 Laurel Hill Boulevard
            Flushing, New York 11377-7396

PHONE NUMBER: (718) 786-8000

RECORDS: Calvary does not have records for interments prior to 1852 and may not have much information about this burial ground.

RESOURCES: Ardolina, Rosemary Muscarella. *Old Calvary Cemetery: New Yorkers Carved in Stone.* Bowie, Md: Heritage Books, 1996. (gravestone inscriptions)

Frost, Josephine C. trans. *Long Island Cemetery Inscriptions.* vol. 1. Brooklyn, N.Y. March 1912. (gravestone inscriptions)

Meigs, Alice H., ed., and The Topographical Bureau, comps. *Description of Private and Family Cemeteries in the Borough of Queens.* Jamaica, N.Y.: The Queens Borough Public Library, 1932. (gravestone inscriptions and maps)

Cypress Hills Cemetery

CATEGORY: Non-sectarian
YEARS OF USE: 1 May 1849 to date
LOCATION: 833 Jamaica Avenue, north side, between Cypress Hills Street and Lincoln Avenue, East New York, Brooklyn.
HISTORY: With the development of for-profit cemeteries in the mid-nineteenth century, a group of investors purchased several hundred acres on the Queens-Brooklyn border for the creation of Cypress Hills Cemetery. Investor C. Edward Lester promoted the new cemetery through newspaper articles and pamphlets that boasted about Cypress Hill's "charming rural scene."

In 1866, the *New York Times* concurred, writing that, "the view from the crown of the hill... is one of the finest on Long Island." The paper further observed that the cemetery appealed to the middle class because the lots were more affordable that those at competing Green-Wood Cemetery.

A variety of benevolent, humane, and social groups purchased plots: the Bank Clerk's Association; the Journalistic Fraternity; and the Metropolitan Police Board are just three. Ecclesiastical groups purchased plots as well. Cypress Hills received 35,000 bodies from Manhattan churchyards alone after its opening in 1849.

Despite numerous removals to Cypress Hills Cemetery, the burial ground has authorized disinterments of its own. In 1931, three Chinese Societies received permission to exhume 309 bodies, buried there between 1902 and 1913, for removal to China.

The cemetery has also lost its share of land. In 1914, Cypress Hills sold eighty-five acres to neighboring Mount Lebanon Cemetery. It lost property when the Interborough Parkway (Jackie Robinson Parkway) was created in 1932. Finally, the United States Government and the State of New York acquired land from Cypress Hills Cemetery for the creation of Cypress Hills National Cemetery.

Baseball-player Jackie Robinson and actress Mae West are among the celebrities buried here.
MAILING ADDRESS: Cypress Hills Cemetery
                        833 Jamaica Avenue
                        Brooklyn, New York 11208-1593
PHONE NUMBER: (718) 277-2900
RECORDS: Records are housed on site. Write for searches.
RESOURCES: *Cypress Hills Cemetery.* Brooklyn, N.Y.: Cypress Hills

Cemetery, 1880. (extensive list of plot owners and location of plot, maps, rules, and history of cemetery)

"Cypress Hills Cemetery, Jamaica Avenue and Crescent Street, Brooklyn, New York." *Cemetery, Church, and Town Records of New York State*. vol. 234. Washington, D.C.: Daughters of the American Revolution, 1960-1961, 48. (Darrow family interments in lots 181 and 244)

"The Forgotten Dead: Many Neglected Graves in Cypress Hills Cemetery." *The Brooklyn Daily Eagle*, 13 August 1893, p. 8, col. 7. (description of Methodist and Chinese plots)

Kraska, Kurt T. *The History of Cypress Hills Cemetery and Its Permanent Residents*. Queens, N.Y.: Woodhaven Cultural and Historical Society, 198–.

"Our Cities of the Dead." *The Brooklyn Daily Eagle*, 28 April 1895, p. 28, col. 1. (burials in the New York Press plot; other notable burials)

Cypress Hills National Cemetery

CATEGORY: Military
YEARS OF USE: 1862 to 1954
LOCATION: 625 Jamaica Avenue, north side of the avenue between Highland Park and Salem Fields Cemetery, East New York, Brooklyn.
HISTORY: Cypress Hills National Cemetery was originally established as a burial ground for Union soldiers and their Confederate prisoners who died in military hospitals and camps in and around New York City during the Civil War. Union soldiers were buried in the western section of the cemetery on either side of "Cypress Way" beginning in April 1862.

An estimated 20,000 veterans from the Civil War and later wars are interred here. Sailors buried in the United States Naval Hospital Cemetery were reinterred here in 1926. The cemetery is now full.
MAILING ADDRESS: Cypress Hills National Cemetery
                 c/o Long Island National Cemetery
                 2040 Wellwood Avenue
                 Farmingdale, New York 11735-1211
PHONE NUMBER: (516) 454-4949
RECORDS: Information is available through the Long Island National Cemetery. Availability of in-depth searches will be determined on a case-by-case basis.
RESOURCES: Holt, Dean W. *American Military Cemeteries*. Jefferson, N.C.: McFarland and Company, Inc., 1992.

Reamy, Martha, and William, comps. *Index to the Roll of Honor*. Reprint. Baltimore, Md.: Genealogical Publishing Company, 1995. (Note: Use with United States Quartermaster's *Roll of Honor*.)

United States Quartermaster's Department. *Roll of Honor: Names of Soldiers who Died in Defense of the American Union, Interred in National Cemeteries*. vols. 13, 16. Reprint. Baltimore, Md.: Genealogical Publishing Company, 1994. (Note: The list of "colored" troops in vol. 13 begins on p. 56.)

Delafield Family Burial Ground

CATEGORY: Private
YEARS OF USE: nineteenth century
LOCATION: East side of Vernon Boulevard, between 35th Avenue and 36th Avenue, Astoria, Queens.
HISTORY: This burial ground was a circular plot east of the John Delafield House, later called the George Brooks House. The house was erected in 1791 and demolished in June of 1886. The fate of the cemetery is unknown.
MAILING ADDRESS: N/A
PHONE NUMBER: N/A
RECORDS: N/A
RESOURCES: N/A

Delaplaine Family Burial Ground
See Bergen Family Burial Ground.

Douglass Memorial Park Cemetery, Frederick
See Frederick Douglass Memorial Park Cemetery.

Douglaston Zion Churchyard

CATEGORY: Protestant Episcopal
YEARS OF USE: Gravestones date 1800 to 1935
LOCATION: 243-01 Northern Boulevard, north side of the boulevard between Douglaston Parkway and 243rd Street, Douglaston, Queens.
HISTORY: The Douglaston Zion Church dates back to 1830, but the grave-yard is known to be older. It is presumed to be the only burial ground in the Little Neck area of Queens.

This cemetery is for the exclusive use of present or former members of the church. Remains from the Waters Cemetery were reinterred here between 1930 and 1938.

Bloodgood H. Cutter, the poet who was celebrated as the "poet lariat" of Mark Twain's *Innocents Abroad,* is among those buried here.

MAILING ADDRESS: Douglaston Zion Episcopal Church
                 243-01 Northern Boulevard
                 Flushing, New York 11362-1161
PHONE NUMBER: (718) 225-0466
RECORDS: N/A
RESOURCES: Frost, Josephine C. trans. *Long Island Cemetery Inscriptions.* vol. 6. Brooklyn, N.Y. 1904. (Douglaston Zion Church gravestone inscriptions)

Haviland, Frank. *Zion Episcopal Churchyard Inscriptions, Douglaston, Long Island.* Manuscript. Brooklyn, N.Y.: Brooklyn Historical Society, 1904. (interments to 1904)

Records 1830-1880 and Cemetery Inscriptions, Zion Episcopal Church, Douglaston, Queens County, New York. Queens, N.Y.: Greater Ridgewood Historical Society, 1970. (church registers; gravestone inscriptions)

Stryker-Rodda, Kenn, trans. "Records of Zion Church of Little Neck at Douglaston, Queens County, New York, 1830 to 1880." *The New York Genealogical and Biographical Record* 98, no. 1 (January 1967): 39–46. Continued in numbers 2 and 3. (funerals; burials in churchyard)

Joseph Rodman Drake Cemetery
See Hunt Family Burial Ground.

Duryea Farm Cemetery

CATEGORY: Private
YEARS OF USE: Before 1919
LOCATION: 30th Avenue, between 83rd Street and 84th Street, Woodside, Queens.
HISTORY: By 1919, the only evidence of this burial ground was a brick vault, several feet below ground, with crops growing on it. The headstones were totally obliterated.
MAILING ADDRESS: N/A
PHONE NUMBER: N/A
RECORDS: N/A
RESOURCES: Powell, Charles U., comp. and Alice H. Meigs, ed. *Description of Private and Family Cemeteries in the Borough of Queens.* City of New York, Borough of Queens, Topographical Bureau. Jamaica, N.Y.: Queens Borough Public Library, 1932. (map)

Dyckman-Nagle Cemetery

CATEGORY: Private

YEARS OF USE: Known burials 1801 to 1908

LOCATION: West 212th Street, south side, between 9th and 10th Avenues, Manhattan.

HISTORY: A bookkeeper and woodcutter by trade, Jan Dyckman traveled from Germany to New York in 1661. He joined with Jan Nagle to create a three hundred-acre farm, one of the largest in Manhattan. The farm remained in the Dyckman family for over two hundred years.

In 1905, the Dyckman remains, excepting Staats Morris Dyckman and his immediate family, were removed and may have been taken to Oakland Cemetery in Yonkers. In 1926, the City of New York disinterred the rest of the cemetery. Of the 417 bodies that were removed, only 67 were identified (51 by way of nameplates), among them Concklins, Hadleys, and Vermilyeas. The remains were taken to Lot 16150 in Woodlawn Cemetery.

MAILING ADDRESS: c/o Woodlawn Cemetery
    233rd Street and Webster Avenue
    Bronx, New York 10471

PHONE NUMBER: (718) 920-0500

RECORDS: Woodlawn's records are stored on-site.

RESOURCES: "Alphabetical List of Known Dead Removed from Nagle Cemetery." *Cemetery, Church, and Town Records of New York State.* vol. 61. Washington, D.C.: Daughters of the American Revolution, 1934, 12–13.

Edsall, Thomas H. "Inscriptions from the Dyckman Burial Ground." *The New York Genealogical and Biographical Record.* 21, no. 2 (April 1890): 81–83. (gravestone inscriptions)

Haacker, Fred C. "Dyckman-Nagle Cemetery, New York City." *The Detroit Society for Genealogical Research Magazine.* 18, no. 4 (April 1955): 111–112. (alphabetical list of dead identified by name plates on coffins)

Haacker, Fred C., comp. *Burials in the Dyckman-Nagle Burial Ground, and the Berrian Graveyards, Near Kingsbridge, New York City.* Manuscript. New York: U.S. History, Local History and Genealogy Division, New York Public Library, 1954. (gravestone inscriptions; reburials; alphabetical list of dead identified by name plates on coffins)

East Bank Cemetery

CATEGORY: Jewish
YEARS OF USE: 1803
LOCATION: North side of West 13th Street, between 6th Avenue and 7th Avenue, Manhattan.
HISTORY: Congregation Shearith Israel purchased this property in 1803 and planned to use it for the burial of the victims of contagious disease. Wolfe Pollock, who died of yellow fever on 10 October 1803, was the first and only person buried here.

A short time later, New York City announced the extension of West Thirteenth Street, a development that was going to run right through the middle of the new burial ground. Congregation Shearith Israel purchased land for its Milligan Street Cemetery a short time later. Wolfe Pollock was transferred to the new grounds on 16 March 1805.

East Bank Cemetery is also known as the Thirteenth Street Cemetery.
MAILING ADDRESS: N/A
PHONE NUMBER: N/A
RECORDS: N/A
RESOURCES: de Sola Pool, Rev. Dr. David. *Portraits Etched in Stone: Early Jewish Settlers 1682 to 1831*. New York: Columbia University Press, 1952, 121–22. (map, history)

Eighteenth Street Methodist Episcopal Churchyard and Vaults

CATEGORY: Methodist Episcopal
YEARS OF USE: circa 1836 to 1851

LOCATION: 305-7 West 18th Street, north side of the street, between 8th and 9th Avenues, extending to 19th Street, Manhattan.

HISTORY: The 18th Street Methodist Episcopal Church was established in 1828. Its services were held in a small, wooden building on West 20th Street between 8th Avenue and 9th Avenue. Interments in the churchyard probably continued until New York City banned burials below 86th Street in 1851.

In 1885, the congregation decided to enlarge and remodel the church. To pay for the work, they decided to empty the one hundred and twenty eight vaults in the churchyard and sell the property. The congregation had some difficulty convincing the owners of the private vaults to agree to the disinterment, and work on the removals did not begin until November 1886. An estimated three hundred bodies were removed to Woodlawn Cemetery lots 5687 and 5689 to 5703.

Records indicate that the public vaults behind the parsonage were never disturbed, apparently forgotten. The congregation merged with the Metropolitan-Duane Church in 1945.

The old 18th Street Church was demolished the week of 13 March 1950 for construction of a six-story apartment building. Bones, along with eleven skulls, were unearthed on 24 March and were estimated to be between one hundred and one hundred fifty years old. The new congregation voted to assume responsibility for the remains. They were reinterred in a cemetery plot owned by the church.

MAILING ADDRESS: c/o Metropolitan-Duane United Methodist Church
201 West 13th Street
New York, New York 10011-7795
PHONE NUMBER: (212) 243-5740
RECORDS: N/A
RESOURCES: N/A

Eleventh Street Cemetery, East

CATEGORY: Roman Catholic
YEARS OF USE: circa 1832 to 1849
LOCATION: East side of 1st Avenue, between 11th Street and 12th Street, extending almost to Avenue A, Manhattan.
HISTORY: In March of 1909, the five thousand bodies in the 11th Street Cemetery were removed to Calvary Cemetery, Section 4B of the Old (or "First") Division. No records were kept at the time of reburial, and the names and dates of death of those who were reinterred are not known to Calvary Cemetery.
MAILING ADDRESS: c/o Calvary Cemetery
49-02 Laurel Hills Boulevard
Flushing, New York 11377-7396
PHONE NUMBER: (718) 786-8000

RECORDS: The only confirmed reburial is that of Lorenzo Da Ponte, librettist for Mozart, but the exact location of his grave at Calvary Cemetery is unknown.

RESOURCES: *Arthur J. Delaney, Plaintiff, Against the Trustees of Saint Patrick's Cathedral in the City of New York. Plaintiff's Statement of His Case and Points of Law for an Injunction... To Restrain Defendants From Removing the Human Remains from Saint Patrick's Cemetery, in East 11th Street, in the City of New York.* New York: C.G. Burgoyne, 1883.

Eleventh Street Cemetery, West
See Milligan Street Cemetery.

Eliot Avenue Cemetery

CATEGORY: Private

YEARS OF USE: Gravestones date 1812 to 1857

LOCATION: At the Southwest corner of the intersection of Queens Boulevard and Eliot Avenue, Elmhurst, Queens.

HISTORY: Members of the Frederick, Gorsline, Hamilton, and Jones families were named on the four remaining gravestones in 1919. The Long Island Expressway covers the site today.

MAILING ADDRESS: N/A

PHONE NUMBER: N/A

RECORDS: N/A

RESOURCES: Frost, Josephine C. trans. *Long Island Cemetery Inscriptions.* vol. 1.   Brooklyn, N.Y. March 1912. (gravestone inscriptions)

Powell, Charles U., comp., and Alice H. Meigs, ed. *Description of Private and Family Cemeteries in the Borough of Queens.* City of New York, Borough of Queens, Topographical Bureau. Jamaica, N.Y.: Queens Borough Public Library, 1932. (gravestone inscriptions and maps)

Ellis-Winant Family Burial Ground
See Winant Family Burial Ground.

Evergreen Cemetery
See Cemetery of the Evergreens.

Factoryville Cemetery
See Staten Island Cemetery.
See Trinity Chapel Burial Ground.

Fairview Cemetery

CATEGORY: Non-sectarian
YEARS OF USE: circa 1889 to date
LOCATION: 1852 Victory Boulevard, south side of the street between
Mountainview Avenue and Lester Street, Castleton Corners, Staten Island.
HISTORY: N/A
MAILING ADDRESS: Fairview Cemetery Association
 1852 Victory Boulevard
 Staten Island, New York 10314-3514
PHONE NUMBER: (718) 448-9140
RECORDS: Fairview Cemetery records are housed on-site. There is a fee for
searches.
RESOURCES: N/A

Famine Cemetery
See Our Lady of Mount Carmel Churchyard.

Farm Colony Cemetery
See New York City Farm Colony Cemetery.

Ferris Family Burial Ground

CATEGORY: Private
YEARS OF USE: 1700s to 1914
LOCATION: Commerce Avenue, between Westchester Avenue and Ferris Place,
Westchester Square, Bronx.
HISTORY: The remains in James Ferris' vault were removed to Trinity Church
Cemetery, Manhattan, in 1900. The remains in Benjamin Ferris' vault were
removed to Kensico Cemetery, Westchester County, in 1928. The rest of the
cemetery was restored in 1973 by members of the local community.
MAILING ADDRESS: N/A
PHONE NUMBER: N/A
RECORDS: N/A
RESOURCES: N/A

Fiftieth Street Cemetery

CATEGORY: Public
YEARS OF USE: 1836 to 1843
LOCATION: 49th to 50th Streets, between 3rd and Park Avenues, Manhattan.
The Waldorf Astoria Hotel now occupies part of the site.
HISTORY: New York City's public cemetery at 50th Street was never popular
with its neighbors. At a hearing in City Hall with the New York City Common
Council, one alderman commented, "No one could now pass within a quarter
mile... without being suffocated with the effluvia emitted from the ground."

The Superintendent of the Deaf and Dumb Asylum, just one block away,
is said to have complained vehemently about the odor.

The problem may have arisen from the method of burial. An article in
the *New York Herald* explained: "The Coroner, while on the grounds, took
occasion to look at the mode of burial in this cemetery, and his investigations
resulted in the discovery of a number of trenches about one hundred feet
long, twenty feet deep, and about seven feet wide. Into these trenches the
coffins are placed in layers and not covered with earth until the trenches are
filled. We are informed by the officers attached to the Coroner's office that
there were hundreds, if not thousands, of these coffins exposed to public
view. Who is to blame in this matter? Somebody, surely, is obnoxious to
loud censure. It is, indeed, shameful."

The 50th Street Cemetery closed a short time later. In 1858, 100,000
bodies were removed to the new public cemetery at the southern tip of
Ward's Island.
MAILING ADDRESS: N/A
PHONE NUMBER: N/A
RECORDS: N/A
RESOURCES: N/A

First Baptist Church Cemetery, Manhattan

CATEGORY: Baptist
YEARS OF USE: circa 1815 to 1851
LOCATION: North side of Houston Street between First and Second Avenues,
Manhattan.
HISTORY: The First Baptist Church, Gold Street, was organized in 1728. The
congregation moved to a church at the corner of Broome and Elizabeth
Streets in 1842, and remained there for about thirty years.

The cemetery was used until 1851, when a ban on burials below 86th
Street prevented further interments. The bodies were removed about 1861,
possibly to Cypress Hills Cemetery where the congregation owns a plot, and
the land was sold two years later.
MAILING ADDRESS: First Baptist Church
                    265 West 79th Street
                    New York, New York 10024
PHONE NUMBER: (718) 724-5600
RECORDS: N/A
RESOURCES: *Cypress Hills Cemetery*. Brooklyn, N.Y.: Cypress Hills
Cemetery, 1880. (extensive list of plot owners and location of plot, maps,
rules, and history of cemetery)

First Baptist Church Cemetery, Staten Island
See Lake Cemetery.

First Calvary Cemetery
See Calvary Cemetery.

First Collegiate Reformed Churchyard, Harlem
See Harlem Reformed Dutch Churchyard and Vaults.

First Free Congregational Churchyard
See Bethel Baptist Churchyard and Burial Vaults.

First German Methodist Cemetery
See Linden Hill Methodist Cemetery.

First Methodist Church of Jamaica Cemetery

CATEGORY: Methodist Episcopal
YEARS OF USE: Gravestones date 1816 to 1933
LOCATION: Southwest corner of Liberty Avenue and Guy R. Brewer Boulevard,
Jamaica, Queens. The cemetery is on the grounds of York College.
HISTORY: The First Methodist Church of Jamaica was organized in 1807. Its

cemetery was given to them in 1850 as a gift of Obediah P. and Susan Leech, along with Abraham D. and Eliza Snedeker.

The congregation abandoned its cemetery about 1970. The burial ground has been severely vandalized by drug users. Garbage litters the lot, and its headstones are overturned. There is ample evidence to suggest that Satan worshippers mine the yard for bones. The Reverend John H. Cole, pastor of the First Methodist Church, told the *New York Times* in 1995 that his congregation is just too poor to take responsibility for the grounds. "The city and community need to take responsibility for it," Cole said. "We are not a rich church. We represent folk who are in the same shape as the cemetery." The Queens Historical Society has since taken interest in restoration of the grounds.

Obediah and Susan Leech are buried here, along with numerous members of the Dunn and Holland families. Abraham and Eliza Snedeker may be buried in nearby Prospect Cemetery. Burials are thought to have ended in 1912, but handwritten notes in *Cemetery Inscriptions from the Methodist Cemetery at Jamaica, New York*, in the Long Island Division of the Queens Borough Central Library, indicate that burials took place until 1933.

MAILING ADDRESS: First United Methodist Church
                 9131 191st Street
                 Jamaica, New York 11423-2812

PHONE NUMBER: (718) 465-6126

RECORDS: The church registers include deaths 1864 to 1883.

RESOURCES: Eardeley, William A., trans. *Cemeteries in Kings and Queens Counties, Long Island, New York: 1753 to 1913*. vol. 1. Brooklyn, N.Y. June 13, 1914. (gravestone inscriptions)

Frost, Josephine C. trans. *Long Island Cemetery Inscriptions*. vol. 15. Brooklyn, N.Y. August 1911. (gravestone inscriptions)

First Moravian Church Cemetery

CATEGORY: Moravian (United Brethren)

YEARS OF USE: 1754 to 1816

LOCATION: Mott Street, corner Pell Street, Manhattan.

HISTORY: The bodies in this burial ground were removed to Moravian Cemetery, Staten Island, circa 1845.

MAILING ADDRESS: Moravian Cemetery
                 2205 Richmond Road
                 Staten Island, New York 10306-2557

PHONE NUMBER: (718) 351-0136

RECORDS: The cemetery's records are housed on-site. They are also available on microfilm at the Staten Island Institute of Arts and Sciences.

RESOURCES: N/A

First Presbyterian Church Cemetery

See Presbyterian Cemetery, East Houston Street.

First Presbyterian Churchyard of the Bronx

CATEGORY: Presbyterian

YEARS OF USE: nineteenth century

LOCATION: 3051 East Tremont Avenue, near Dudley Avenue, Throgg's Neck, Bronx.

HISTORY: The First Presbyterian Church of Throgg's Neck was organized in 1855. Its church was destroyed by fire in 1870. The congregation worshipped at the nearby Friends' Meeting House until their new church was completed in 1883.

MAILING ADDRESS: First Presbyterian Church
3051 East Tremont Avenue
Bronx, New York 10461-5721

PHONE NUMBER: (718) 829-5326

RECORDS: The church records may have been destroyed in the 1870 fire.

RESOURCES: N/A

First Presbyterian Churchyard of Newtown

Category: Presbyterian

YEARS OF USE: circa 1723 to circa 1929

LOCATION: North side of Queens Boulevard, opposite 54th Avenue, Elmhurst, Queens.

HISTORY: The Fish family donated land to the First Presbyterian Church of Newtown in 1715 and buried Jonathan Fish there in 1723. Over the years, the church served the local community, as well as soldiers stationed at nearby Fort Greene. Church records contain the name, rank, and regiment of soldiers in its congregation beginning in 1775.

On 12 and 13 November 1901, the church removed the remains of its early ministers from the Newtown Village Cemetery to its churchyard. Buried with them are members of the Cornell, Corsline, Furman, Leverich, Luyster, Low, Moore, Morell, and Woodhull families.

In 1958, the congregation discussed selling the churchyard to developers for construction of an apartment complex. They made plans to remove the bodies to the Cemetery of the Evergreens.

MAILING ADDRESS: Presbyterian Church of Newtown
5404 Seabury Street
Flushing, New York 11373-4498

PHONE NUMBER: (718) 429-9508

RECORDS: The Church does not have death records prior to 1728, for the period during the Revolutionary War, or for the year 1810.

RESOURCES: Frost, Josephine C. trans. *Long Island Cemetery Inscriptions*, vol. 4 (March 1912). (gravestone inscriptions)

Haviland, Frank. *All Inscriptions in the Presbyterian Churchyard, Newtown*. Manuscript. Brooklyn, N.Y.: Brooklyn Historical Society, 1904. (gravestone inscriptions)

Powell, Charles U., comp., and Alice H. Meigs, ed. *Description of Private and Family Cemeteries in the Borough of Queens*. City of New York, Borough of Queens, Topographical Bureau. Jamaica, N.Y.: Queens Borough Public Library, 1975 supplement. (gravestone inscriptions)

White, Arthur. trans. "Records of the Presbyterian Church, Newtown (now Elmhurst), Queens County, Long Island, New York: A List of All Deaths Recorded on the Books of the Newtown Presbyterian Church of Elmhurst, Long Island from 1728 to 1882." *The New York Genealogical and Biographical Society Collections*, 1928: 48–64.

First Presbyterian Churchyard and Vaults

Category: Presbyterian
YEARS OF USE: 1717 to 1823
LOCATION: 5 Wall Street, north side of the street between Nassau Street and Broadway, Manhattan.
HISTORY: The First Presbyterian Church formed in 1716 and erected its first church in 1719. Its trustees authorized the construction of burial vaults in front of the church in 1800, only to empty them twenty-five years later when the property was sold to developers. The graveyard was removed in 1844.
MAILING ADDRESS: First Presbyterian Church
    12 West 12th Street
    New York, New York 10011-8690
PHONE NUMBER: (212) 675-6150
RECORDS: Prior to 1809, the records of the First Presbyterian Church include those of the Brick Presbyterian Church and the Rutgers Presbyterian Church.
RESOURCES: *First Presbyterian Church Deaths, 1786 to 1804.* Manuscript NY-24, at the New York Genealogical and Biographical Society. New York, New York.

Disosway, Gabriel P. *The Earliest Churches of New York City and its Vicinity*. New York: J. G. Gregory, 1865. (register of deaths between January 1786 and July 1804)

First Reformed Dutch Churchyard of Brooklyn

Category: Reformed Dutch
YEARS OF USE: circa 1662 to 1849
LOCATION: Fulton Street, between Bridge Street and Smith Street, Williamsburg, Brooklyn.

HISTORY: The First Reformed Dutch Church of Brooklyn was organized in 1660 and erected its first church six years later on Fulton Street. Burials in the yard predate construction of the church. One worshipper asked the church elders for permission to enclose his wife's grave with a fence in 1662.

In 1807, the congregation built a new church on nearby Joralemon Street, but continued to use its old churchyard. Use of the yard came to an end in 1849 when burials were prohibited within the Brooklyn city limits. About 1865, the church removed the bodies and gravestones to the Cedar Dell section of Green-Wood Cemetery. The property was sold a short time later.

MAILING ADDRESS: c/o Gardner Sage Library
                    New Brunswick Theological Seminary
                    21 Seminary Place
                    New Brunswick, New Jersey 08901-1187

PHONE NUMBER: (908) 247-5243

RECORDS: Original church records are now housed at the Gardner Sage Library in New Brunswick, New Jersey. Copies of post-1785 records are at the New York Genealogical and Biographical Society. Some records were taken to England during the Revolutionary War and have never been recovered.

RESOURCES: E., F. J. "Old Burial Grounds. Cemeteries in Brooklyn and the County Towns." *The Brooklyn Eagle*, 29 August 1886, p. 9, col. 3. (cemetery history)

Hazelton, Henry Isham. *The Boroughs of Brooklyn and Queens and the Counties of Nassau and Suffolk, Long Island, New York.* New York: Lewis Historical Publishing Company, Inc., 1925, 1181–1182. (reprint of Walt Whitman's description of grounds)

Murphy, Henry Cruse. "Memoranda Taken from the Tombstones in the Old Dutch Burying Ground in Fulton Street, near Smith Street." *Long Island Historical Society Quarterly* 1, no. 3 (July 1939): 82–86. (gravestones inscriptions copied in 1862)

Ronk, Daniel T. *First Reformed Church of Brooklyn Tombstone Inscriptions, Copied From Their Lot in Green-Wood Cemetery.* Manuscript. New York: U.S. History, Local History and Genealogy Division, New York Public Library, 1920.

First Reformed Dutch Churchyard of Newtown

CATEGORY: Reformed Dutch

YEARS OF USE: Gravestones date 1794 to 1933

LOCATION: 85-15 Broadway, east side of the street between Corona Avenue and 51st Avenue, Elmhurst, Queens.

HISTORY: The First Reformed Dutch Church of Newtown and its graveyard were established on land given by Peter Berrien in 1731. Gravestones to the memory of the Devevoise, Rapalye, and Remsen families are predominant in the churchyard.

MAILING ADDRESS: Reformed Church of Newtown
                 49-20 87th Street
                 Flushing, New York 11373-3949
PHONE NUMBER: (718) 592-4466
RECORDS: Registers include deaths back to 1764. Early records may be in
Dutch.
RESOURCES: Debevoise, Richard Gosmond, ed. *Records of the Newtown
Reformed Church*. Brooklyn, N.Y.: Published by the author, 1935. (deaths,
1866–1935)
     Frost, Josephine C. trans. *Long Island Cemetery Inscriptions*. Brooklyn,
New York. vol. 4. March 1912. (Gravestone Inscriptions)
     Haviland, Frank. *Complete Inscriptions from the Churchyard of the
Dutch Reformed Church of Newtown*. manuscript. Brooklyn, N.Y.:
Brooklyn Historical Society, 1904. (gravestone inscriptions)
     Powell, Charles U., comp., and Alice H. Meigs, ed. *Description of Private
and Family Cemeteries in the Borough of Queens*. City of New York,
Borough of Queens, Topographical Bureau. Jamaica, N.Y.: Queens Borough
Public Library, 1975 supplement. (gravestone inscriptions)

Fish Family Burial Ground

CATEGORY: Private
YEARS OF USE: eighteenth to nineteenth century
LOCATION: On the grounds now occupied by LaGuardia Airport, Astoria,
Queens.
HISTORY: This burial ground was established circa 1715 for the family of
Samuel Fish. In 1882, William Munsell wrote that it was "in a field a few
yards east of the [William] Palmer Cottage" and noted that John Fish's head-
stone read "In memory of John Fish who died 2nd day July 1793, aged 73."
Munsell remarked that there was not a headstone for Fish's wife, but that his
daughter and her husband were buried there. Members of the Fish family
were also interred in the Alsop Family Burial Ground and in the First
Presbyterian Churchyard of Newtown.
     Forty-six members of the Fish family were buried in the Fish Family
Burial Ground. When the bodies were disinterred for construction of
LaGuardia Airport in 1938, the gravestones were illegible. The bodies were
taken to Saint Michael's Cemetery.
MAILING ADDRESS: c/o Saint Michael's Cemetery and Mausoleums
                 72-02 Astoria Boulevard
                 Flushing, New York 11370-1094
PHONE NUMBER: (718) 278-3240
RECORDS: Saint Michael's records are housed on-site.
RESOURCES: N/A

Flatbush Reformed Dutch Churchyard

CATEGORY: Reformed Dutch
YEARS OF USE: circa 1657 to circa 1913
LOCATION: 890 Flatbush Avenue, southwest corner of Church Avenue, Flatbush, Brooklyn.
HISTORY: The Flatbush Reformed Dutch Church was established in 1654. Members of the Bergen, Cortelyou, Leffert, Lott, and Vanderbilt families were buried in the churchyard before interments stopped about 1913.
MAILING ADDRESS: Flatbush Reformed Church
890 Flatbush Avenue
Brooklyn, New York 11226-4018
PHONE NUMBER: (718) 284-5140
RECORDS: Records are in Dutch prior to 1783. The church may have a blueprint of the cemetery from 1900.
RESOURCES: *Cemetery, Church, and Town Records of New York State*. vol. 108. Washington, D.C.: Daughters of the American Revolution, 1937-1938, 8–24. (gravestone inscriptions)

E., F. J. "Old Burial Grounds. Cemeteries in Brooklyn and the County Towns." *The Brooklyn Eagle*, 29 August 1886, p. 9, col. 3. (gravestone inscription of Charles and Elizabeth Clarkson)

Eardeley, William Applebie, trans. *Dutch Reformed Cemetery Inscriptions, Flatbush, Kings County, New York, 1754 to 1913*. Brooklyn, N.Y., 1913.

Frost, Josephine C. trans. *Inscriptions from the Reformed Dutch Churchyard at Flatbush, Brooklyn, New York, 1797 to 1855*. Brooklyn, New York. vol. 2, 1914.

Van Cleef, Frank L., trans. and ed. *Records of the Reformed Protestant Dutch Church of Flatbush*. Brooklyn, N.Y., 1915. Manuscript. (burial fees, 1657–1724)

Flatlands Reformed Dutch Churchyard

CATEGORY: Reformed Dutch
YEARS OF USE: circa 1663 to date
LOCATION: 3931 King's Highway, between Flatbush Avenue and Overbaugh Place, Flatlands, Brooklyn.
HISTORY: The Flatlands Reformed Dutch Church was established on 9 February 1654 at the direction of Peter Stuyvesant, Governor of New Amsterdam. The original church was erected in 1663 with stocks and a whipping post in the front yard. By 1910, burials were limited to the owners of plots or graves.
MAILING ADDRESS: Flatlands Reformed Church
3931 Kings Highway
Brooklyn, New York 11234-2336

PHONE NUMBER: (718) 252-5540
RECORDS: Records prior to 1783 are in Dutch. Vital records begin in 1747.
RESOURCES: E., F. J. "Old Burial Grounds. Cemeteries in Brooklyn and
the County Towns." *The Brooklyn Eagle*, 29 August 1886, p. 9, col. 3.
(church history; some gravestone inscriptions)

Frost, Josephine C. trans. *Long Island Cemetery Inscriptions*. Brooklyn,
New York. vol. 12, 1914. (Gravestone Inscriptions)

"Inscriptions on the Tombstones in and around the Churchyard in the
Village of Flatlands, Kings County, New York, 1707 to 1877." *Kings County
Genealogical Club Collection* 1, no. 2 (1 July 1882): 17–29. (alphabetical list
of gravestone inscriptions)

Flatlands Town Cemetery

CATEGORY: Public
YEARS OF USE: Gravestones date 1832 to 1902
LOCATION: East side of Avenue J, between Remsen Avenue and East 92nd
Street, Canarsie, Brooklyn. The cemetery is bisected by East 91st Street.
HISTORY: In 1842, the Town of Flatlands purchased one acre of land from
John and Catherine Remsen for use as a cemetery.

Part of the cemetery was lost when New York City ran East 91st Street
through the middle of it. Davis, Denton, Fortmeier, and Gosline were among
those names found on the 89 gravestones still standing in 1915.

New York City took title to the cemetery in 1948. When the Board of
Estimate decided to sell it at public auction in 1964, Grace Church expressed
interest in purchasing and restoring the property. The Church indicated that
it would fence, landscape, and generally preserve the cemetery.

This cemetery is mistakenly listed on some city records as "Indian
Cemetery." It is across the street from its successor, Canarsie Cemetery.
MAILING ADDRESS: N/A
PHONE NUMBER: N/A
RECORDS: N/A
RESOURCES: Eardeley, William Applebie, trans. *Cemeteries in Kings and
Queens Counties, Long Island, New York: 1793 to 1902*. vol. 2, March
1916. Brooklyn, New York. (gravestone inscriptions)

Flushing Cemetery

CATEGORY: Non-sectarian
YEARS OF USE: 1853 to Date
LOCATION: 163-06 46th Avenue, between 164th Street and Fresh Meadow
Lane, Flushing, Queens.
HISTORY: The jazz musician Louis Armstrong and politicians Adam Clayton
Powell Jr. and Sr. are buried here.

MAILING ADDRESS: Flushing Cemetery
                         163-06 46th Avenue
                         Flushing, New York 11358-3241
PHONE NUMBER: (718) 359-0100
RECORDS: Records are housed at the cemetery.
RESOURCES: Heiser, Evelyn M. *Cemetery Lot-Holders and Interments for 1862 to 1868, Flushing.* Manuscript. Brooklyn Historical Society. Brooklyn, New York. (taken from newspapers)
    Tennent, John Hooper, and Marjorie Beverly Tennent, comps. *The Lawrence Family Letters of Willow Bank, Flushing, New York, 1846 to 1896.* Bowie, Md.: Heritage Books, Inc., 1996, 223, 229–34. (Bogert, Bowne and Lawrence family gravestone inscriptions and plots)

Fordham Manor Reformed Dutch Church Cemetery
See Berrian Family Burial Ground.

Fordham University Cemetery
See Corsa Family Burial Ground.

Fordham University Chapel Cemetery

CATEGORY: Roman Catholic
YEARS OF USE: 1848 to 1909
LOCATION: West side of the Priests' Residence, Fordham University, Rose Hill Campus, Bronx.
HISTORY: This cemetery, in the northwest section of the campus, contains the remains of one hundred fifty men, primarily Jesuit priests who worked as instructors at the University. It was moved to this site in 1889 from its original spot in a wooded grove at Southern Boulevard, the site of the New York Botanical Garden. The tombstones were of Vermont marble and, as such, are mostly illegible today.
MAILING ADDRESS: c/o Fordham University Archivist
                         Fordham University-Rose Hill Campus
                         441 East Fordham Road
                         Bronx, New York 10458-9993
PHONE NUMBER: (718) 817-3560
RECORDS: In 1971, the cemetery records contained burial lists; brief biographies of several men; a plan of the cemetery showing where each man was buried; and miscellaneous correspondence. Burials prior to 1889 were recorded in a small notebook showing the date of birth, nationality, occupation, date studies began, and date of death.
RESOURCES: Falco, Nicholas. "The Old Cemetery in Fordham University." *Bronx County Historical Society Journal* 8, no. 1 (January 1971): 20–25. (photos; limited genealogical data)

Forsyth Street Methodist Episcopal Churchyard

CATEGORY: Methodist Episcopal
YEARS OF USE: circa 1789 to 1823
LOCATION: 12 Forsyth Street, on the east side of the street between Bayard and Walker Streets, Manhattan. This site is currently the on-ramp to the Manhattan Bridge.
HISTORY: The Forsyth Street Methodist Episcopal Church was established in 1789. Although burials in the churchyard probably stopped following an 1823 prohibition on interments below Grand Street in Manhattan, it wasn't until the 1851 ban on burials below 86th Street that the trustees of the Forsyth Street Church decided to move their dead to a plot in Cypress Hills Cemetery. The removals began in 1854 and lasted for two years. The *Brooklyn Daily Eagle* interviewed a watchman who stated that the bones and coffins were buried in trenches, while the best headstones were "put up to look good."

This church was also known as the Second Methodist Episcopal Church. The congregation disbanded in 1904.
MAILING ADDRESS: c/o Cypress Hills Cemetery
            833 Jamaica Avenue
            Brooklyn, New York 11208-1593
PHONE NUMBER: (718) 277-2900
RECORDS: Cypress Hills Cemetery prefers written requests for searches.
RESOURCES: *Cypress Hills Cemetery*. Brooklyn, N.Y.: Cypress Hills Cemetery, 1880. (extensive list of plot owners and location of plot, maps, rules, and history of cemetery)

"The Forgotten Dead: Many Neglected Graves in Cypress Hills Cemetery." *The Brooklyn Daily Eagle*, 13 August 1893, p. 8, col. 7. (description of the Methodist plot)

Fort Columbus Cemetery
See Governors Island Cemetery.

Fort Hamilton Cemetery

CATEGORY: Military
YEARS OF USE: 1862 to 1866
LOCATION: United States Government Reservation at the intersection of the Varrazano-Narrows Bridge and the Shore Parkway, Bay Ridge, Brooklyn.
HISTORY: Construction on Fort Hamilton was completed in 1831. Captain Robert E. Lee, post engineer, supervised expansion of the fort's gun platform ten years later. During the Civil War, volunteer Union soldiers trained at Fort Hamilton, and its sister installation, Fort Lafayette, became a prison for Confederate prisoners-of-war.

During the 1800s, the Fort had no chapel and was affiliated with nearby Saint John's Episcopal Church.

Approximately 100 soldiers were buried here during the Civil War: only a third of them were identified.

MAILING ADDRESS: N/A
PHONE NUMBER: N/A
RECORDS: N/A
RESOURCES: Reamy, Martha, and William, comps. *Index to the Roll of Honor*. Reprint. Baltimore, Md.: Genealogical Publishing Company, 1995. (Note: Use with United States Quartermaster's *Roll of Honor*)

United States Quartermaster's Department. *Roll of Honor: Names of Soldiers who Died in Defense of the American Union, Interred in National Cemeteries*. vol. 10. Reprint. Baltimore, Md.: Genealogical Publishing Company, 1994.

Fort Totten Cemetery

CATEGORY: Military
YEARS OF USE: Civil War
LOCATION: Fort Totten, Totten Avenue and Cross Island Parkway, Bay Terrace, Queens.
HISTORY: Land for Fort Totten was acquired by the United States Government in 1857. Construction began five years later, but was abandoned in 1864 due to technological advancements that made stone forts obsolete. Between 1864 and 1865, Grant Hospital was located here to treat members of the Union Army. Four unknown soldiers were buried in the cemetery at that time.

Fort Totten is also known as Willett's Point.
MAILING ADDRESS: N/A
PHONE NUMBER: N/A
RECORDS: N/A
RESOURCES: Holt, Dean W. *American Military Cemeteries*. Jefferson, N.C.: McFarland and Company, Inc., 1992.

Reamy, Martha and William, comps. *Index to the Roll of Honor*. Reprint. Baltimore, Md.: Genealogical Publishing Company, 1995. (Note: Use with United States Quartermaster's *Roll of Honor*.)

United States Quartermaster's Department. *Roll of Honor: Names of Soldiers who Died in Defense of the American Union, Interred in National Cemeteries*. vol. 10. Reprint. Genealogical Publishing Company, 1994, 9.

Forty-Fifth Street Cemetery

CATEGORY: Public
YEARS OF USE: circa 1845 to 1851

LOCATION: North side of West 45th Street, between 10th and 11th Avenues, Manhattan.

HISTORY: The 45th Street Cemetery was used by the City of New York between 1845 and 1851, possibly for the dead of Bellevue Hospital.   Burials presumably came to an end with the 1851 ban on interments south of 86th Street in Manhattan, and with the opening of Ward's Island Cemetery in June of 1852.

The bodies in this cemetery may have been removed to Ward's Island Cemetery in 1858, along with bodies from the Fiftieth Street Cemetery.

MAILING ADDRESS: N/A

PHONE NUMBER: N/A

RECORDS: N/A

RESOURCES: N/A

Forty-Fourth Street Cemetery and Vaults

CATEGORY: Methodist Episcopal

YEARS OF USE: circa 1843 to 1851

LOCATION: South side of West 44th Street, between 8th and 9th Avenues, Manhattan.

HISTORY: This cemetery was used as a general burial ground by the Methodist Episcopal churches of New York. Interments most likely came to an end with the 1851 ban on burials below 86th Street in Manhattan.

The bodies may be reinterred in Cypress Hills Cemetery where several New York City Methodist churches have plots.

MAILING ADDRESS: N/A

PHONE NUMBER: N/A

RECORDS: N/A

RESOURCES: N/A

Fountain Cemetery
(See also Clove Meeting House Cemetery.)

CATEGORY: N/A

YEARS OF USE: 1865 to 1911+

LOCATION: At the dead end of Tompkins Court, south of Richmond Terrace and adjacent to Staten Island Cemetery, West New Brighton, Staten Island.

HISTORY: Observers note that most of the gravestones in Fountain Cemetery are from the nineteenth century. The graveyard was abandoned sometime after 1911, but Friends of Abandoned Cemeteries of Staten Island has taken an interest in the grounds.

This cemetery is also known as the Van Street Burial Plot.

MAILING ADDRESS: Fountain Cemetery
                    c/o Friends of Abandoned Cemeteries of Staten Island

140 Tysen Street
Staten Island, New York 10301-1120

PHONE NUMBER: N/A

RECORDS: Friends of Abandoned Cemeteries of Staten Island maintains a database of records from this cemetery. An interment list has been posted on the Richmond County RootsWeb project Web site. The address is: <http://www.rootsweb.com/~nyrichmo>

RESOURCES: "Some Civil War Burials at Fountain Cemetery." *The FACSI Newsletter* 15, issue 3, (Winter 1998–1999). (burials of Civil War vets)

Vosburgh, Royden W., editor and transcriber, *Staten Island Gravestone Inscriptions*, vol. 1, New York City, March 1924 (typed manuscript). An interment list has been posted on the Richmond County RootsWeb project Web site. The address is: <http://www.rootsweb.com/~nyrichmo>

Fountain Family Burial Ground
(See also Clove Meeting House Cemetery.)

CATEGORY: Private

YEARS OF USE: 1750 to 1820

LOCATION: In a field south of Old Town Road and east of the Staten Island Rail Road, Dongan Hills, Staten Island.

HISTORY: Ship-Builder Cornelius Fountain and his wife, Elizabeth, are buried here.

This cemetery may be the burial ground referred to in the 23 May 1738 deed regarding the sale of property on Old Town Road to John Garretson. It might also be the burial place of Hendric Garretson who died in November 1818 and was buried on "Colonel Garretson's farm."

About 1900, the cemetery was leveled and the gravestones were taken to an unspecified location.

MAILING ADDRESS: N/A

PHONE NUMBER: N/A

RECORDS: N/A

RESOURCES: Davis, William T. "Homestead Graves." *Proceedings of the Natural Science Association of Staten Island*. Staten Island, New York. Special Number 9, December 1889. (Gravestone Inscriptions)

Fourth Calvary Cemetery
See Calvary Cemetery.

Fox Cemetery
See Friends' Burial Ground, Bronx.

Frederick Douglass Memorial Park Cemetery

CATEGORY: African, Non-sectarian
YEARS OF USE: 1935 to date
LOCATION: 3201 Amboy Road, between Montreal Avenue and Oceanview
Cemetery, Richmond, Staten Island.
HISTORY: Rodney Dade, a prominent African-American funeral director,
wanted to open a cemetery for the exclusive use of African-Americans. He
realized his dream in 1935. Today, Dade's cemetery is open to people of all
races.
MAILING ADDRESS: Frederick Douglass Memorial Park Cemetery
                 3201 Amboy Road
                 Staten Island, New York 10306-2703
PHONE NUMBER: (718) 351-0764
RECORDS: Burial records are stored at the cemetery.
RESOURCES: N/A

French Huguenot Churchyard
French Church of Saint Espirit
See l'Eglise of St. Espirit Cemetery.

Fresh Pond Crematory

CATEGORY: Non-sectarian
YEARS OF USE: 1883 to date
LOCATION: Mount Olivet Crescent and 62nd Avenue, opposite Lutheran
Cemetery, Middle Village, Queens.
HISTORY: Fresh Pond Crematory was constructed in the form of a Grecian
Temple with an ornamental marble front. In 1895, the *Brooklyn Daily Eagle*
reported that there had been 1,101 cremations since the company's incep-
tion. Half of those were identified as persons born in Germany, three-quar-
ters of them male.
    The cremated remains were deposited in ornamental urns.
MAILING ADDRESS: Fresh Pond Crematory
                 61-40 Mount Olivet Crescent
                 Flushing, New York 11379-1045
PHONE NUMBER: (212) 821-9700
RECORDS: N/A
RESOURCES: N/A

Friends' Burial Ground, Bronx

CATEGORY: Quaker
YEARS OF USE: N/A

LOCATION: 2450 Westchester Avenue, adjacent to Saint Peter's Churchyard, Westchester Bronx.

HISTORY: This cemetery is also known as Fox Cemetery.

MAILING ADDRESS: c/o Saint Peter's Episcopal Church
2500 Westchester Avenue
Bronx, New York 10461-4588

PHONE NUMBER: (718) 931-9270

RECORDS: Tombstones were not permitted in Quaker cemeteries until 1852: if a tombstone bears a death date prior to 1852, it was probably erected by a family member at a much later date.

RESOURCES: N/A

Friends' Meeting House Cemetery

CATEGORY: Quaker

YEARS OF USE: circa 1694 to 1893; Gravestones date 1821 to 1893

LOCATION: 137-16 Northern Boulevard, on the south side of the street, east of Main Street, Flushing, Queens.

HISTORY: This meeting house has been in continuous use since its erection in 1694, excepting 1776 to 1783, when it was taken by the British for use as a barn, hospital, and prison during the Revolutionary War.

MAILING ADDRESS: Friends' Meeting House
137-16 Northern Boulevard
Flushing, New York 11354-4122

PHONE NUMBER: (718) 358-9636

RECORDS: Gravestones were not permitted in Quaker cemeteries until 1852: if a tombstone bears a death date prior to 1852, it was probably erected by a family member at a much later date.

RESOURCES: *Flushing Monthly Meeting, New York: Births and Deaths 1801 to 1880.* (Salt Lake City: Genealogical Society of Utah, 1950), microfilm no. 17,354. (death records)

Flushing Monthly Meeting, New York: Births, Deaths, and Marriages 1640 to 1798. (Salt Lake City: Genealogical Society of Utah, 1950), microfilm no. 17,376. (death records)

"Flushing Quaker Meeting House Graveyard." *Cemetery, Church, and Town Records of New York State.* vol. 25. Washington, D.C.: Daughters of the American Revolution, 1958-1959, 164–169. (gravestone inscriptions; index)

Frost, Josephine C. trans. *Long Island Cemetery Inscriptions.* Brooklyn, New York. 1904. vol. 5. (gravestone inscriptions)

Haviland, Frank. *Quaker Tombstones of Long Island.* Manuscript. Brooklyn Historical Society. Brooklyn, New York. 1904. (gravestone inscriptions)

Powell, Charles U., comp., and Alice H. Meigs, ed. *Description of Private and Family Cemeteries in the Borough of Queens*. City of New York, Borough of Queens, Topographical Bureau. Jamaica, N.Y.: Queens Borough Public Library, 1975 supplement. (gravestone inscriptions)

Garretson Burial Ground
See Fountain Family Burial Ground.

Gate of Heaven Cemetery
See Cemetery of the Gate of Heaven.

German Burial Ground
See Most Holy Trinity Cemetery.

German Lutheran Burial Ground
See Saint Matthew's burial grounds.

German Reformed Dutch Churchyard and Cemetery

CATEGORY: Reformed Dutch
YEARS OF USE: circa 1758 to 1847
LOCATION: West side of Forsyth Street, between Walker Street and Bayard Street, Manhattan. Current site of the entrance to the Manhattan Bridge.
HISTORY: The remains in the German Reformed Churchyard were removed to Green-Wood Cemetery in January of 1847, along with remains from the German Reformed Church Cemetery on 12th Street, Manhattan. The exact location of the 12th Street burial ground is unclear.

The German Reformed Church disbanded in 1968.
MAILING ADDRESS: c/o Gardner Sage Library
New Brunswick Theological Seminary
21 Seminary Place
New Brunswick, New Jersey 08901-1187
PHONE NUMBER: (908) 247-5243

RECORDS: The German Reformed Church records, 1823 to 1968, are housed
at the Gardner Sage Library. The New York Historical Society has the
church's account book which contains payments for funeral and burials, 1785
to 1835.
RESOURCES: Farrell, Charles, trans. "Records of the German Reformed
Church of New York." *The New York Genealogical and Biographical Record*
128, no. 3 (July 1997): 164–166. Continued in its next issue. (deaths,
1764–1803; some reinterments)

Gilhooley's Burial Plot
See African Methodist Episcopal Church Cemetery, Seneca Village.
See All Angels' Church Cemetery.

Gorsline Family Burial Ground
See Eliot Avenue Cemetery.

Governors Island Cemetery

CATEGORY: Military
YEARS OF USE: circa 1710 to 1865
LOCATION: Governors Island, New York Harbor, New York.
HISTORY: Located just five hundred yards from the southern tip of
Manhattan, Governors Island has been an integral part of New York City his-
tory from its earliest days as a colony.

The island was purchased from the Manahata Indians in 1637 for nothing more than two axe-heads and a few other trinkets. It became a retreat
for colonial leaders, including Lord Cornbury, a cousin of Queen Anne, who
built a villa upon the island with colonial tax money. Hundreds of German
Protestant refugees arrived at the Port of New York in 1710, suffering from
the plague: they were quarantined in Cornbury's villa. Although many died
and were buried upon the island, John Peter Zenger was among those who
survived. Zenger was the publisher of the *New York Weekly Journal* who, in
1735, stood up for freedom of speech in the press.

British and French troops were stationed on Governors Island during the
French and Indian War. Continental troops occupied the Island for a time
during the Revolution, but the British captured it in 1776 and held it until
the end of the war in 1783.

New York City used the island for quarantine between 1794 and 1799.

During the Civil War, Governors Island served as a recruiting depot for
Union Soldiers and as a prison camp. Over 1,500 Confederate prisoners-of-
war were housed in the island's Castle Williams. Those Confederates convicted of espionage, and awaiting execution, were held on the island in a
building near Fort Columbus.

In 1900, construction forced the removal of an estimated three hundred bodies from the island's cemetery to Cypress Hills National Cemetery in Queens. Of them, the earliest known date of death is 1797. Thirty-one were casualties of the Civil War.

MAILING ADDRESS: Cypress Hills National Cemetery
c/o Long Island National Cemetery
2040 Wellwood Avenue
Farmingdale, New York 11735-1211

PHONE NUMBER: (516) 454-4949

RECORDS: Information is available through the Long Island National Cemetery. Availability of in-depth searches will be determined on a case-by-case basis.

RESOURCES: Reamy, Martha and William, compilers. *Index to the Roll of Honor*. Reprint. Baltimore, Md.: Genealogical Publishing Company, 1995. (Note: Use with United States Quartermaster's *Roll of Honor*.)

United States Quartermaster's Department. *Roll of Honor: Names of Soldiers who Died in Defense of the American Union, Interred in National Cemeteries*. vol. 10. Reprint. Baltimore, Md.: Genealogical Publishing Company, 1994, 8–9.

Grace Episcopal Churchyard

CATEGORY: Protestant Episcopal

YEARS OF USE: 1734 to 1908

LOCATION: 155-03 Jamaica Avenue, between 153rd Street and Parsons Boulevard, Jamaica, Queens.

HISTORY: Grace Episcopal Church, formed 1702, erected its first church building in April of 1734. That building was destroyed by fire on 1 January 1861, and the present building was erected a short time later.

Rufus King, a Federalist Statesman, member of the Continental Congress, and father of a New York Governor, is buried here. His former home is down the street at 150-03 Jamaica Avenue.

MAILING ADDRESS: Grace Episcopal Church
155-24 90th Avenue
Jamaica, New York 11432

PHONE NUMBER: (718) 291-4901

RECORDS: N/A

RESOURCES: Betts, Reverend Beverley R. "Inscriptions from the Tombstones in the Parish Churchyard at Jamaica, Long Island." *The New York Genealogical and Biographical Record* 7, no. 1 (January 1876): 18.

Frost, Josephine C, trans. *Account Book of Aaron Van Nostrand (Chairmaker 1767) Sexton for Grave Digging, Bell Ringing, Pall, and Attendings at the Grace Episcopal Church of Jamaica, Long Island, New York: 1773 to 1820*. Brooklyn, New York. 1913. (names people who paid for burial services)

Frost, Josephine C., trans. *Baptisms, Marriages, and Funerals Recorded at Grace Episcopal Church Jamaica, Long Island, New York: 1769 to 1853.* Brooklyn, New York. 1913. Pages 89 to 101 (funerals, 1790–1830)

Frost, Josephine C. trans. *Long Island Cemetery Inscriptions, Flatlands, Brooklyn, New York.* Brooklyn, New York. vol. 15, August 1911. (Gravestone Inscriptions)

"Episcopal Church Cemetery, Jamaica, Long Island, New York." *The New York Genealogical and Biographical Record* 28, no. 1 (January 1897): 56–57.

Hoffman, William L. "Parish of Jamaica Grace Episcopal Church, Queens." *Yesteryears* 15, no. 58 (Winter 1971): 105. (limited gravestone inscriptions for Willett family)

Grand Street Presbyterian Church Cemetery
See Scotch Presbyterian Church Cemetery.

Graniteville First Baptist Churchyard
See Lake Cemetery.

Grant's Tomb

CATEGORY: Private
YEARS OF USE: 1897 and 1902
LOCATION: 122nd Street and Riverside Drive, Manhattan.
HISTORY: Yes, President Ulysses S. Grant is buried here, as is his wife. It is the largest mausoleum in the United States and has panoramic views of the Hudson River.
MAILING ADDRESS: N/A
PHONE NUMBER: N/A
RECORDS: President Ulysses S. Grant was born 27 April 1822 in Point Pleasant, Ohio. After his death on 23 July 1885 at Mount McGregor, New York, his remains were placed in a temporary vault in Riverside Park until a permanent monument could be erected. On 27 April 1897, Grant's birthday, the tomb was dedicated in a ceremony attended by his widow, the former Julia Dent, and President William McKinley. Grant is the only president buried in New York City. Julia Dent Grant was born 18 February 1826 in Saint Louis, Missouri. She died 14 December 1902 in Washington, D.C., and is interred beside her husband.
RESOURCES: Culbertson, Judi and Tom Randall. *Permanent New Yorkers: A Biographical Guide to the Cemeteries of New York.* Chelsea, Vt.: Chelsea Green Publishing Company, 1987. (description of mausoleum)

Gravesend Reformed Dutch Church Cemetery

CATEGORY: Public, Reformed Dutch
YEARS OF USE: circa 1650 to 1917
LOCATION: In the triangle formed by Gravesend Neck Road, McDonald Avenue, and Van Sicklen Street, Gravesend, Brooklyn.
HISTORY: Gravesend was settled in 1643 by a flock of religious dissenters lead by Lady Deborah Moody of Massachusetts. Early documents show that they established this cemetery as early as 1650. Lady Moody is supposed to be buried here, but the exact location of her grave is unknown. All of the seventeenth century gravestones are gone.

The Reformed Dutch Church chose the village cemetery as its burial ground when the congregation was established in 1654. Nearly every member of the church owned a plot. The congregation abandoned the graveyard about 1810.

The cemetery was subsequently taken over by the Town of Gravesend. Gravesend became part of the City of Brooklyn in 1894. In 1898, Brooklyn became part of New York City, and New York City assumed control of the cemetery.

By 1901, burials were limited to those who already owned graves or plots, principally the descendants of Gravesend's original settlers. New York City tried to give the cemetery back to the Reformed Dutch Church in 1917. That overture was rebuffed, and the grounds are now fenced and locked.

This burial ground is also called Gravesend Town Cemetery, Gravesend-Van Sicklen Cemetery, and Old Gravesend Cemetery.
MAILING ADDRESS: Trinity Tabernacle of Gravesend
                  121 Gravesend Neck Road
                  Brooklyn, New York 11223-4708
PHONE NUMBER: (718) 998-7827
RECORDS: Vital records date back to 1714
RESOURCES: Frost, Josephine C. trans. *Cemetery Inscriptions, Gravesend, Brooklyn, New York.* Brooklyn, New York. vol. 11, 1914.

"Inscriptions on the Tombstones in and Around the Churchyard in the Village of Gravesend, Kings County, New York." *Kings County Genealogical Club Collections,* vol. 1, no. 3 (August 1, 1882). (gravestone inscriptions)

"Seek Funds to Preserve Old Gravesend Cemetery." *The Brooklyn Daily Eagle,* 22 July 1917. (limited list of burials)

Stillwell, William H. *History of the Reformed Protestant Dutch Church of Gravesend, Kings County, New York.* Brooklyn, N.Y.: Brooklyn Citizen Job Printers, 1892. Printed for the Consistory. (alphabetical list of deaths)

Gravesend-Van Sicklen Cemetery
See Gravesend Reformed Dutch Church Cemetery.

Gravesend Village Cemetery

See Gravesend Reformed Dutch Church Cemetery.

Greene Street Methodist Episcopal Church Cemetery

CATEGORY: Methodist Episcopal
YEARS OF USE: circa 1837 to 1851
LOCATION: North side of 36th Street between 8th and 9th Avenues,
Manhattan.
HISTORY: The Greene Street Methodist Episcopal Church was organized in
1831. The congregation erected its first church on Greene Street, between
Broome Street and Spring Street, where it remained until 1874. They
merged with the Washington Square Methodist Episcopal Church in 1893.

Interments in its cemetery probably came to an end with the 1851 ban on
burials below 86th Street in Manhattan.
MAILING ADDRESS: c/o Washington Square United Methodist Church
          133 West Fourth Street
          New York, New York 10012-1095
PHONE NUMBER: (212) 777-2528
RECORDS: N/A
RESOURCES: N/A

Greene Street Methodist Episcopal Churchyard and Vaults

CATEGORY: Methodist Episcopal
YEARS OF USE: circa 1831 to 1851
LOCATION: Church at Greene Street, between Broome and Spring Streets,
Manhattan.
HISTORY: The Greene Street Methodist Episcopal Church was organized in
1831. The congregation erected its first church on Greene Street, where it
remained until 1874. They merged with the Washington Square Methodist
Episcopal Church in 1893.

Interments in the churchyard probably came to an end with the 1851 ban
on burials below 86th Street in Manhattan.
MAILING ADDRESS: c/o Washington Square United Methodist Church
          133 West Fourth Street
          New York, New York 10012-1095
PHONE NUMBER: (212) 777-2528
RECORDS: N/A
RESOURCES: N/A

Greenwich Village Methodist Episcopal
Church Cemetery and Vaults

See Bedford Street Methodist Episcopal Church Cemetery and Vaults.

Green-Wood Cemetery

CATEGORY: Non-Sectarian
YEARS OF USE: 1840 to date
LOCATION: Fifth Avenue, opposite 25th Street, Brooklyn.
HISTORY: "It is the ambition of the New Yorker to live on Fifth Avenue, to take his airings in The [Central] Park, and to sleep with his fathers in Green-Wood," wrote the *New York Times* in 1866. "It would need a volume... to mention by name all the elaborate monuments and tombs that have been erected. Money has been lavished quite as freely upon the dead as upon the living. Ten thousand dollars is not an uncommon expenditure upon a burial plot and its adornments, and in some cases five or six times that sum." Indeed, monuments and mausoleums take the shape of Egyptian pyramids, Greek temples, sinking steamboats, mangled railroad cars, fire hydrants, angels, and empty chairs and beds.

Once called "the largest and handsomest [cemetery] in the vicinity of New York," Green-Wood's beauty ultimately inspired the contest to design Manhattan's Central Park. Designed by David Bates Douglass, and modeled after Mount Auburn Cemetery in Cambridge, Massachusetts, the 478-acre cemetery was seen "as a rural retreat where visitors could contemplate death as a reconciliation with nature." Douglass' plan included trees, flowers, shrubbery, ponds, streams, a lake, and more than twenty miles of winding paths with views of Manhattan and New York Harbor. Richard Upjohn, architect of Trinity Church, designed the Main Gate. Erected in 1861, the gate was made of brownstone and crowned with multi-colored slate shingles. Spires, turrets, finials, crockets, and gables distinguish the structure in the gothic revival style.

There have been over 600,000 interments at Green-Wood. Among those buried here are former New York City Mayor, William "Boss" Tweed; the inventor Samuel F. B. Morse; the newspaper publisher and presidential candidate Horace Greeley; the conductor Leonard Bernstein; and birth control advocate Margaret Sanger.
MAILING ADDRESS: Green-Wood Cemetery
                  Fifth Avenue and 25th Street
                  Brooklyn, New York 11232-1690
PHONE NUMBER: (718) 768-7300
RECORDS: Records are held at the cemetery's office. Requests may be made on-site or by mail.
RESOURCES: Bell, Bill. "Stiff Lesson on Gray Line Tour." *New York Daily News*, 27 October 1997, City Central section. (notable burials)

Brower, Effie. *In Memoriam: Green-Wood Leaves*. Brooklyn, N.Y.: author imprint, 1878.

Green-Wood Cemetery, Catalogue of Proprietors, to August 1, 1884. Brooklyn, N.Y., Printed for the Cemetery. (alphabetical list of 24,758 lot owners)

Groussett, Agnes M., trans. "Horn, Randolph, Story, Teimann and Allied Families." *New York State Miscellaneous Records, District X*, New York. Washington, D.C.: Daughters of the American Revolution, 1978, 4–8. (related interments)

Moos, Dorothy A., trans. "Cemetery Records of New York and New Jersey, 1824 to 1973." *Church and Cemetery Records from New Jersey.* Washington, D.C.: Daughters of the American Revolution, 1979. (Concklin, Smith, and Reid burials in lot 7778, section 58)

"Our Cities of the Dead: Millions of People are at Rest in Them." *The Brooklyn Daily Eagle*, 28 April 1895, p. 28, col. 1. (notable gravestones)

Hallett Family Burial Ground

CATEGORY: Private
YEARS OF USE: circa 1724 to 1861
LOCATION: Main Street, Astoria, Queens.
HISTORY: In 1905, the Hallett family sold its ancestral estate to developers and moved the remains of its family burial ground to Mount Olivet Cemetery. Samuel Hallett, who died on 27 December 1724, was the earliest known burial.

William Hallett (Samuel's nephew), his pregnant wife, and five children were murdered in their sleep on 24 January 1708. Their two slaves, a man and a woman, were accused and convicted of the crime within two weeks. Both were executed. The female slave was burned at the stake, while the man "hung in gibbets and placed astride a sharp iron and in a state of delirium which ensued, believing himself to be on horseback, would urge forward his animal while the blood oozing from his lacerated flesh streamed to the ground."

William's family was buried in one grave, possibly in the Hallett Family Burial Ground. It is not known if they were among those removed to Mount Olivet Cemetery.
MAILING ADDRESS: c/o Mount Olivet Cemetery
65-40 Grand Avenue
Flushing, New York 11378-2423
PHONE NUMBER: (718) 326-1777
RECORDS: Mount Olivet Cemetery prefers written requests for information. The *Long Island Daily Star* may have published the Hallett gravestone inscriptions in May of 1884, day and page unknown.
RESOURCES: Riker, James. "Historical Notes of Newtown." *The Long*

Island Collection. vol. 3. Queens Borough Public Library. Jamaica, N.Y.,
1941, 445. (gravestone inscriptions, 1731–1764)

Harlem Reformed Dutch Churchyard and Vaults

CATEGORY: Reformed Dutch
YEARS OF USE: circa 1660 to 1835
LOCATION: West side of First Avenue, between 124th Street and 125th Street,
Manhattan.
HISTORY: The Harlem Reformed Dutch Church is the oldest church on the
northern end of Manhattan. Its worship services were established in
November of 1660, and its first church building was completed in 1667.
During the Revolutionary War, the church was destroyed, and a new one was
built upon the site. Burial vaults were constructed at this time.
     The churchyard and vaults remained untouched until 1881, when the
congregation decided to move the church building and sell portions of its
property. The remains in its burial ground were removed to Woodlawn
Cemetery, lots 1061 to 1068.
     This church was also known as the First Collegiate Reformed Church of
Harlem. The Elmendorf Reformed Church is its successor.
MAILING ADDRESS: Elmendorf Reformed Church
                 171 East 121st Street
                 New York, New York 10035-3588
PHONE NUMBER: (212) 534-5856
RECORDS: No separate records before 1806: prior to that time, records are
part of the Collegiate Church (or common) registers.
RESOURCES: "Burials in the Dutch Church of New York City, 1804 to 1813."
The New York Genealogical and Biographical Record 75 (July 1944): 127.
     Disinterments From Vaults and Churchyard, 1869 to 1875. Manuscript at
the New York Genealogical and Biographical Society. New York, New York.
File "NYC-Churches-Dutch Reformed-Harlem-Cemetery."
     Records of the Collegiate Churches, Burials 1727 to 1804. Manuscript
#NY-53 at the New York Genealogical and Biographical Society. New York,
New York. (dates of death and burial)
     White, Mrs. William R. "Records of the Reformed Dutch Church of
Harlem." *The New York Genealogical and Biographical Record* 118 (October
1987): 217–222. (payments for burials, 1816–1827)
     Year Book of the Holland Society of New York. New York, 1899,
139 –211. (alphabetized list of deaths, 1727–1803)

Harris Family Burial Ground

CATEGORY: Private
YEARS OF USE: Gravestone dated 1850

LOCATION: "Back of a little cottage on the Rossville Road," Rossville, Staten Island.
HISTORY: A marble gravestone was erected to the memory of Celia Harris, who died on 23 February 1850 at the age of fifty-one years, six months, and twenty days.
MAILING ADDRESS: N/A
PHONE NUMBER: N/A
RECORDS: N/A
RESOURCES: Davis, William T. "Homestead Graves." *Proceedings of the Natural Science Association of Staten Island.* Staten Island, New York. Special Number 9, December 1889. (Gravestone Inscription)

Hart Island Cemetery

CATEGORY: Public
YEARS OF USE: April 20, 1869 to date
LOCATION: Hart Island, east of City Island, Long Island Sound, Bronx.
HISTORY: Louisa Van Slyke died in Charity Hospital without family or friends to claim her body. On 20 April 1869, she became the first person buried in Hart Island Cemetery. One million others are buried with her. Today, Hart Island Cemetery is the largest potter's field in the United States.

Inmates from the prison on Riker's Island receive the dead, shipped to Hart Island on a ferry run by the Department of Corrections. The deceased's name and identification number are both carved into the coffin. A packet with other identifying information is attached to the coffin, and the deceased's name is again marked upon it, in indelible ink.

Most of those buried here are indigent persons who arrive from public institutions. Very few of them are Jewish. Several burial societies exist to inter the remains of indigent Jews in private cemeteries.

The remains of all unidentified bodies are sent to Hart Island for interment after being photographed at the morgue. John and Jane Does constitute one-tenth of all burials. Approximately one hundred bodies are identified by relatives or friends each year. A body can be disinterred for up to eight years after burial.

The cemetery is dotted with white markers, each denoting a mass burial of 150 bodies laid out in two rows, three coffins deep. None of the dead have personal grave markers, but there are two large monuments dedicated to all. A granite cross, erected in 1902, is inscribed "He Calleth His Children by Name." A thirty-foot memorial was erected in 1948. The word "PEACE" is inscribed on one side in faded gold letters.

An elaborate stone fence surrounds a sixteen-foot obelisk dedicated to the Union soldiers who died on Hart Island during the Civil War. The island was used as a training ground for fifty-thousand soldiers—those that died here died from disease, not battle. These men were buried in a small cemetery on the island before the public cemetery was established. Each soldier had his own grave with a stone giving his name, regiment, age, and date of death. Their remains were exhumed in the twentieth century and reburied in national and private cemeteries. Some were taken to the West Farms Presbyterian Churchyard in the Bronx.

Over the years, various sections of the the island were developed by private and government entities. One speculator attempted to open an amusement park in 1925. He constructed a dance hall, boardwalk, and eight boarding houses before New York City purchased his share of the island, putting an end to the project. The carcasses of other development projects still dot the landscape: a rotting jail, a broken greenhouse, an empty Catholic Church, a crumbling street, and empty Nike missile silos. The cemetery continues to spread across the island and around these ruins as gravediggers clear the land for new burials.

Although Hart Island is not open to the public, a group affiliated with Saint Benedict's Roman Catholic Church in the Bronx travels to the Island each May, on Ascension Thursday, to say prayers for the dead.

MAILING ADDRESS: c/o The Municipal Archives
                  31 Chambers Street, Room 103
                  New York, New York 10007-1210
PHONE NUMBER: (212) 788-8582
RECORDS: Burial registers are turned over to the Municipal Archives when disinterment is no longer possible.
RESOURCES: Hunt, Melinda and Joel Sternfeld, "Hart Island," 1998, Scalo, Zurich–Berlin–New York. (history of cemetery, interviews with gravediggers, extensive collection of photographs). Researchers can also view photos of the cemetery on the New York City Web site located at
    <www.ci.nyc.ny.us/html/doc/html/hart.html>.

Hedger-Edwards Cemetery
See West Farms Reformed Dutch Cemetery.

Hegney Place Cemetery
May refer to Morrisania Cemetery.

Hicks Burial Ground
See Waters Cemetery.

Hillside Cemetery

CATEGORY: Baptist
YEARS OF USE: 1829 to date
LOCATION: Richmond Avenue, south of Hillside Street, adjoining Baron Hirsch Cemetery, Mariner's Harbor, Staten Island.

HISTORY: The Union Avenue Baptist Church was erected in 1829, an extension of the Clove Meeting House. Hillside Cemetery was its burial ground.

The cemetery is currently operated and cared for by the Willowbrook Park Baptist Church.

MAILING ADDRESS: Hillside Cemetery
c/o Willowbrook Park Baptist Church
1780 Richmond Avenue
Staten Island, New York 10314-3994

PHONE NUMBER: (718) 698-1318

RECORDS: Researchers should check the Staten Island RootsWeb page, on the Internet, to see if this cemetery has been added to their cemetery database. The address is
<http://www.rootsweb.com/~nyrichmo>.

RESOURCES: Vosburgh, Royden W., editor and transcriber, *Staten Island Gravestone Inscriptions*. vol. 1. New York City, March 1924 (typed manuscript). An interment list has been posted on the Richmond County RootsWeb project Web site. The address is:
<http://www.rootsweb.com/~nyrichmo>

Holmes-Perine Family Burial Ground

CATEGORY: Private

YEARS OF USE: Gravestones date 1777 to 1823

LOCATION: Justin Avenue, west of Hylan Boulevard, Great Kills, Staten Island.

HISTORY: The Stillwell-Perine House was purchased by the Perine family in 1764 and remained in their possession until 1913. The Barton Homestead was erected in 1789. Members of both families are interred in this nearby burial ground, along with members of the Holmes and Wood families.

By 1930, the gravestones were gone, and the yard was neatly planted with roses.

MAILING ADDRESS: N/A

PHONE NUMBER: N/A

RECORDS: N/A

RESOURCES: Davis, William T. "Homestead Graves." *Proceedings of the Natural Science Association of Staten Island*. Staten Island, New York. Special Number 9, December 1889. (Gravestone Inscriptions)

Morris, Ira K. *Morris's Memorial History of Staten Island, New York*. vol. 2. West New Brighton, Staten Island: Memorial Publishing Company, New York: 1900, 108–9. (genealogical data taken from tombstones, county records, and church records)

Holy Cross Cemetery

CATEGORY: Roman Catholic
YEARS OF USE: July 1849 to date
LOCATION: East side of Brooklyn Avenue, Cortelyou Road and Snyder
Avenue, Flatbush, Brooklyn.
HISTORY: Holy Cross Cemetery, of the Diocese of Brooklyn, was established
in 1849 during a cholera epidemic. Six thousand graves were opened during
the second half of the year: 278 of them in a single week. The original plot
was gradually enlarged with additional purchases, but by 1904, the cemetery
was near capacity.

Prior to the opening of Holy Cross Cemetery, members of the Roman
Catholic faith in Brooklyn were buried in Saint James' Churchyard, or in the
Roman Catholic section of the Wallabout Cemetery. Remains from the
Wallabout Cemetery were reinterred here in 1857.
MAILING ADDRESS: The Holy Cross Cemetery
       3620 Tilden Avenue
       Brooklyn, New York 11203-4032
PHONE NUMBER: (718) 284-4520
RECORDS: Records are housed at the cemetery.
RESOURCES: "Old Burial Grounds. Cemeteries in Brooklyn and the
County Towns." *The Brooklyn Eagle*, 29 August 1886, p. 9, col. 3. (grave-
stone inscription of Ann Lime)

Silinonte, Joseph M. *Tombstones of the Irish Born: Cemetery of the
Holy Cross, Flatbush, Brooklyn*. Concord, Ontario: Becker Associates, 1992.
(limited gravestone inscriptions)

Holy Trinity Cemetery
See Trinity Church Cemetery and Vaults.

Homestead Cemetery
See Southside Cemetery.

Houston Street Burial Ground
of the Society of Friends

CATEGORY: Quaker
YEARS OF USE: circa 1825 to 1848
LOCATION: 105-107 East Houston Street, south side of the street between
Chrystie Street and the Bowery, Manhattan.
HISTORY: The Houston Street Burial Ground of the Society of Friends was
used by all Friends in the City of New York. It was discontinued in 1848 and
the remains were removed to Prospect Park Cemetery. The property was
sold to Trinity Corporation for the construction of Saint Augustine's Chapel.

MAILING ADDRESS: c/o Friends' Historical Library
                          Swarthmore College
                          500 College Avenue
                          Swarthmore, Pennsylvania 19081-1399
PHONE NUMBER: (610) 328-8000
RECORDS: Original records are now housed at the Friends' Historical Library
of Swarthmore College. Tombstones were not permitted in Quaker cemeter-
ies until 1852.
RESOURCES: *New York Monthly Meeting, New York City: Births and
Deaths 1827 to 1904.* Salt Lake City: Genealogical Society of Utah, 1950,
microfilm number 17,380.

Huguenot Cemetery

CATEGORY: Reformed Dutch
YEARS OF USE: circa 1851 to 1913
LOCATION: Amboy Road and Huguenot Avenue, Prince's Bay, Staten Island.
HISTORY: The Reformed Protestant Dutch Church of the Huguenots was
organized in 1849. The congregation erected its first church in 1851 and
remained at the same location until 1940.

Land in their one-acre cemetery was sporadically sold off and put to
other use. Disinterments began in the late nineteenth century. The Jessup
family moved its dead to the Moravian Cemetery on 20 October 1885; the
MacFarland Family sent its dead to Moravian Cemetery on 3 August 1896;
and by 1913, the last of the bodies were transferred to Woodrow United
Methodist Churchyard.

This cemetery is also known as the Reformed Protestant Dutch Cemetery
of Staten Island.
MAILING ADDRESS: Huguenot Reformed Church
                          5501 Amboy Road
                          Staten Island, New York 10312-3999
PHONE NUMBER: (718) 356-3737
RECORDS: Vital records date back to 1849.
RESOURCES: Vosburgh, Royden Woodward, trans. and ed. *Records of the
Reformed Protestant Dutch Church, Westfield, Staten Island.* Staten Island,
N.Y., November 1923. Manuscript. (deaths and funerals, 1852–1872, 1917;
gravestone inscriptions 1852–1880)

Humboldt Street Cemetery
See Bushwick Reformed Protestant Dutch Churchyard.

Hungarian Union Field of the Mutual Benevolent Society

CATEGORY: Jewish, Hungarian
YEARS OF USE: 1865 to date
LOCATION: 8229 Cypress Avenue, north side of the avenue between Union
Field Cemetery and Cypress Hills Street, Glendale, Queens.
HISTORY: N/A
MAILING ADDRESS: Hungarian Cemetery
                            8299 Cypress Avenue
                            Flushing, New York 11385-6716
PHONE NUMBER: (718) 366-3434
RECORDS: Cemetery records are housed on-site.
RESOURCES: N/A

Hunt Family Burial Ground

CATEGORY: Private
YEARS OF USE: Gravestones date 1749 to 1881
LOCATION: Drake Park, Hunts Point and Oak Point Avenues, Bronx.
HISTORY: The Hunt Family Burial Ground is within Drake Park, named for
Joseph Rodman Drake, a poet who was buried there in 1820. Members of
the Hunt, Leggett, and Willett families are buried there as well. A slave bur-
ial ground was situated on the opposite side of the street.
MAILING ADDRESS: N/A
PHONE NUMBER: N/A
RECORDS: N/A
RESOURCES: *Cemetery, Church, and Town Records of New York State.* vol.
9. Washington, D.C. Daughters of the American Revolution, 1927, 237–238.
(gravestone inscriptions)

Indian Cemetery

See Canarsie Cemetery and/or Flatlands Town Cemetery.

Indian Hill Burial Ground

CATEGORY: Military, Native American
YEARS OF USE: 31 August 1778
LOCATION: Within Van Cortlandt Park, at Oneida Avenue and East 238th Street, Bronx.
HISTORY: This is the burial ground of Chief Ninhan and seventeen Patriot Stockbridge Indians who were killed in an ambush near 233rd Street by the British during the Revolutionary War.

    The Daughters of the American Revolution erected a six-foot bronze and fieldstone monument to the memory of Chief Ninhan in 1906.
MAILING ADDRESS: N/A
PHONE NUMBER: N/A
RECORDS: N/A
RESOURCES: N/A

Irish Church Cemetery

See Presbyterian Cemetery, West 25th Street.

Iron Hill Cemetery

See Burbanck Family Burial Ground.

Jacobson Burial Vault

See Van Der Vanter Burial Vault.

Jesuit Cemetery

See Fordham University Chapel Cemetery.

John Street Methodist Episcopal Churchyard

CATEGORY: Methodist Episcopal
YEARS OF USE: circa 1766 to no later than 1823
LOCATION: 44 John Street, between William Street and Nassau Street, Manhattan.
HISTORY: The John Street Methodist Episcopal Church was erected in 1768, the first Methodist Church in the United States. The congregation is still at the same location today.

The church was also known as Wesley Chapel.
MAILING ADDRESS: John Street United Methodist Church
              44 John Street
              New York, New York 10038-3714
PHONE NUMBER: (212) 269-0014
RECORDS: N/A
RESOURCES: *Cemetery, Church, and Town Records of New York State.* vol. 105. Washington, D.C.: Daughters of the American Revolution, 1938, 163–174. (inscriptions from marble tablets)

The New York Genealogical and Biographical Society Collection 11 (1916): 361. (deaths, 1840–1841)

The New York Genealogical and Biographical Society Collection 21 (1926): 680. (Interments, 1785–1787)

Journeay Family Burial Ground and Vault

CATEGORY: Private

YEARS OF USE: Gravestones date 1760 to 1845

LOCATION: Carlton Boulevard and Halpen Avenue, west of the intersection, Annadale, Staten Island.

HISTORY: Albert Journeay Sr., in his will proved 24 September 1860, ordered his "executors to purchase a plot of land in Saint Andrew's Churchyard... for the interment of members of my family... " He then gave to his "sons Edward and Albert the plot used for a burial place on my farm, Westfield, and a free passage thereto forever to be used for such of my father's family as may desire to be interred there."

When historian William T. Davis visited the plot in the late 1880s, there were only ten gravestones standing. They memorialized members of the Furman, Hedden, Journeay, Pearson, and Randolph families. Today, the burial ground is abandoned: one vandalized gravestone remains.

Friends of Abandoned Cemeteries of Staten Island reports that the cemetery is within the proposed Arden Heights Woods Park and has contacted city officials in a bid to protect the property.

MAILING ADDRESS: N/A

PHONE NUMBER: N/A

RECORDS: N/A

RESOURCES: Davis, William T. "Homestead Graves." *Proceedings of the Natural Science Association of Staten Island.* Staten Island, New York. Special Number 9, December 1889. (gravestone inscriptions)

Ketchum's Hill Burial Ground
See Bedell-Decker Family Burial Ground.

Kingsbridge Burial Ground

CATEGORY: Private
YEARS OF USE: Gravestones date 1794 to 1807
LOCATION: Within Van Cortlandt Park, between Van Cortlandt Mansion and Van Cortlandt Lake, Bronx.
HISTORY: Members of the Ackerman, Berrian, Bashford, and Warner families are known to be buried in this cemetery. Most of the graves were marked by rough fieldstones. In some cases, the initials of the deceased were engraved into stone, while formal monuments were erected for others.

The New York City and Northern Railroad was cut through the northern end of the plot circa 1890, where African-American slaves are thought to be buried.

MAILING ADDRESS: c/o Van Cortlandt House Museum
                 Van Cortlandt Park
                 Broadway and West 246th Street
                 Bronx, New York 10471
PHONE NUMBER: (718) 543-3344
RECORDS: N/A
RESOURCES: Edsall, Thomas H. "Old Burial Grounds in Westchester County, New York." *The New York Genealogical and Biographical Record* 20, no. 2 (April 1889): 67–8. (gravestone inscriptions; limited genealogy)

Kip Family Burial Ground

CATEGORY: Private
YEARS OF USE: Prior to 1831
LOCATION: Kip's Bay, Manhattan.
HISTORY: The area near Second Avenue and East Thirty-fifth Street, Manhattan, was the site of the Jacobus Kip farm, "a goodly estate, covering one-hundred and fifty acres and comprising meadow, woodland and stream." It extended all the way to the East River. In 1655, Kip built a mansion of imported brick for his wife, Marie de la Montagne; the house stood on the farm for almost 200 years. The house was torn down, and the property sold for development, in 1851. The remains in the family burial ground were reinterred in the New York City Marble Cemetery, Manhattan.
MAILING ADDRESS: N/A
PHONE NUMBER: N/A
RECORDS: N/A
RESOURCES: "An Old Cemetery: Sketch of a Notable Landmark." *The New York Times*, 18 May 1875, p. 8, col. 1. (partial list of vault owners)
     King, Moses. "The New York City Marble Cemetery." *King's Handbook of New York City*. Boston, Mass., 1893. Reissued. New York: Benjamin Blom Inc., 1972, 510–511. (photo; some burials)

Knollwood Park Cemetery

CATEGORY: Jewish
YEARS OF USE: 1947 to date
LOCATION: 5780 Cooper Avenue, south side of the Avenue between Cemetery of the Evergreens and Cypress Avenue, Ridgewood, Queens.
HISTORY: N/A
MAILING ADDRESS: Knollwood Park Cemetery
                 5780 Cooper Avenue
                 Flushing, New York 11385-6069
PHONE NUMBER: (718) 386-6700
RECORDS: The cemetery records are housed on-site.
RESOURCES: N/A

Cornelius Kreuzer Family Burial Ground and Vault

CATEGORY: Private
YEARS OF USE: Gravestones date 1760 to 1815
LOCATION: Richmond Terrace, between Elizabeth Street and Bement Avenue, Livingston, Staten Island.
HISTORY: The Kreuzer-Pelton House, at the corner of Richmond Terrace and Pelton Avenue, was purchased by Cornelius Kreuzer in 1751. Kreuzer occu-

pied the house until his death in 1807. He is interred in the family burial ground along with his wife, Beliche, who died in 1815.

Although the Kreuzer family maintained the right to use the cemetery after the estate was sold, circa 1832, they never exercised that right. The cemetery's gravestones were laid on the ground and covered with sod. At one point, a family member may have pulled the stones up and copied down the inscriptions, but the location of that list is unknown.

The grounds were eventually occupied by the Staten Island Athletic Club. Friends of Abandoned Cemeteries of Staten Island reports that the graveyard is now beneath a disused gas station.

This cemetery is also known as the Cruser Family Burial Ground.

MAILING ADDRESS: N/A

PHONE NUMBER: N/A

RECORDS: N/A

RESOURCES: Davis, William T. "Homestead Graves." *Proceedings of the Natural Science Association of Staten Island*. Staten Island, New York. Special Number 9, December 1889. (gravestone inscriptions)

Lane, Doris. "The Cruser Family Burying Ground: A Most Abandoned Cemetery." *The FACSI Newsletter*, vol. 14, issue 1 (Spring 1997). (history of cemetery, list of burials, sources of information)

Lake Cemetery

CATEGORY: Baptist
YEARS OF USE: circa 1842 to 1949
LOCATION: Southwest corner of Willow Brook Road and Forest Avenue, Graniteville, Staten Island.
HISTORY: Lake Cemetery began as the burial ground of the Graniteville First Baptist Church, established in 1830 by the Reverend Samuel White. The congregation moved to a new location in 1842, but kept this property for use as a burial ground.

When Reverend White died in 1863, he was buried in the White family vault in the church cemetery. The congregation went into a slow decline without his leadership. They disbanded in 1882 and sold the cemetery in 1899, presumably to the Lake family.

The cemetery was subsequently acquired by the Christ Mission Methodist Church of Staten Island. They sold the property to Christ Mission Rehoboth Pentecostal Church in 1961. There have been very few burials in Lake Cemetery since 1949, and over the years, the grounds fell into a state of neglect. Ownership of the property is now in question.

Friends of Abandoned Cemeteries of Staten Island took an interest in Lake Cemetery. They regularly inspect and clean it. Records from this burial ground were the first entered into their database of burials in abandoned cemeteries on Staten Island.

This cemetery is also known as Silvie's Cemetery.
MAILING ADDRESS: Lake Cemetery
                c/o Friends of Abandoned Cemeteries of Staten Island
                140 Tysen Street
                Staten Island, New York 10301-1120

PHONE NUMBER: N/A
RECORDS: Friends of Abandoned Cemeteries of Staten Island has created a computerized database of Lake Cemetery records. An interment list has been posted on the Richmond County RootsWeb project Web site. The address is: <http://www.rootsweb.com/~nyrichmo>
RESOURCES: N/A

Lake Family Burial Ground

CATEGORY: Private
YEARS OF USE: Gravestones date 1783 to 1841
LOCATION: Site of the Oakwood Beach Sewage Treatment Plant, between Tarlton Street and the Gateway National Recreation Area, Oakwood, Staten Island.
HISTORY: The Lake Family Burial Ground was a short distance from the Lake Family Homestead, erected 1786. Most of the gravestones in the cemetery were broken when historian William T. Davis visited the grounds in the late 1880s. Nearly all of the stones were dedicated to members of the Lake family, but the Androvette, DuBois, Marsh, and Mersereau families were represented as well.

Davis noted that there was a slave cemetery in the woods behind the homestead, though none of the graves were marked. He stated that a female slave named "Blacky Time" was the last person buried in that cemetery.

Friends of Abandoned Cemeteries of Staten Island reports that the Lake Family Burial Ground is no longer extant.
MAILING ADDRESS: N/A
PHONE NUMBER: N/A
RECORDS: N/A
RESOURCES: Davis, William T. "Homestead Graves." *Proceedings of the Natural Science Association of Staten Island.* Staten Island, New York. Special Number 9, December 1889. (gravestone inscriptions)

Lawrence Family Burial Ground

CATEGORY: Private
YEARS OF USE: 1832 to 1939
LOCATION: 216th Street at 42nd Avenue, Bayside, Queens.
HISTORY: The Lawrence family acquired this property in 1645, but they didn't use it as a graveyard until 1832. In 1840, Effingham Lawrence, a judge, created a deed that allowed any member of the Lawrence family to be buried there, prohibited sale of the grounds, and forbade removal of bodies. Forty-eight members of the Lawrence family were buried there, including Cornelius W. Lawrence, New York City's mayor between 1834 and 1837, and Frederick Newbold Lawrence, former president of the New York Stock Exchange.

After the last burial in 1939, the cemetery was neglected and ultimately abandoned. It was vandalized and used as a trash dump. New York City illegally seized the cemetery for non-payment of taxes in the early 1950s, but dropped the claim in 1954. To add to the unrest of the Lawrence family, Judge Effingham Lawrence's grave was opened by neighborhood boys in 1957.

A 1963 title search led the City of New York to Philip Lawrence of Bernardsville, New Jersey. Mr. Lawrence, who was then a retired real estate and insurance salesman, told the *New York Times*, "it's just one of those awful things that we're very much ashamed of."

The Bayside Historical Society has since organized to transform the burial ground into the Lawrence Memorial Park of Bayside. In 1975, new research showed that members of the Eccles and Gilman families were buried with the Lawrences.

MAILING ADDRESS: Lawrence Family Cemetery
                                c/o Queens Historical Society
                                Kingsland Homestead
                                143-35 37th Avenue
                                Flushing, New York 11354-5729
PHONE NUMBER: (718) 939-0647
RECORDS: N/A
RESOURCES: Frost, Josephine C. trans. *Long Island Cemetery Inscriptions*. Brooklyn, New York. vol. One, March 1913. (gravestone inscriptions)

    Powell, Charles U., comp., and Alice H. Meigs, ed. *Description of Private and Family Cemeteries in the Borough of Queens*. City of New York, Borough of Queens, Topographical Bureau. Jamaica, N.Y.: Queens Borough Public Library, 1932 and 1975 supplements. (gravestone inscriptions and maps) (Note: 1975 edition has eight additional names.)

Lawrence Manor Burial Ground

CATEGORY: Private
YEARS OF USE: 1703 to 1975
LOCATION: 35-10 20th Road, southeast corner of 35th Street, Astoria, Queens.
HISTORY: This private burial ground is final resting place of nearly one hundred members of the Lawrence family. Among them are distinguished Revolutionary War soldiers and statesmen. They include Major John Lawrence, a Patriot soldier, member of the Provincial Congress of 1776, and member of the convention that created the New York State Constitution; John Lawrence, a Revolutionary War officer and Town Supervisor of Newtown; Nathaniel Lawrence, a ratifier of the United States Constitution; and William T. Lawrence, a member of the United States Congress.

In 1915, the cemetery was restored after some years of neglect. Its stone fence and wrought iron gate were repaired, and the grounds were planted with flowers. There were plans to purchase the surrounding property and convert it into a park as a historic site for future generations. The cemetery is now a New York City Landmark.

Members of the Duthie, Hartman, Sackett, Suydam, Van Sinderen, and Wells families are buried with the Lawrences. Oliver Lawrence, who died in 1975, was the last person buried in the cemetery.

MAILING ADDRESS: Lawrence Manor Burial Ground
                        c/o Queens Historical Society
                        Kingsland Homestead
                        143-35 37th Avenue
                        Flushing, New York 11354-5727

PHONE NUMBER: (718) 939-0647

RECORDS: N/A

RESOURCES: Clines, Francis X. "About New York: On Bringing Life Among the Dead." *The New York Times*, 5 November 1977, p. 19, col. 1. (gravestone inscriptions; post-1932 burials; family history)

"Many Soldiers Rest in Lawrence Plot." *The Long Island Daily Press*, 7 February 1937. (list of notable burials)

Martin, Mary Lawrence. "Lawrence Family Cemetery, Long Island, New York." *Daughters of the American Revolution Magazine* 49, no. 5 (November 1916): 340–342. (vital records, photos, and burial notes)

Poweli, Charles U., comp., and Alice H. Meigs, ed. *Description of Private and Family Cemeteries in the Borough of Queens*. City of New York, Borough of Queens, Topographical Bureau. Jamaica, N.Y.: Queens Borough Public Library, 1932. (gravestone inscriptions and maps)

Leake and Watts Orphan Home Cemetery

CATEGORY: Institutional

YEARS OF USE: circa 1843 to 1851

LOCATION: South of 40th Street, Manhattan.

HISTORY: Leake and Watts Orphan Home opened in 1843 as an asylum for impoverished orphans between the ages of three and twelve. It was situated at West 113th Street, Manhattan, on property purchased from New York Hospital.

In a report written by the Board of Assistant Aldermen in 1849, Leake and Watts was named as the owner of a cemetery south of 40th Street in Manhattan. This may be mistaken for a cemetery located on their upper west-side property, at the southeast corner of 9th Avenue and West 110th Street, Manhattan.

In 1899, the *Brooklyn Eagle* reported that the Leake and Watts Orphan Home "has a plot in Saint Michael's Cemetery."

A representative of the Home states that they do not have record of a cemetery in Manhattan, nor are they aware of a plot in Saint Michael's Cemetery.

MAILING ADDRESS: Leake and Watts Children's Home
                 463 Hawthorne Avenue
                 Yonkers, New York 10705-3498
PHONE NUMBER: (914) 963-5220
RECORDS: N/A
RESOURCES: *Report of the Special Committee on the Subject of Interments South of 40th Street in the City of New York.* Board of Assistant Aldermen. New York, New York. Documents Number 2 and 5, July 12th and July 19th, 1849. (identifies cemetery)

Le Comte Family Burial Ground

CATEGORY: Private
YEARS OF USE: circa 1700
LOCATION: Le Comte Estate, Richmond Valley, Staten Island.
HISTORY: In his will dated October 2, 1697, John Le Comte instructed his executors to bury him in the garden near his house. The exact location of his home is unknown.
MAILING ADDRESS: N/A
PHONE NUMBER: N/A
RECORDS: N/A
RESOURCES: N/A

Leffert Family Burial Ground

CATEGORY: Private
YEARS OF USE: Gravestones date 1762 to 1859
LOCATION: Current site of Halsey Street, between Bedford Avenue and Arlington Place, Bedford-Stuyvesant, Brooklyn.
HISTORY: According to an article in *The Brooklyn Daily Eagle*, the Leffert Family Burial Ground stood in a grove of trees "a few hundred yards back of the Rem Leffert house." Members of the Leffert, Rapalye, Remsen, and Vandervoort families were among those buried there.

The bodies were removed to Green-Wood Cemetery sometime prior to the article's publication on 25 June 1893.
MAILING ADDRESS: c/o Green-Wood Cemetery
                 Fifth Avenue and 25th Street
                 Brooklyn, New York 11232-1690
PHONE NUMBER: (718) 768-7300
RECORDS: Green-Wood's records are held at the cemetery's office. Requests may be made on-site or by mail.
RESOURCES: Bergen, Teunis G. "The Leffert Burying Ground." *The Long Island Historical Society Quarterly* 4, no. 1 (January 1942): 21–22. (gravestone inscriptions)

l'Eglise of Saint Espirit Churchyard and Vaults

CATEGORY: French Huguenot, Protestant Episcopal
YEARS OF USE: 1704 to 1830
LOCATION: Northeast corner of Nassau Street and Pine Street, Manhattan.
HISTORY: l'Eglise of Saint Espirit dates back to 1688. In 1704, the congregation erected a church on the north side of Pine Street. Its graveyard was behind the church building.

The church building and graveyard were sold about 1831. The remains were removed to a vault in the graveyard of Saint Mark's Church, Manhattan.

MAILING ADDRESS: French Church of Saint Espirit
                  111 East 60th Street, or 50th Street
                  New York, New York 10022-1113 (if 60)
PHONE NUMBER: (212) 838-5680 (if 60)
RECORDS: Photocopies of the church registers are located at the New York Historical Society.
RESOURCES: Wittmeyer, Reverend Alfred V., ed. *Registers of the Births, Marriages, and Deaths of the Eglise Française à la Nouvelle York from 1688 to 1804.* Collections of the Huguenot Society of America. vol. 1. New York: The Huguenot Society of America, 1886. Printed for the Consistory.

Leonard Street Methodist Episcopal Churchyard

CATEGORY: Methodist Episcopal
YEARS OF USE: N/A
LOCATION: Leonard Street, between Grand Street and Powers Street, Williamsburg, Brooklyn.
HISTORY: The Leonard Street Methodist Episcopal Church was established in 1845. After a ban on burials below 86th Street in Manhattan, the trustees of the First Methodist Circuit decided to move their dead to a plot in Cypress Hills Cemetery. The removals began in 1854 and lasted for two years. The *Brooklyn Daily Eagle* interviewed a watchman who stated that the bones and coffins were buried in trenches, while the best headstones were "put up to look good."
MAILING ADDRESS: c/o Cypress Hills Cemetery
                 833 Jamaica Avenue
                 Brooklyn, New York 11208-1593
PHONE NUMBER: (718) 277-2900
RECORDS: Cypress Hills Cemetery prefers written requests for searches.
RESOURCES: *Cypress Hills Cemetery.* Brooklyn, N.Y.: Cypress Hills Cemetery, 1880. (extensive list of plot owners and location of plot, maps, rules, and history of cemetery)

"The Forgotten Dead: Many Neglected Graves in Cypress Hills Cemetery." *The Brooklyn Daily Eagle*, 13 August 1893, p. 8, col. 7.

Leverich Family Burial Ground

CATEGORY: Private
YEARS OF USE: Gravestones date 1765 to 1818
LOCATION: Leverich Street and 71st Street, Jackson Heights, Queens.
HISTORY: The Leverich Family Burial Ground was situated directly across the street from the Leverich Homestead. There is no sign of the cemetery today, and there is no evidence to suggest that the bodies were removed. The gravestone of James Hazard, who died 1765, was taken to Saint James Episcopal Church in 1925.
MAILING ADDRESS: N/A
PHONE NUMBER: N/A
RECORDS: N/A
RESOURCES: Powell, Charles U., comp., and Alice H. Meigs, ed.
Description of Private and Family Cemeteries in the Borough of Queens. City of New York, Borough of Queens, Topographical Bureau. Jamaica, N.Y.: Queens Borough Public Library, 1975 supplement. (gravestone inscriptions)
    Frost, Josephine C. trans. *Long Island Cemetery Inscriptions.* Brooklyn, New York. vol. 1. March 1912. (gravestone inscriptions)

Linden Hill Cemetery of Central Synagogue

CATEGORY: Jewish
YEARS OF USE: 1850 to date
LOCATION: 55-22 Metropolitan Avenue, south side between Starr Street and Stanhope Street, Ridgewood, Queens.
HISTORY: This cemetery was established in 1850 by Congregation Ahavath (Ahawath) Chesed of Manhattan.
MAILING ADDRESS: Linden Hill Jewish Cemetery
                   201 East Broadway
                   New York, New York 10002-5593
PHONE NUMBER: (212) 477-2800
RECORDS: Write to the cemetery's Manhattan office for burial information. Most records have been computerized. If a burial is not in the computer, the office will do additional research using records that are stored at the cemetery.
RESOURCES: N/A

Linden Hill Methodist Cemetery

CATEGORY: Methodist Episcopal, Non-sectarian
YEARS OF USE: 1852 to date
LOCATION: 323 Woodward Avenue, Ridgewood, Queens.
HISTORY: Linden Hill Methodist Cemetery was established by the First

German Methodist Episcopal Church, Manhattan. The cemetery is non-sectarian, and a large number of Jews are buried here.

This cemetery is also known as the Methodist Episcopal Cemetery.

MAILING ADDRESS: Linden Hill Methodist Cemetery
                 323 Woodward Avenue
                 Flushing, Queens 11385-1162

PHONE NUMBER: (718) 821-6480

RECORDS: Records are stored at the cemetery.

RESOURCES: N/A

Little Green Street Burial Ground of the Society of Friends

CATEGORY: Quaker

YEARS OF USE: circa 1700 to 1823

LOCATION: Little Green Street (now Liberty Place), between Maiden Lane and Liberty Street, Manhattan.

HISTORY: The Friends' Meeting House at Little Green Street was erected in 1700, the first in New York City. In September 1825, the New York City Common Council gave the congregation permission to remove the bodies in their graveyard, on condition that they do it by March 1826. The remains were placed in a vault at the Houston Street Burial Ground.

The property later became known as Thoburn's Garden.

MAILING ADDRESS: c/o Friends' Historical Library
                 Swarthmore College
                 500 College Avenue
                 Swarthmore, Pennsylvania 19081-1399

PHONE NUMBER: (610) 328-8000

RECORDS: Original records are now housed at the Friends' Historical Library of Swarthmore College. Gravestones were not permitted in Quaker cemeteries until 1852.

RESOURCES: *Flushing Monthly Meeting, New York: Births, Deaths, and Marriages 1640 to 1796.* (Salt Lake City: Genealogical Society of Utah), microfilm no. 17,376.

Lott Family Burial Ground

See Wyckoff-Snedicker Cemetery.

Lutheran Cemetery

CATEGORY: Lutheran, Non-sectarian

YEARS OF USE: 1850 to date

LOCATION: 67-29 Metropolitan Avenue, at 69th Street, Middle Village, Queens.

HISTORY: The pastors of Saint Matthew's and Saint Paul's Lutheran Churches in Manhattan united in 1850 to establish this cemetery. Although its founders were Lutheran, this cemetery was never formally associated with the Lutheran Church and contains burials of all faiths.

The oldest section of the cemetery was frequently used by German immigrants. Many people buried in this section were removed by their descendants in the mid-1900s to more fashionable cemeteries or to cemeteries in other parts of the country.

MAILING ADDRESS: Lutheran Cemetery
                 67-29 Metropolitan Avenue
                 Flushing, New York 11379-1683

PHONE NUMBER: (718) 821-1750

RECORDS: There is a fee for searches. Replies may take several months. Records include information on those bodies that have been removed.

RESOURCES: *Saint Matthew's Church, Interments in Lutheran Cemetery, Middle Village, 1851 to 1866.* (New York: New York Genealogical and Biographical Society), microfilm no. 32.1, reel no. 3.

Thompson, Gloria G. "The Lutheran Cemetery at Queens, New York." *The German Genealogical Society of America Bulletin* 2, issue 2 (February 1988): 17. (detailed description of the cemetery's "old" section)

Luyster Family Burial Ground

CATEGORY: Private

YEARS OF USE: circa 1695 to 1816

LOCATION: Vicinity of the Marine Air Terminal, LaGuardia Airport, Astoria, Queens.

HISTORY: Peter C. Luyster, patriarch of this family, came to New York in 1656 from Holland. He died in 1695 and may have been buried on his son's property. Historian William Munsell wrote in 1882 that the "cemetery is dismantled and potatoes and cabbage grown over several generations of the dead, and of the ancient house of Luyster, only a heap of family tombstones remain."

Of the thirty-six gravestones standing in 1932, only twenty-five were left in 1938 when the remains of the Luyster family were disinterred for construction of LaGuardia Airport and removed to Saint Michael's Cemetery.

MAILING ADDRESS: c/o Saint Michael's Cemetery and Mausoleums
                 72-02 Astoria Boulevard
                 Flushing, New York 11370-1094

PHONE NUMBER: (718) 278-3240

RECORDS: Saint Michael's records are housed on-site.

RESOURCES: Powell, Charles U., comp., and Alice H. Meigs, ed. *Description of Private and Family Cemeteries in the Borough of Queens.* City of New York, Borough of Queens, Topographical Bureau. Jamaica, N.Y.: Queens Borough Public Library, 1932. (gravestone inscriptions and maps)

Macedonia African Methodist
Episcopal Churchyard

CATEGORY: African, Methodist Episcopal

YEARS OF USE: 1838 to 1909

LOCATION: South side of 37th Avenue, between Main Street and Union Street, about one hundred feet from the street, Flushing, Queens.

HISTORY: Although the Macedonia African Methodist Episcopal Churchyard dates back to 1811, the congregation didn't erect its first church until 1838. The churchyard was in use from that time until burials ended in 1909. Two hundred bodies were removed from the churchyard and reinterred in a common grave beneath the church building when the congregation decided to enlarge the edifice in 1931.

   In 1949, the congregation opposed the demolition of their church for use as a parking lot because more than two hundred people were buried under the church. They lost the battle, and the bodies were taken to Flushing Cemetery.

MAILING ADDRESS: Macedonia AME Church
                3722 Union Street
                Flushing, New York 11354-4192

PHONE NUMBER: (718) 353-5870

RECORDS: The death register dates back to 1811.

RESOURCES: Powell, Charles U., comp., and Alice H. Meigs, ed. *Description of Private and Family Cemeteries in the Borough of Queens.* City of New York, Borough of Queens, Topographical Bureau. Jamaica, N.Y.: Queens Borough Public Library, 1975 supplement. (map)

Machpelah Cemetery, Queens

CATEGORY: Non-Sectarian
YEARS OF USE: 1840 to date
LOCATION: 82-30 Cypress Hills Street, between Beth-El Cemetery and
Hungarian Cemetery, Glendale, Queens.
HISTORY: Machpelah Cemetery was founded in 1855 and is now owned by
the Congregation Beth-El in Manhattan. Although many of those buried
here were of the Jewish faith, the cemetery is non-sectarian.

Magician Harry Houdini was buried in Machpelah Cemetery following
his death on 31 October 1929.
MAILING ADDRESS: Machpelah Cemetery
                  201 East Broadway
                  New York, New York 10002-5593
PHONE NUMBER: (718) 366-5959
RECORDS: Machpelah's records are housed in the New York City Office.
RESOURCES: N/A

Madison Square Cemetery

CATEGORY: Public
YEARS OF USE: 1794 to 1797
LOCATION: Madison Square, Manhattan.
HISTORY: The Madison Square Cemetery opened in October 1794 as the
burial ground of Bellevue Hospital and the New York City Almshouse. It
lasted only three years, serving as the public burial ground during the yellow
fever epidemic of 1796, which took 1,300 lives in two months. The cemetery was closed in May 1797.

Madison Square was subsequently ceded to the United States government
for construction of an arsenal. In 1847, it became Madison Square Park.
The bodies were not removed.
MAILING ADDRESS: N/A
PHONE NUMBER: N/A
RECORDS: N/A
RESOURCES: N/A

Maimonides Cemetery

CATEGORY: Jewish
YEARS OF USE: 1854 to date
LOCATION: 895 Jamaica Avenue, between Mount Hope Cemetery and
Cypress Hills Cemetery, Brooklyn.
HISTORY: N/A

MAILING ADDRESS: c/o Maimonides Cemetery
                 90 Elmont Avenue
                 Elmont, New York 11003-1224
PHONE NUMBER: (718) 347-0095
RECORDS: Records are at the office in Elmont, Nassau County.
RESOURCES: N/A

Maple Grove Cemetery

CATEGORY: Non-sectarian
YEARS OF USE: 1875 to date
LOCATION: 83-15 Kew Gardens Road, east side of the road between 83rd
Avenue and 86th Road, Kew Gardens, Queens.
HISTORY: Maple Grove Cemetery was established in 1875 "for the purpose
of laying out and constructing an appropriate and beautiful burial place for
the dead, in which lots might be sold at a comparatively low price."
    Missionary Ann Wilkins and Actor George Jones are both buried here.
MAILING ADDRESS: Maple Grove Cemetery
                  83-15 Kew Gardens Road
                  Kew Gardens, New York 11415-1920
PHONE NUMBER: (718) 544-3600
RECORDS: The cemetery records are housed on-site.
RESOURCES: N/A

Marble Cemetery
See New York City Marble Cemetery.
See New York Marble Cemetery.

Marine Cemetery

CATEGORY: Institutional, Seamen
YEARS OF USE: circa 1850 to 1900
LOCATION: Silver Lake Golf Course.
HISTORY: N/A
MAILING ADDRESS: N/A
PHONE NUMBER: N/A
RECORDS: N/A
RESOURCES: Vosburgh, Royden W., editor and transcriber, "Staten Island
Gravestone Inscriptions," vol. 2, New York City, April 1925 (typed manu-
script). An interment list has been posted on the Richmond County
RootsWeb project Web site. The address is
<http://www.rootsweb.com/~nyrichmo>

Mariner's Family Asylum Cemetery

CATEGORY: Institutional, Seamen
YEARS OF USE: circa 1880 to 1920
LOCATION: 119 Tompkins Avenue, between Tompkins Street and Vanderbilt Avenue, Stapleton, Staten Island.
HISTORY: Organized and incorporated in 1843, "the Old Ladies Home" housed "the aged and destitute widows, wives, mothers, sisters, and daughters of seamen sixty years of age or over of the Port of New York." The cemetery is no longer extant.
MAILING ADDRESS: c/o Friends of Abandoned Cemeteries of Staten Island
                    140 Tysen Avenue
                    Staten Island, New York 10301-1120
PHONE NUMBER: N/A
RECORDS: N/A
RESOURCES: N/A

Martin's Field Cemetery
See Colored Cemetery of Flushing.

Meretz Cemetery
See Washington Cemetery.

Merrell Family Burial Ground

CATEGORY: Private
YEARS OF USE: Gravestones date 1794 to circa 1889
LOCATION: North side of Merrell Avenue, between Richmond Avenue and Hillman Avenue, Bulls Head, Staten Island.
HISTORY: Surrounded by a wooden fence on three sides and a "neat stone wall" on the fourth, the Merrell Family Burial Ground is the final resting place of the Braisted, Decker, Martin, Merrell, and Owen families. The cemetery is owned by descendants of the Merrell family, but it was abandoned some years ago.

Friends of Abandoned Cemeteries of Staten Island has taken an interest in the cemetery. The group worked with the developer of a nearby housing project to assure preservation of the grounds.

The Merrell Family Burial Ground is also known as the Braisted Family Burial Ground.
MAILING ADDRESS: Friends of Abandoned Cemeteries of Staten Island
                    140 Tysen Street
                    Staten Island, New York 10301-1120
PHONE NUMBER: N/A
RECORDS: Researchers should check the Staten Island RootsWeb page, on the

Internet, to see if this cemetery has been added to their cemetery database. The address is <http://www.rootsweb.com/~nyrichmo>.

RESOURCES: Davis, William T. "Homestead Graves." *Proceedings of the Natural Science Association of Staten Island.* Staten Island, New York. Special Number 9, December 1889. (gravestone inscriptions)

Vosburgh, Royden W., editor and transcriber, "Staten Island Gravestone Inscriptions," vol. 1, New York City, March 1924 (typed manuscript). An interment list has been posted on the Richmond County RootsWeb project Web site. The address is: <http://www.rootsweb.com/~nyrichmo>

Methodist Cemetery, Brooklyn

CATEGORY: Methodist Episcopal
YEARS OF USE: Pre-1834
LOCATION: In the area bounded by Union, Lorimer, and Grand and Devoe, Williamsburg, Brooklyn.
HISTORY: In March 1944, construction workers unearthed human bones and skulls while excavating a sewer line. Maps and deeds in the King's County Hall of Records revealed that the site was the former cemetery of the Methodist Episcopal Church. In 1834, church elders divided the property into building lots. The last lot was sold in 1874.
MAILING ADDRESS: N/A
PHONE NUMBER: N/A
RECORDS: N/A
RESOURCES: "Old Skulls and Bones Give Bluebeard Scare to Boro." *The Brooklyn Eagle*, 17 March 1944, p. 22, col. 4. (identifies cemetery)

Methodist Cemetery, Manhattan

CATEGORY: Methodist Episcopal, Independent Methodist
YEARS OF USE: circa 1805 to 1851
LOCATION: In the center of the block bounded by First Street, Second Street, First Avenue and Second Avenue, Manhattan.
HISTORY: City directories and maps indicate that this cemetery began as a common burial ground for New York City's Methodist Episcopal churches. By the 1840s, it appeared to be used almost exclusively by The Methodist Society, an independent Methodist church founded by Samuel Stillwell in 1820. The Methodist Society is also known as "Stillwell's Church" and as "The Saviour's Church."

Henry Worrall, in his will proved 5 May 1849, wrote, "I also give and bequeath unto my aforesaid wife and nine children in perpetuity all that certain piece of ground lying and being in the tenth ward of the City of New York between the 1st and 2nd Avenues and 1st and 2nd Streets, known on a map of burial ground belonging to Samuel Stillwell by numbers 82 and 84."

Worrall might have foreseen the eventual demise of this cemetery, for he went on to ask that the bodies of his three deceased children be removed from this burial ground to a new plot in Green-Wood Cemetery, the same plot where he asked to be buried.

The Methodist Cemetery probably closed in 1851, when New York City banned interments south of 86th Street. Bodies from this burial ground were among the 15,000 removed from New York City Methodist cemeteries to a plot in Cypress Hills Cemetery between 1854 and 1856.

Some graves may have been missed during the removal. In 1891, the New York State legislature authorized the "Board of Education in the City of New York... to remove the human remains buried in the old burying ground, between 1st and 2nd Streets and 1st and 2nd Avenues in said city... and to reinter the same in any cemetery or burying-ground selected by or under the direction of the said Board of Education." It isn't clear how many graves remained, when the removal took place, or where the bodies were reinterred.

MAILING ADDRESS: N/A

PHONE NUMBER: N/A

RECORDS: Methodist burial records, prior to 1815, are part of the Methodist Collection at the New York Public Library, Rare Books and Manuscripts Division, 5th Avenue and 42nd Street, New York, New York.

RESOURCES: *Laws Passed at the 114th Legislature*. chapter 137. Albany, N.Y.: Banks & Brothers, 1891. (identifies cemetery)

Methodist Society Cemetery
See Methodist Cemetery, Manhattan.

Micheau Family Burial Ground

CATEGORY: Private

YEARS OF USE: Gravestones dated 1751 to 1789

LOCATION: Near Jefferson Boulevard, corner Woodrow Road, Arden Heights, Staten Island.

HISTORY: There are three known interments in the Micheau Family Burial Ground. Paul Micheau, a prominent Staten Islander who served in the colonial assembly from 1748 to his death in 1751, was buried here, along with Martha Mersereau and Mary Pollion.

MAILING ADDRESS: N/A

PHONE NUMBER: N/A

RECORDS: N/A

RESOURCES: Davis, William T. "Homestead Graves." *Proceedings of the Natural Science Association of Staten Island*. Staten Island, New York. Special Number 9, December 1889. (gravestone inscriptions)

Midddagh Family Burial Ground

CATEGORY: Private
YEARS OF USE: circa 1816
LOCATION: West side of Clinton Street, corner Pierrepont Street, Brooklyn Heights, Brooklyn.
HISTORY: Following the Civil War, one member of the Middagh family launched a campaign to change the street names in her neighborhood, mostly named for the old families of Brooklyn. She tore down the city street signs and replaced them with new ones displaying botanical names like Orchard, Orange, Cranberry, and Willow. Whenever the city restored its street signs, Miss Middagh tore them down and put hers back up. The City of Brooklyn finally gave in and changed the street names officially. One street, however, still bears the name of the Middagh family. It is situated five blocks north of the old family burial ground.
MAILING ADDRESS: N/A
PHONE NUMBER: N/A
RECORDS: N/A
RESOURCES: N/A

Middle Dutch Churchyard and Vaults

CATEGORY: Reformed Dutch
YEARS OF USE: 1729 to circa 1844
LOCATION: East side of Nassau Street, between Cedar Street and Liberty Street, Manhattan.
HISTORY: Interments in the graveyard of the Middle Dutch Church generally ended with the 1823 ban on burials south of Grand Street in Manhattan. However, some well-to-do families paid the penalty of $250 per infraction and continued to use their private burial vaults. In 1827, the widening of Nassau Street eliminated six vaults. A few years later, the widening of Cedar Street took another portion of the churchyard.

The Middle Dutch Church moved to a new building on Lafayette Place in 1839, and to its present location in 1891. The remains in the old churchyard were removed to an unspecified location, and the property was sold for development.
MAILING ADDRESS: Middle Collegiate Church
                50 East 7th Street
                New York, New York 10003-8497
PHONE NUMBER: (212) 477-0666
RECORDS: 13 January 1733, the church ruled that "in the Church Master's Book shall be recorded the name of each buyer of a grave." Records for the Middle Dutch Church are part of the Collegiate Church Register (or common register).
RESOURCES: "Burials in the Dutch Church of New York City, 1804 to

1813." *The New York Genealogical and Biographical Record*, vol. 75 (July 1944). (continued in subsequent issues)

Records of the Collegiate Churches, Burials 1727 to 1804. (New York: New York Genealogical and Biographical Society), manuscript #NY-53. (dates of death and burial)

Records of the Collegiate Churches, Burials 1814 to 1820. Manuscript at The New York Genealogical and Biographical Society. New York, New York. File "New York City-Churches-Dutch."

Year Book of the Holland Society of New York. New York, New York. 1899. Pages 139 to 211. (alphabetized list of deaths 1727 to 1803)

Milligan Street Cemetery

CATEGORY: Jewish
YEARS OF USE: 1805 to 1829
LOCATION: 76 West 11th Street, between 5th and 6th Avenues, Manhattan.
HISTORY: Congregation Shearith Israel's second cemetery was consecrated on March 16, 1805. At first, the burial ground was used for those who did not have family ties to the cemetery at Chatham Square. It went into regular use when the 1823 ban on burials below Grand Street closed the Chatham Square Cemetery.

The Milligan Street Cemetery closed in 1829. A portion of the property was taken for the extension of 11th Street the following year. This burial ground is also known as the 11th Street Cemetery.
MAILING ADDRESS: c/o Congregation Shearith Israel
                8 West 70th Street
                New York, New York 10023-4601
PHONE NUMBER: (212) 873-0300
RECORDS: N/A
RESOURCES: de Sola Pool, Rev. Dr. David. *Portraits Etched in Stone: Early Jewish Settlers 1682 to 1831.* New York: Columbia University Press, 1952, 123–130. (history)

Phillips, Rosalie S. "A Burial Place for the Jewish Nation Forever." *Publications of the American Jewish Historical Society* no. 18 (1909): 93–122. (gravestone inscriptions and list of removals)

Mokom Sholom Cemetery

CATEGORY: Jewish
YEARS OF USE: 1865 to date
LOCATION: 80-07 Pitkin Avenue, east side of the street between Bayside Cemetery and 80th Street, Ozone Park, Queens.
HISTORY: Mokom Sholom Cemetery was established in 1865 by Congregation Darech Amuno. The congregation set aside the northern sec-

tion of the grounds for the free burial of indigent Jews. This section was used until 1901, when free burials were discontinued. There were approximately 12,000 interments in the "free area" between 1865 and 1901.

Between 1961 and 1962, Congregation Darech Amuno removed a large number of gravestones from the free area "in an attempt to beautify the cemetery." The cemetery was then sold to a Rabbi Applebaum, stating in its deed that 1,500 new graves could be sold in the northern section of the cemetery. The New York State Attorney General eventually accused Rabbi Applebaum of misappropriating funds and gross neglect of the cemetery. The cemetery was taken over by the state.

Mokom Sholom Cemetery is now managed by David Jacobson, head of United Hebrew Congregation. Controversy over the removal of headstones and use of the free burial ground continues today.

The cemetery is sometimes confused with Bayside Cemetery and Acacia Cemetery.

MAILING ADDRESS: Mokom Sholom Cemetery
                  80-07 Pitkin Avenue
                  Jamaica, New York 11417-1228
PHONE NUMBER: (718) 845-6030
RECORDS: The Mokom Sholom Cemetery Recording Project is working to record the name of everyone buried in Mokom Sholom Cemetery through the use of cemetery records, death certificates, obituaries, wills, family histories, and gravestones.
RESOURCES: The Mokom Sholom Cemetery Recording Project's list of names is distributed as MOKOMCEM.EXE and is available on the Internet at
   <ftp://ftp.cac.psu.edu/pub/genealogy/text/jewish/mokomcem.exe>.

Montefiore Cemetery

CATEGORY: Jewish
YEARS OF USE: 1908 to date
LOCATION: 121-83 Springfield Boulevard, east side of the boulevard between 130th Avenue and Francis Lewis Boulevard, Cambria Heights, Queens.
HISTORY: Montefiore Cemetery may have been named for Sir Moses Montefiore, a former Sheriff of London. Springfield Cemetery is within its grounds.
MAILING ADDRESS: Montefiore Cemetery
                  121-83 Springfield Boulevard
                  Jamaica, New York 11413-1158
PHONE NUMBER: (718) 528-1700
RECORDS: N/A
RESOURCES: N/A

Moore-Jackson Family Burial Ground

CATEGORY: Private

YEARS OF USE: Gravestones date 1733 to 1867

LOCATION: The cemetery is in the triangular island formed by 51st Street, 54th Street, and 31st Avenue to 32nd Avenue, Woodside, Queens.

HISTORY: The Moore-Jackson Family Burial Ground contains the descendants of the Reverend John Moore, a Loyalist who housed British troops on his estate during the Revolution and who was later implicated in a plot to kidnap George Washington.

Part of the cemetery was sold to the Jackson family, but toward the end of the 1800s, it fell into disrepair. The Works Progress Administration cleaned the lot during the 1940s. About ten years later, New York City illegally seized the cemetery for non-payment of taxes. When it realized the error, the City tried to give the burial ground back to the family, but was unable to locate any descendants.

The Queens Historical Society has identified one descendant, Ann Ellis. The Historical Society hopes that Ms. Ellis will sign the cemetery over to them for the creation of the Moore-Jackson Cemetery Corporation.

MAILING ADDRESS: Moore-Jackson Cemetery
c/o The Queens Historical Society
Kingsland Homestead
143-35 37th Avenue
Flushing, New York 11354-5729

PHONE NUMBER: (718) 939-0647

RECORDS: N/A

RESOURCES: Frost, Josephine C. trans. *Long Island Cemetery Inscriptions.* Vol. 1. March 1912. Brooklyn, New York. (gravestone inscriptions)

Powell, Charles U., comp., and Alice H. Meigs, ed. *Description of Private and Family Cemeteries in the Borough of Queens.* City of New York, Borough of Queens, Topographical Bureau. Jamaica, N.Y.: Queens Borough Public Library, 1932. (gravestone inscriptions and map)

Moravian Cemetery

CATEGORY: Moravian, Non-Sectarian

YEARS OF USE: circa 1723 to date

LOCATION: 2205 Richmond Road, north side of the road between Altamont Street and Todt Hill Road, New Dorp, Staten Island.

HISTORY: This site was used as a public cemetery for at least thirty-five years before it was taken over by the New Dorp Moravian Church circa 1758. The earliest extant gravestone is thought to be that of Colonel Nicholas Britten, who died in 1740, but there are reports of other gravestones that date back to 1710.

The cemetery was used as a burial ground for English soldiers during colonial times. In the section set aside for the exclusive use of the Moravians in 1763, the dead were segregated according to sex. This practice ended in 1819. The rest of the cemetery is non-sectarian.

Moravian Cemetery was completely free of charge until 1819, when it began to charge for the opening and closing of graves. In 1826, the cemetery began to sell plots and graves.

The Vanderbilt Mausoleum is situated a short distance west of the church. It cost one million dollars when it was erected in the summer of 1885. Commodore Cornelius Vanderbilt and his son, William, are among those interred in the mausoleum. The family patriarch, Jacob Vanderbilt, his wife, and their son, are buried in an adjoining plot.

MAILING ADDRESS: Moravian Cemetery
　　　　　　　　2205 Richmond Road
　　　　　　　　Staten Island, New York 10306-2557
PHONE NUMBER:　(718) 351-0136
RECORDS: The cemetery's records are housed on-site. They are also available on microfilm at the Staten Island Institute of Arts and Sciences.
RESOURCES:　"Staten Island Church Records." *Collections of the New York Genealogical and Biographical Society* 4 (1909): 210–240. (deaths and burials, 1758–1862)

Morgan Family Burial Ground

CATEGORY: Private
YEARS OF USE: Gravestones date 1795 to 1865
LOCATION: One-half mile north of Arthur Kill Road, opposite Arden Avenue, Arden Heights, Staten Island.
HISTORY: The Morgan Family Burial Ground was situated a short distance from the family homestead. Among those buried in it were members of the Hanmer, Hill, Karr, and LaForge families.

Friends of Abandoned Cemeteries on Staten Island reports that the graveyard is no longer extant.
MAILING ADDRESS: N/A
PHONE NUMBER:　N/A
RECORDS: N/A
RESOURCES:　Davis, William T. "Homestead Graves." *Proceedings of the Natural Science Association of Staten Island.* Staten Island, New York. Special Number 9, December 1889. (Gravestone Inscriptions)

Morrell Family Burial Ground

CATEGORY: Private
YEARS OF USE: Gravestone dated 1816

LOCATION: South side of 39th Avenue, between 50th Street and Woodside Avenue, Woodside, Queens.
HISTORY: There were seven interments in this little burial ground. John Morrell, who died in 1816, was the only one memorialized by a gravestone.
MAILING ADDRESS: N/A
PHONE NUMBER: N/A
RECORDS: N/A
RESOURCES: N/A

Morrisania Cemetery

CATEGORY: Public
YEARS OF USE: Circa 1848 to 1868
LOCATION: Saint Mary's Park, at the intersection of Saint Mary's Avenue and 149th Street, Mott Haven, Bronx.
HISTORY: This cemetery was once the public burial ground of the Town of Morrisania. It contained the members of many local families, as well as one hundred fifty members of The Sons of Liberty who fought in the Civil War.

Burials ended in 1868, when the extension of Saint Ann's Avenue cut the cemetery in half. The displaced bodies were reinterred in Woodlawn Cemetery, lots 1698 to 1707.   Others were taken to Green-Wood Cemetery.

In December 1903, the New York City Board of Estimate and Apportionment ruled that "for a long time back, the place has been filthy and unsightly" and passed a resolution to convert the grounds into Saint Mary's Park. The burial ground is also known as Bensonia Cemetery.
MAILING ADDRESS: N/A
PHONE NUMBER: N/A
RECORDS: N/A
RESOURCES: N/A

Most Holy Trinity Cemetery
See also Trinity Cemetery.

CATEGORY: Roman Catholic
YEARS OF USE: circa 1850 to date
LOCATION: 675 Central Avenue, between Chauncey Street and Cemetery of the Evergreens, Bedford-Stuyvesant, Brooklyn.
HISTORY: Most Holy Trinity Cemetery does not permit stone grave markers—only those of wood or galvanized iron. Many are inscribed with German verses. At the turn of the century, children's graves were often decorated with toys, so that when their parents came to visit, they were reminded "vividly" of their child.

This cemetery is also known as the German Burial Ground and as Raffeiner Cemetery.

MAILING ADDRESS: c/o Saint John's Cemetery
                  80-01 Metropolitan Avenue
                  Flushing, New York 11379-2991
PHONE NUMBER: (718) 894-4888
RECORDS: Most Holy Trinity Cemetery retains ownership of the graves and
plots—there are no individual owners. Its burial records are kept in the
offices of Saint John's Cemetery.
RESOURCES: N/A

Mott Family Burial Ground

CATEGORY: Private
YEARS OF USE: Gravestones date 1826 to 1877
LOCATION: North of Maspeth Avenue, near 55th Street, Maspeth, Queens.
HISTORY: On 10 January 1950, the Flushing Friends Meeting was authorized
to remove the bodies in the Mott Family Burial Ground and reinter them in
Prospect Park Cemetery. There were thirteen graves in the cemetery, seven
identifiable by gravestones.
MAILING ADDRESS: N/A
PHONE NUMBER: (718) 287-3400 for permission to enter Prospect Park
Cemetery and occasional tours.
RECORDS: N/A
RESOURCES: Powell, Charles U., comp., and Alice H. Meigs, ed.
Description of Private and Family Cemeteries in the Borough of Queens. City
of New York, Borough of Queens, Topographical Bureau. Jamaica, N.Y.:
Queens Borough Public Library, 1932 and 1975 supplements. (gravestone
inscriptions and map)

Mount Carmel Cemetery

CATEGORY: Jewish
YEARS OF USE: 1902 to date
LOCATION: 8345 Cypress Hills Street, southeast corner of Cooper Avenue,
Glendale, Queens.
HISTORY: The old section of the cemetery is known as "Mount Carmel
Cemetery." The new section is "New Mount Carmel Cemetery." The old
and new sections are separated by Mount Neboh Cemetery.
MAILING ADDRESS: Mount Carmel Cemetery
                  83-45 Cypress Hills Street
                  Flushing, Queens 11385-6895
PHONE NUMBER: (718) 366-5900
RECORDS: Cemetery records are housed on-site.
RESOURCES: N/A

Mount Hebron Cemetery

CATEGORY: Jewish
YEARS OF USE: 14 April 1909 to date
LOCATION: 130-04 Horace Harding Expressway, south side of the highway between the Van Wyck Expressway and Cedar Grove Cemetery, Flushing, Queens.
HISTORY: Mount Hebron Cemetery is owned by Cedar Grove Cemetery.
MAILING ADDRESS: Mount Hebron Cemetery
                 130-04 Horace Harding Expressway
                 Flushing, New York 11367-1027
PHONE NUMBER: (718) 939-9405
RECORDS: Mount Hebron's Cemetery records include the first and last names of the decedent, age, date of death, and date of burial.
RESOURCES: N/A

Mount Hope Cemetery

CATEGORY: Jewish
YEARS OF USE: Pre-1890 to date
LOCATION: 895 Jamaica Avenue, north side of the Avenue between Maimonides Cemetery and Dexter Court, East New York, Brooklyn.
HISTORY: The plots were all sold, primarily to families, by 1934.
MAILING ADDRESS: c/o Maimonides Cemetery
                 Post Office Box 125
                 Elmont, New York 11003-1224
PHONE NUMBER: (516) 347-0095
RECORDS: Mount Hope Cemetery's records are housed at Maimonides Cemetery in Elmont, Nassau County.
RESOURCES: Moos, Dorothy A., transcriber. "Cemetery Records of New York and New Jersey, 1824 to 1973." *Church and Cemetery Records from New Jersey*. Washington, D.C.: Daughters of the American Revolution, 1979. (Gross and Moos burials in lot 23, 1907–1973)

Moos, Dorothy A., trans. "Cemetery Records of New York and New Jersey, 1824 to 1973." *Church and Cemetery Records from New Jersey*. Washington, D.C.: Daughters of the American Revolution, 1979. (Goldsmith and Mark burials in lot 24, 1891–1940)

Mount Judah Cemetery

CATEGORY: Jewish
YEARS OF USE: 1912 to date
LOCATION: Cypress Avenue, between Cemetery of the Evergreens and the
Interborough Parkway (Jackie Robinson Parkway), Ridgewood, Queens.
HISTORY: N/A
MAILING ADDRESS: Mount Judah Cemetery
                 Post Office Box 177
                 Ridgewood, New York 11385-0177
PHONE NUMBER: (718) 821-1060
RECORDS: The cemetery records are housed on-site.
RESOURCES: N/A

Mount Lebanon Cemetery

CATEGORY: Jewish
YEARS OF USE: 1911 to date
LOCATION: 78-00 Myrtle Avenue, on the south side of the avenue, between
Cypress Hills Cemetery and Forest Park Golf Course, Glendale, Queens.
HISTORY: N/A
MAILING ADDRESS: Mount Lebanon Cemetery
                 78-00 Myrtle Avenue
                 Flushing, New York 11385-7494
PHONE NUMBER: (718) 821-0200
RECORDS: Although interment and care records are computerized, many of
the names are so similar that researchers must supply the exact details of the
deceased's parentage in order to determine the correct record. Requests for
information should be made in writing.
RESOURCES: N/A

Mount Loretto Home Cemetery

CATEGORY: Institutional, Roman Catholic
YEARS OF USE: circa 1880 to 1910
LOCATION: 361 Sharrott Avenue, between Bedell Street and Hylan Boulevard,
Pleasantville, Staten Island.
HISTORY: This cemetery is located on the grounds of Mount Loretto, owned
by the Mission of the Immaculate Virgin for the Protection of Homeless and
Destitute Children in Manhattan. The Mission at Mount Loretto began as an
asylum for homeless newsboys from Manhattan. It later sheltered Saint
Elizabeth's Home, for orphaned girls; Saint Joseph's Asylum, for blind girls;
and several trade schools for "senior" boys. Today, it is an asylum for children of broken homes.

Children were buried in the Home's cemetery providing there were no relatives to claim the body. If there were known relatives, the interment had to be made in another cemetery.

In 1979, part of Mount Loretto was taken for use as Cemetery of the Resurrection.

MAILING ADDRESS: Mission of the Immaculate Virgin
6581 Hylan Boulevard
Staten Island, New York 10309-3830

PHONE NUMBER: (718) 984-1500

RECORDS: N/A

RESOURCES: N/A

Mount Neboh Cemetery

CATEGORY: Jewish

YEARS OF USE: 1886 to 1913+

LOCATION: 82-07 Cypress Hills Street, east side of the street between the new and old sections of Mount Carmel Cemetery, Glendale, Queens.

HISTORY: N/A

MAILING ADDRESS: Mount Neboh Cemetery
82-07 Cypress Hills Street
Flushing, New York 11385-6898

PHONE NUMBER: (718) 366-4141

RECORDS: N/A

RESOURCES: N/A

Mount Olivet Cemetery and Mausoleum

CATEGORY: Non-sectarian, Protestant Episcopal

YEARS OF USE: 1850 to date

LOCATION: 65-40 Grand Avenue, south side of the avenue between 69th Street and Mount Olivet Crescent, Maspeth, Queens.

HISTORY: In 1851, Mount Olivet Cemetery ruled that its burial ground was "specifically for the use of the Protestant Episcopal Church, no other funeral service will be allowed within its limits than that of the said church, but this regulation is not to be understood as requiring that the persons buried shall be members of the Episcopal Church or that the burial service shall be performed at their interment."

The Betts Family Burial Ground is within Mount Olivet Cemetery's limits. *The New York Times* reports that the oldest Japanese-American burial vaults are at Mount Olivet Cemetery.

MAILING ADDRESS: Mount Olivet Cemetery
65-40 Grand Avenue
Flushing, New York 11378-2423

PHONE NUMBER: (718) 326-1777
RECORDS: The cemetery records are housed on-site. Written requests for information are preferred.
RESOURCES: N/A

Mount Pleasant Cemetery
See Citizens' Union-Mount Pleasant Cemetery.

Mount Richmond Cemetery

CATEGORY: Jewish
YEARS OF USE: circa 1910 to date
LOCATION: 420 Clarke Avenue, southwest side of the avenue, between Arthur Kill Road and Cotter Avenue, Richmondtown, Staten Island.
HISTORY: Founded by The Hebrew Free Burial Association as a successor to Silver Lake Cemetery, Mount Richmond Cemetery is the final resting place of Jewish immigrants "who made it to our shores, but never made it up the ladder."

In a letter to *The FACSI Newsletter*, Sandra Wiesel, Administrator of the Hebrew Free Burial Association, wrote that "in the years since the Iron Curtain was first opened to Soviet Jews, many have been buried in our cemetery. We bury those who have outlived their savings; people who have stayed in the old neighborhood when everyone else moved... the homeless... those who have fallen through the safety net."

Mount Richmond Cemetery is the largest free Jewish cemetery in the world, outside of Israel. Often, there isn't enough money to buy headstones, but the cemetery is currently trying to raise enough funds to buy headstones for 20,000 existing graves.

A portion of the cemetery was set aside for the bodies of people whose Jewishness is in question.
MAILING ADDRESS: Mount Richmond Cemetery
                 420 Clarke Avenue
                 Staten Island, New York 10306-6139
PHONE NUMBER: (718) 667-0915
RECORDS: N/A
RESOURCES: Crane, Fred. "The Hebrew Free Burial Association: Silver Lake and Mount Richmond Cemeteries." *The FACSI Newsletter*, vol. 14, issue 2/3, (Summer/Fall 1997). (vignette)

Mount Saint Mary Cemetery

CATEGORY: Roman Catholic
YEARS OF USE: 1900 to date
LOCATION: 172-00 Booth Memorial Avenue, south side of the avenue,

between 164th Street and Fresh Meadow Lane, Flushing, Queens.
HISTORY: Mount Saint Mary Cemetery is owned by Saint Michael's Church in Flushing. The cemetery is also known as Saint Mary's Cemetery.
MAILING ADDRESS: c/o Saint John's Cemetery
80-01 Metropolitan Avenue
Flushing, New York 11379-2991
PHONE NUMBER: (718) 894-4888
RECORDS: Cemetery records for the Diocese of Brooklyn are kept in the offices of Saint John's Cemetery. Requests for information must be in writing.
RESOURCES: N/A

Mount Saint Vincent Cemetery

CATEGORY: Roman Catholic
YEARS OF USE: circa 1856 to 1956
LOCATION: On the grounds of the College of Mount Saint Vincent, West 261st Street and Riverdale Avenue, North Riverdale, Bronx.
HISTORY: Approximately one hundred fifty nuns were buried in this cemetery, set aside for the exclusive use of the Sisters of Charity of Mount Saint Vincent.
MAILING ADDRESS: College of Mount Saint Vincent
6301 Riverdale Avenue
Bronx, New York 10471-1093
PHONE NUMBER: (718) 549-8000
RECORDS: N/A
RESOURCES: N/A

Mount Zion Cemetery

CATEGORY: Jewish
YEARS OF USE: 1893 to date
LOCATION: 5963 54th Avenue, Maspeth, Queens. Bounded by Maurice Avenue, Tyler Avenue, New Calvary Cemetery, and 54th Avenue.
HISTORY: N/A
MAILING ADDRESS: Mount Zion Cemetery
5963 54th Avenue
Flushing, New York 11378-1298
PHONE NUMBER: (718) 335-2500
RECORDS: Mount Zion Cemetery's records are housed on-site.
RESOURCES: N/A

Mutual Benevolent Society Cemetery
See Hungarian Union Field of the Mutual Benevolent Society.

Nagle Cemetery
See Dykman-Nagle Cemetery.

Nassau Street Cemetery
See Middle Dutch Church Yard and Vaults.

National Cemetery
See Cypress Hills National Cemetery.

Negroes' Burial Ground
See African Burial Ground.

New Burial Place
(Without the Gate of the City)

CATEGORY: Public
YEARS OF USE: circa 1662 to 1821
LOCATION: Northern section of Trinity Churchyard on Wall Street, between Broadway and Trinity Place, Manhattan.
HISTORY: In 1662, the Director General of New Netherland granted the Burgomasters of New Amsterdam a parcel of land for use as the "new" public burial ground.

Trinity Church erected its first house of worship on property next to the cemetery in 1697. Six years later, the cemetery was given to Trinity Church on condition that the city be allowed to continue using it as a public burial ground.

Burials were discontinued in 1821 when New York City passed an ordinance prohibiting burials south of Grand Street in Manhattan.

MAILING ADDRESS: N/A
PHONE NUMBER: N/A
RECORDS: N/A
RESOURCES: N/A

New Dutch Churchyard and Vaults
See Middle Dutch Meeting House Yard and Vaults.

New Lots Private Cemetery

CATEGORY: Private, Reformed Dutch
YEARS OF USE: circa 1780 to date
LOCATION: North and south sides of New Lots Avenue, between Barrey Street and Schenck Avenue, East New York, Brooklyn.
HISTORY: There are nearly seven hundred people buried in this cemetery. Most of them are descended from the original Dutch settlers of Kings County and their slaves. Slaves were apparently buried on the north side of the street, while their Dutch masters were buried on the south side, near the Reformed Church, erected 1823.

Some of the graves in the cemetery were disturbed with the widening of New Lots Avenue. According to one story, passers-by could see exposed bones on the side of the road until about 1895. Some of those buried on the north side of the street may have been reinterred near the Church due to building and road construction.

There are forty-five family plots and one general plot, designated for use by "the poor."
MAILING ADDRESS: New Lots Reformed Church
            653 Schenck Avenue
            Brooklyn, New York 11207-7312
PHONE NUMBER: (718) 232-3455
RECORDS: A list of plot owners, and the surnames of those buried in each plot, has been posted on the internet at:
    <http://www.nycgenweb.com/NewLots.htm>
RESOURCES: Bergen, Teunis G. "Inscriptions from the Burying Grounds of the Protestant Reformed Dutch Church of New Lots." *Long Island Historical Society Quarterly* 2, no. 2 (April 1940): 52–54. (alphabetical list of gravestone inscriptions)

Frost, Josephine C. trans. *Long Island Cemetery Inscriptions.* Brooklyn, New York. vol. 9, 1914. (gravestone inscriptions 1781 to 1878)

List, Mrs. Herbert V. "Inscriptions from the Burying Ground of the Protestant Dutch Reformed Church of New Lots." *Cemetery, Church, and Town Records of New York State.* vol. 489. Washington, D.C.: Daughters of the American Revolution, 1978, 87–95. (gravestone inscriptions)

"The Old Dutch Cemetery in East New York: A Landmark Which Has

Almost Disappeared. Its Grass Grown Graves and Its Defaced Headstones—
The Hands of the Vandal and of Father Time Have Been Busy." *The
Brooklyn Daily Eagle*, 5 August 1900, p. 28, col. 1. (gravestone inscriptions;
description of cemetery; photos; love story of Anna Van Patten)

New Montefiore Cemetery
See Montefiore Cemetery.

New Mount Carmel Cemetery
See Mount Carmel Cemetery.

New Springville Cemetery
See Asbury Methodist Episcopal Churchyard and Cemetery.

Newtown Cemetery
See Old Newtown Cemetery.

New Union Fields Cemetery
See Beth-El Cemetery.

New Utrecht Reformed Dutch Church Cemetery

CATEGORY: Reformed Dutch
YEARS OF USE: circa 1789 to 1879
LOCATION: 16th Avenue, between 84th Street and 85th Street, Bensonhurst,
Brooklyn.
HISTORY: This cemetery is the burial ground of the New Utrecht Reformed
Dutch Church, organized in 1677. The northwest corner of the cemetery
was fenced off for use as a slave burial ground. The graveyard surrounded
the church until 1826, when a new church building was erected about two
blocks east of the original site.
MAILING ADDRESS: New Utrecht Reformed Church
                 1827 84th Street
                 Brooklyn, New York 11214-2914
PHONE NUMBER: (718) 232-9500
RECORDS: N/A
RESOURCES: Brooks, Willis. "Old Church Graveyard in a Sad State of
Neglect: New Utrecht Dutch Reformed Church Committee Making an
Effort to Restore It." *The Brooklyn Eagle*, 24 December 1905, p. 7, col. 1.
(gravestone inscriptions, genealogies, church history, list of slave owners, bur-
ial of Jack Hicks)
   *Huntington, Edna. Later Inscriptions from the Burial Ground of the
Protestant Reformed Dutch Church of New Utrecht*. Manuscript. Brooklyn
Historical Society. Brooklyn, New York. (BHS closed indefinitely)

"Inscriptions on Tombstones in the Cemetery of the Reformed Dutch Church, New Utrecht, Long Island, 1814 to 1880." *Kings County Genealogical Club Collections*. vol. 1, no. 1 (1 June 1882). (alphabetical list of gravestone inscriptions)

New York City Farm Colony Cemetery

CATEGORY: Institutional, Public
YEARS OF USE: 1830 to circa 1910
LOCATION: Northern grounds of the New York City Farm Colony, west side of Brielle Avenue between Eastman Avenue and Walcott Avenue, Castleton Corners, Staten Island.
HISTORY: In 1825, Richmond County purchased land for use as the Richmond County Cemetery. The land around the cemetery was eventually taken by the City of New York for use as the New York City Farm Colony. Opened in 1904, the Farm Colony was an asylum for aging, able-bodied individuals who were formerly sent to the home for the aged on Blackwell's Island.

The Farm Colony was soon joined by the Richmond County Hospital for Communicable Diseases and by Sea View Hospital, a treatment center for tuberculosis patients, now a home for the elderly.

Although hundreds of people were buried in the Farm Colony Cemetery, there were less than a dozen gravestones standing in 1900. The oldest gravestone was marked 1862. Friends of Abandoned Cemeteries of Staten Island reports that the cemetery has been abandoned. There is only one gravestone standing today.
MAILING ADDRESS: N/A
PHONE NUMBER: N/A
RECORDS: N/A
RESOURCES: N/A

New York City Hall Cemetery
See African Burial Ground.

New York City Marble Cemetery

CATEGORY: Non-sectarian
YEARS OF USE: 1832 to date
LOCATION: 52 to 74 East 2nd Street, between 1st and 2nd Avenues, Manhattan.
HISTORY: Following the success of its sister cemetery, the New York Marble Cemetery, vaults in this burial ground were snapped up prior to its completion. In many instances, the remains of several generations of one family were reinterred here, as were those of the Kip family, whose remains were

removed from their private family burial ground in Kip's Bay.

Marble monuments and headstones memorialize the notable families who are buried here. Among them are the Fish, Lenox, Ogden, Roosevelt, Varian, and Willett families. President James Monroe was among the first to be interred here. His remains were removed to Hollywood Cemetery, Richmond, Virginia, in 1858.

The cemetery is visible from the street. It is surrounded by an iron fence and locked at all times, and casual visitors are not permitted. The cemetery trustees plan to restore the grounds.

MAILING ADDRESS: N/A

PHONE NUMBER: N/A

RECORDS: The New York City Marble Cemetery does not maintain an office and therefore cannot field requests for information. The New York Historical Society and The New York Genealogical and Biographical Society both maintain copies of the cemetery records.

Many of the early cemetery records were destroyed by fire. Cemetery trustees were able to reconstruct most of them.

RESOURCES: "An Old Cemetery: Sketch of a Notable Landmark." *The New York Times*, 18 May 1875, p. 8, col. 1. (partial list of vault owners)

King, Moses. "The New York City Marble Cemetery." *King's Handbook of New York City*. Boston, Mass., 1893. Reissued. New York: Benjamin Blom Inc., 1972, 510–511. (vignette, photo)

New York Marble Cemetery

CATEGORY: Non-sectarian

YEARS OF USE: 1830 to 1937

LOCATION: Central portion of the block bounded by East 2nd and East 3rd Streets, between 2nd Avenue and the Bowery, Manhattan.

HISTORY: When New York City passed legislation banning burials in earthen graves, several enterprising investors created New York City's first marble cemetery. They built one hundred fifty six underground vaults of Tuckahoe Marble and marketed the cemetery as a "place of interment for gentlemen." Members of the Beekman, Hoyt, Mott, Scribner, Tallmadge, and Varick families are represented among the 2,000 recorded burials.

Marble plaques set into the cemetery's north and south walls memorialize each family. The cemetery cannot be seen from the street, and its entrance is discreetly hidden behind an iron gate and a heavy wooden door on Second Avenue, near Second Street. Both are closed and locked at all times.

As rural cemeteries became increasing popular, family members removed their relatives to new locations. Approximately one-fourth of those interred in the Marble Cemetery were removed—many went to Green-Wood Cemetery in Brooklyn.

Although the burial ground has been designated a New York City Landmark, and is listed on the National Register of Historic Places, its masonry and marble are in need of repair. Cemetery trustees hope to accomplish the restoration in stages. They also hope to publish a "definitive list of persons interred, together with identifying biographical information, in 1999."

This cemetery is just one block from its sister cemetery, the New York City Marble Cemetery.

MAILING ADDRESS: N/A

PHONE NUMBER: N/A

RECORDS: The New York Marble Cemetery does not maintain an office or phone and cannot field requests for information. Most of the cemetery's papers were given to the New York Historical Society, along with two burial registers and a vault list. The register information varies, but may include the deceased's name, birth date, birthplace, date of death, cause of death, and names of the vault owner, sexton, and attending physician. The vault list was compiled about 1870 and contains the name and date of interment of each person, as well as reinterment notes. Burials and reinterments after 1870 were not always recorded in the vault list.

The New York Genealogical and Biographical Society maintains copies of some records.

RESOURCES: Brown, Anne W., comp. *The New York Marble Cemetery, Interments 1830 to 1937*. Kinship. Rhinebeck, New York. Anticipated 1999.

King, Moses. "The New York Marble Cemetery." *King's Handbook of New York City*. Boston, Mass., 1893. Reissued. New York: Benjamin Blom Inc., 1972, 506. (photo)

Two typewritten transcriptions of the vault list and an alphabetical list of interments are available from the Family History Center of The Church of Jesus Christ of Latter-day Saints on microfilms #001777 and #1862779. The cemetery trustees caution that the vault lists are incomplete in the first case and illegible in the second case. The alphabetical list only includes information through 1894. All three items contain misreadings and typographical errors.

New York Nursery and Child's Hospital Cemetery

CATEGORY: Institutional

YEARS OF USE: circa 1921

LOCATION: West side of Melba Street, between Westwood Avenue and Holden Boulevard, Castleton Corners, Staten Island.

HISTORY: New York Nursery and Child's Hospital opened in 1854 as a day-care center in Manhattan, but quickly expanded to include a medical division. A hospital was erected the following year at Lexington Avenue and 51st Street. It provided medical assistance to pregnant women and their infants. The hospital also served as an asylum for destitute children under the age of six, providing them with medical attention, food, clothing, shelter, and education.

The property on Staten Island was purchased in 1870 for use as a branch hospital.

New York Nursery and Child's Hospital merged with New York Hospital-Cornell Medical Center in 1934. An archivist at the hospital writes that their records mention use of "property on Melba Street in Staten Island for the burial of almost two hundred people killed in a fire in 1921... We definitely do not have anything like a record of the burials in any cemetery." The place and exact date of the fire are unspecified, and the report of death by fire may be inaccurate.

Friends of Abandoned Cemeteries of Staten Island reports that the cemetery is no longer extant.

MAILING ADDRESS: c/o Medical Archivist
                 New York Hospital-Cornell Medical Center
                 1300 York Avenue
                 New York, New York 10021-4896
PHONE NUMBER: (212) 746-5454
RECORDS: There are no specific records for the cemetery. Patient records are sparse for this institution and time period.
RESOURCES: N/A

North Baptist Church Cemetery
See Hillside Cemetery.

North Dutch Churchyard

CATEGORY: Reformed Dutch
YEARS OF USE: 1768 to 1823
LOCATION: William Street, between Fulton Street and Ann Street, Manhattan.
HISTORY: The New York City Common Council gave land to the North Dutch Church in October of 1768. The congregation erected its first church the following year and remained at that location for nearly a century.

In 1823, New York City passed an ordinance prohibiting interments south of Grand Street in Manhattan, with a penalty of $250 for each infraction. Some members of the congregation paid that fine.

The North Dutch Church decided to lease its property in 1866. The church building was demolished, and the remains in the churchyard were removed to an unspecified location. The congregation disbanded in 1875. Its papers were deposited in the Gardner Sage Library in New Brunswick, New Jersey.
MAILING ADDRESS: c/o Gardner Sage Library
                 New Brunswick Theological Seminary
                 21 Seminary Place
                 New Brunswick, New Jersey 08901-1187
PHONE NUMBER: (908) 247-5243

RECORDS: Records are part of the Collegiate Church Register (or common register).

RESOURCES: "Burials in the Dutch Church of New York City, 1804 to 1813." *The New York Genealogical and Biographical Record*. vol. 75 (July 1944). Continued in subsequent issues.

Records of the Collegiate Churches, Burials 1727 to 1804. Manuscript #NY-53 at the New York Genealogical and Biographical Society. New York, New York. (dates of death and burial)

Records of the Collegiate Churches, Burials 1814 to 1820. Manuscript at The New York Genealogical and Biographical Society. New York, New York. File "New York City-Churches-Dutch."

Year Book of the Holland Society of New York. New York, New York. 1899. Pages 139 to 211. (alphabetized list of deaths 1727 to 1803)

Northfield Methodist Episcopal Churchyard
See Asbury Methodist Episcopal Churchyard and Cemetery.

Northfield Reformed Dutch Churchyard
See Port Richmond Reformed Dutch Churchyard.

North Shore Cemetery
See Fairview Cemetery.

North Shore Protestant Episcopal Church Cemetery
See Trinity Chapel Burial Ground.

North Side Methodist Episcopal Churchyard
See Saint John's Churchyard.

Oakley Burying Ground
See Blazing Star Burial Ground.

Oceanview Cemetery

CATEGORY: Non-sectarian
YEARS OF USE: 1900 to date
LOCATION: 3315 Amboy Road, west side of the road adjacent to Frederick Douglas Memorial Park Cemetery, Richmond, Staten Island.
HISTORY: Oceanview Cemetery is also known as Valhalla Burial Park. Saint Agnes Cemetery is part of the grounds.
MAILING ADDRESS: Oceanview Cemetery
                        Post Office Box 116
                        Staten Island, New York 10307-0116
PHONE NUMBER: (718) 351-1870
RECORDS: The cemetery's records are housed on-site.
RESOURCES: N/A

Old Clove Baptist Church Cemetery
See Clove Meeting House Cemetery.

Old Farmers' Cemetery
See Southside Cemetery.

Old Flushing Cemetery
See Colored Cemetery of Flushing.

Old John Street Methodist Episcopal Churchyard
See John Street Methodist Episcopal Churchyard.

Old Neck Cemetery
See Asbury Methodist Episcopal Churchyard and Cemetery.

Old Newtown Cemetery

CATEGORY: Public
YEARS OF USE: circa 1652 to circa 1880
LOCATION: East side of 90th Street, between 56th Avenue and 57th Avenue, Elmhurst, Queens.
HISTORY: When the Village of Newtown was settled in 1652, an acre of land was set aside for use as a general cemetery. Plots were given to each of the families in town, including the Fish and Moore families. For over 160 years, this cemetery was the only public cemetery in town.

After 1818, other cemeteries were opened and burials in the Old Newtown Cemetery ceased. Several years later, it reopened as a pauper cemetery, but it was closed again sometime between 1865 and 1880. The cemetery became neglected and was used by a local farmer for his hens, cattle, and horses.

The Presbyterian Church of Elmhurst moved its former pastors, who were buried in the cemetery, to its churchyard on 12 and 13 November 1901. The Field family of Manhattan followed suit and had seven of its family members removed to Mount Olivet Cemetery. The bodies of Mr. and Mrs. Samuel Moore were removed to Mount Olivet Cemetery, and when Toledo Street was cut through the graveyard, another thirty bodies were removed to a common grave in Mount Olivet Cemetery.

About 1932, the New York City Department of Parks converted the cemetery into a playground. The eighty-six surviving gravestones were supposed to be laid on the graves they marked and covered with topsoil.
MAILING ADDRESS: c/o Mount Olivet Cemetery
65-40 Grand Avenue
Flushing, New York 11378-2423
PHONE NUMBER: (718) 326-1777
RECORDS: Mount Olivet Cemetery prefers written requests for information.
RESOURCES: "Bodies of Old Worthies to be Moved in Newtown." *The Brooklyn Daily Eagle*, 10 November 1901, sec. 4, p. 3, col. 5. (gravestone inscriptions)

Frost, Josephine C. trans. *Long Island Cemetery Inscriptions, Flatlands, Brooklyn, New York*. Brooklyn, New York. vol. 12, 1914. (gravestone inscriptions)

McQueen, David. *Index to Queens County Wills 1607 to 1762, with [Inscriptions From The] Town Burial Ground, Newtown*. Brooklyn, N.Y.: Brooklyn Historical Society, 1899, manuscript.

"Over a Century Buried: The Remains of Old Pastors of the Presbyterian Church are Taken from the Old Town Cemetery." *Newtown Register*, 14 November 1901. (gravestone inscriptions, biographies)

Powell, Charles U., comp., and Alice H. Meigs, ed. *Description of Private and Family Cemeteries in the Borough of Queens.* City of New York, Borough of Queens, Topographical Bureau. Jamaica, N.Y.: Queens Borough Public Library, 1932. (gravestone inscriptions and map)

White, Arthur. "In Soil Under New Elmhurst Playground Lie Bones of Many Famous in New York's History: Hamilton Fish Ancestors There." *The Long Island Daily Star*, 4 October 1935. (list of burials, death dates, biographies)

Old Prospect Cemetery
See Prospect Cemetery.

Old Remsen Cemetery
See Remsen Family Burial Ground.

Old Saint Patrick's Cathedral Churchyard and Vaults

CATEGORY: Roman Catholic
YEARS OF USE: circa 1815 to 1851
LOCATION: 263 Mulberry Street, between Prince and East Houston Streets, Manhattan.
HISTORY: The cornerstone for Old Saint Patrick's Cathedral was laid in 1809. The church opened six years later, with burial vaults beneath its edifice, and room for a graveyard. Although the building was destroyed by fire during construction of the new Saint Patrick's Cathedral on Fifth Avenue in 1866, the old church was rebuilt and dedicated just two years later.

Old Saint Patrick's Churchyard is the former burial ground of Pierre Toussaint, a Haitian-born slave, philanthropist, and entrepreneur who is being considered for sainthood. His body was removed to the crypts beneath the new Saint Patrick's Cathedral in 1990, making Toussaint the first layperson to be buried in the new Cathedral.
MAILING ADDRESS: c/o Calvary Cemetery
                         49-02 Laurel Hill Boulevard
                         Woodside, New York 11377-7396
PHONE NUMBER: (718) 786-8000
RECORDS: According to Old Saint Patrick's, church records were destroyed by fire in 1866, but some surviving burial records may be housed at Calvary Cemetery. Records prior to 1820 might be found with those of Saint Peter's Roman Catholic Church.
RESOURCES: "Tombs Under the City." *The New York Times*, 2 August 1896, p. 20, col. 1. (description of vaults, some burials and vault owners)

Photographs of the churchyard are available on the Internet at: <www.oldsaintpatricks.org/views.htm>.

Old Slave Burying Ground

See Cherry Lane Second Asbury African Methodist Episcopal Cemetery.

Old Slave Cemetery

See New Lots Private Cemetery.

Old Springfield Cemetery

See Springfield Cemetery.

Old West Farms Cemetery

See West Farms Reformed Dutch Church Cemetery.

Old West Farms Soldiers' Cemetery

See West Farms Presbyterian Churchyard.

Oliver Street Cemetery

See Chatham Square Cemetery.

One Hundred Third Street Cemetery, West

See Saint Michael's Churchyard and Cemetery.

Our Lady of Mount Carmel Churchyard

CATEGORY: Roman Catholic
YEARS OF USE: Gravestones date 1844 to 1926
LOCATION: West side of 21st Street, between 26th Avenue and 25th Road, Astoria, Queens.
HISTORY: Our Lady of Mount Carmel Church was established in 1840. Its congregation was initially made up of one hundred eighteen persons, sixteen of whom were not Roman Catholic. They secured lots for their church and burial ground and remained at that location for about thirty years.

In 1871, the congregation erected a new church at the intersection of Newtown Avenue and Crescent Street. It continued to use the graveyard and maintained its old church as a Sunday School. By 1881, the congregation peaked at 1,200 members.

The congregation disbanded and abandoned its graveyard about 1940. One hundred and five gravestones were standing in 1935, but since then, most of the stones have been vandalized or destroyed. The information engraved on them was remarkably detailed. A typical stone reads: "In memory of OWEN DUNN, native of Queens County, Ireland, who died December 28, 1859, aged 58 years."

This churchyard is sometimes referred to as "The Famine Cemetery" because those buried here between 1850 and 1880 were exclusively Irish. Nine veterans of the Civil War are buried with them. The grounds were cleaned up and fenced during the summer of 1983 and are now maintained by the Diocese of Brooklyn.

MAILING ADDRESS: c/o Saint John's Cemetery
                            80-01 Metropolitan Avenue
                            Flushing, New York 11379-2991
PHONE NUMBER: (718) 894-4888
RECORDS: Cemetery records for the Diocese of Brooklyn are kept in the offices of Saint John's Cemetery. Requests for information must be in writing.
RESOURCES: Powell, Charles U., comp., and Alice H. Meigs, ed.
Description of Private and Family Cemeteries in the Borough of Queens. City of New York, Borough of Queens, Topographical Bureau. Jamaica, N.Y.: Queens Borough Public Library, 1975 supplement. (gravestone inscriptions and map)

Parsons Family Burial Ground
See Bowne-Parsons Family Burial Ground.

Pasture Hill Burial Ground
See Ferris Family Burial Ground.

Pelham Cemetery

CATEGORY: Non-sectarian
YEARS OF USE: circa 1776 to date
LOCATION: King Avenue, between Ditmars Street and Tier Street, City Island, Bronx, Long Island Sound.
HISTORY: In 1761, a group of enterprising City Island residents tried to turn their island into a port that would rival the Port of New York. That plan obviously failed, but the community enjoyed thriving shipbuilding, sailmaking, and oystering industries.

City Island's cemetery takes it name from Thomas Pell, an Englishman who settled in the Bronx in 1654. Pell's descendants are among those buried in Pelham Cemetery. The cemetery was originally located on Fordham Street, but in 1882, it was removed to its current location on the east side of the island, just north of the ferry slips on Fordham Place.

MAILING ADDRESS: Pelham Cemetery
73 Earley Street
Bronx, New York 10467-1513
Phone: (718) 885-3036
RECORDS: N/A
RESOURCES: N/A

Pell Family Burial Ground

CATEGORY: Private
YEARS OF USE: Gravestones date 1748 to 1790
LOCATION: Shore Road, north of Split Rock Road, Pelham Bay Park, Bronx.
HISTORY: Thomas Pell purchased more than 9,000 acres from the Siwanoy
Indians in 1654. The family mansion, third on the site, was built by Pell's
descendants, Robert and Marie (Lorillard) Bartow. New York City purchased
the house and grounds in 1888 as part of a program to develop parks in the
city. The house stood vacant until 1915, when the International Garden
Club made its headquarters there, restored the house and grounds, and planted gardens.

Thomas Pell's descendants are buried in a small plot behind the house.
There are about eight gravestones.

David Pell Secor, in a letter to the *New York Tribune* in 1903, wrote that
there were many more headstones when he visited the cemetery in the 1860s.
Secor recalled that many of the gravestones had been placed against a stone
wall near the burial ground. In a later report, the Department of Parks
revealed that "the Garden Club said that the site has no bodies, the gravestones were scattered throughout the area and consolidated into one site."

Members of the Pell family are also buried in Pelham Cemetery, in Green-
Wood Cemetery, and in New Rochelle, New York.

This burial ground is also known as the Bartow-Pell Family Burial
Ground.
MAILING ADDRESS: c/o International Garden Club
                 Bartow-Pell Mansion
                 895 Shore Road North
                 Bronx, New York 10464-1030
PHONE NUMBER: (718) 885-1461
RESOURCES: *Cemetery, Church, and Town Records of New York State.* vol.
70. Washington, D.C.: Daughters of the American Revolution, 1935, 1.
(gravestone inscriptions)

Perine-Holmes Family Burial Ground
See Holmes-Perine Family Burial Ground.

Polish National Catholic Cemetery

CATEGORY: Polish National Catholic
YEARS OF USE: circa 1904 to date
LOCATION: 50 Willowbrook Road, west side, Port Richmond, Staten Island.
HISTORY: This well-maintained cemetery is owned by a congregation in
Bayonne, New Jersey. Bayonne is separated from Staten Island by the Kill Van Kull.

MAILING ADDRESS: Heart of Jesus Polish National Catholic Church
290 Avenue E
Bayonne, New Jersey 07002-3757
PHONE NUMBER: (201) 858-4320
RECORDS: N/A
RESOURCES: N/A

Pollock's Grave, Saint Claire
See Amiable Child Monument.

Port Richmond Reformed Dutch Churchyard

CATEGORY: Reformed Dutch
YEARS OF USE: circa 1696 to date
LOCATION: West side of Port Richmond Avenue, south of Richmond Terrace, Port Richmond, Staten Island.
HISTORY: The Reformed Dutch Church at Port Richmond was organized in 1680. Although the church wasn't erected until 1716, the churchyard was in use as early as 1696 and was known as "The Burial Place." Around 1910, the New York City Board of Health banned further interments in the grave-yard with one exception: plot owners may still use the grounds.

This church is also known as the Northfield Reformed Dutch Church and as the Staten Island Reformed Dutch Church.
MAILING ADDRESS: The Reformed Church on Staten Island
54 Richmond Avenue
Staten Island, New York 10302-1334
PHONE NUMBER: (718) 442-7393
RECORDS: The early records are in poor condition. Only a few vital records predate the Revolution.
RESOURCES: Vosburgh, Royden Woodward, trans. *Records of the Reformed Protestant Dutch Church on Staten Island, Richmond County, New York, in the former Town of Northfield, and now the Reformed Church at Port Richmond, in the Borough of Richmond, City of New York.* Staten Island, New York. vol. 2, January 1923. Pages 167 to 245. (photos of several gravestones, gravestone inscriptions)

Presbyterian Cemetery, East Houston Street

CATEGORY: Presbyterian
YEARS OF USE: circa 1803 to 1851
LOCATION: South side of East Houston Street, between Chrystie and Forsyth Streets, Manhattan.
HISTORY: The First Presbyterian Church purchased twenty-four lots from Abraham K. Beekman on 1 April 1803 for use as a cemetery. The cemetery

was jointly owned and used by the First Presbyterian Church, Brick Church, and Rutgers Street Church. Interments probably ended with the 1851 ban on burials below 86th Street in Manhattan.

Most of the bodies and gravestones were removed to Cemetery of the Evergreens sometime between 1856 and 1865. Approximately five hundred bodies were removed to a plot in Cypress Hills Cemetery. The burial ground was sold in 1865.

MAILING ADDRESS: N/A

PHONE NUMBER: N/A

RECORDS: The records of the Brick Presbyterian Church and the Rutgers Street Presbyterian Church will be found with those of the First Presbyterian Church prior to 1809. Thereafter, records are with the individual congregation.

RESOURCES: *Cypress Hills Cemetery*. Brooklyn, N.Y.: Cypress Hills Cemetery, 1880. (extensive list of plot owners and location of plot, maps, rules, and history of cemetery)

Disosway, Gabriel P. *Earliest Churches of New York City and its Vicinity*. 1865. Pages 121 to 163. (register of First Presbyterian Church deaths between January 1786 and July 1804)

Knapp, Shepherd. *Personal Records of the Brick Presbyterian Church in the City of New York, 1809 to 1908*. New York: the church, 1909. (list of deaths)

Roney, Lila James. "Gravestone Inscriptions from the Burial Grounds of the Brick Presbyterian Church." *The New York Genealogical and Biographical Record* 60, no. 1 (January 1929): 8–14.

Presbyterian Cemetery, West 25th Street

CATEGORY: Presbyterian

YEARS OF USE: circa 1837 to 1851

LOCATION: West 25th Street, near 8th Avenue, Manhattan.

HISTORY: The bodies in this cemetery were removed to an unspecified location about 1853. Although the "Irish Church" was located on a portion of the property, it appears that the grounds were used by Presbyterians in general.

MAILING ADDRESS: N/A

PHONE NUMBER: N/A

RECORDS: N/A

RESOURCES: N/A

Presentation Sisters' Cemetery
See Saint Michael's Home Cemetery.

Prospect Cemetery

CATEGORY: Presbyterian, Public

YEARS OF USE: circa 1668 to Date

LOCATION: Southwest corner of 159th Street and Beaver Road, Jamaica, Queens.

HISTORY: Prospect Cemetery began as the burial ground of the Old Stone Church, a Presbyterian congregation on Union Hall Street. In 1668, the cemetery was appropriated for use by the Town of Jamaica. As such, it is Jamaica's first public burial ground and one of the oldest public cemeteries in Queens.

Prospect Cemetery has seen better days. Its trustees, who operate on a $3,000 yearly budget, have not been able to maintain the property, prevent vandalism, or make much needed repairs to broken and crumbling gravestones. The grounds are surrounded by a locked chain link and barbwire fence.

The cemetery chapel is boarded up. The trustees are in need of $300,000 to repair its pews, slate roof, broken stained glass windows, and other structural damage.

Cate Ludlam, President of the Prospect Cemetery Association, told *Newsday* that fifty-three Revolutionary War patriots, forty-three Civil War veterans, three Spanish-American War veterans, and at least one slave are counted among Prospect Cemetery's dead. She added, "It should be preserved for posterity because there are people buried there who fought for the freedoms we enjoy today."

Approximately half of the cemetery's five hundred gravestones date back to the colonial era. They represent some of the earliest European families in Queens: Harriman, Lefferts, Ludlam, Merrick, Simonson, Sutphin, and VanWyk are just a few. The remains of Egbert Benson, the First Attorney General of New York; Revolutionary statesmen Thomas Wicks and Henry Benson; and actor James H. Hackett are also among the thousands buried here.

Cate Ludlam hopes to raise public and private funds to restore the grounds. "I want to make it useful," she said. "I want to be able to open the grounds and the chapel for meditation, acoustic concerts, public meetings and tours."

"People moved away and lost interest in their own family history," she added. "It's a real shame."

MAILING ADDRESS: Prospect Cemetery Association
                     c/o Queens Historical Society
                     Kingsland Homestead
                     143-35 37th Avenue
                     Flushing, New York 11354-5729

PHONE NUMBER: (718) 939-0647

RECORDS: The Prospect Cemetery Association is working to establish a database of burials.

RESOURCES: Frost, Josephine C. trans. *Inscriptions from Prospect Cemetery at Jamaica, Long Island, New York.* Brooklyn, New York. vol. 14, 1910. (gravestone inscriptions) The Long Island Room of the Queens Borough Public Library retains a copy of this book with a 1986 Addendum listing burials November 1942 to 4 January 1962.

Powell, Charles U., comp., and Alice H. Meigs, ed. *Description of Private and Family Cemeteries in the Borough of Queens.* City of New York, Borough of Queens, Topographical Bureau. Jamaica, N.Y.: Queens Borough Public Library, 1975 supplement. (map)

Welker, Mrs. A.S., trans. "Tombstone Inscriptions from Prospect Cemetery, 159th Street, Jamaica, New York." *Cemetery, Church, and Town Records of New York State.* vol. 335. Washington, D.C.: Daughters of the American Revolution, 1969-1970, 68–80. (partial list of gravestone inscriptions)

Winans, George Woodruff. *First Presbyterian Church of Jamaica, New York, 1662-1942.* Jamaica, Long Island: the church, 1943, 156-158. (cemetery history)

Prospect Park Cemetery

CATEGORY: Quaker
YEARS OF USE: 1847 to date
LOCATION: Near Entrance Number 6, 16th Street and Prospect Park Southwest, Park Slope, Brooklyn.
HISTORY: This burial ground is for the exclusive use of the Society of Friends. Simple tombstones, in the Quaker tradition, memorialize the dead. Those persons who wish to visit a grave must schedule an appointment. This cemetery is also known as the Quaker Cemetery.
MAILING ADDRESS: Religious Society of Friends
                 15 Rutherford Place
                 New York, New York 10003-3791
PHONE NUMBER: (212) 777-8866
RECORDS: Tombstones were not permitted in Quaker cemeteries until 1852. If a tombstone bears a death date prior to 1852, it was probably erected by a family member at a much later date.
RESOURCES: Haviland, Frank. *Friends Cemetery in Prospect Park, Brooklyn, New York.* Manuscript. Brooklyn Historical Society. Brooklyn, New York. 1906. (Interments 1847 to 1906)

New York Monthly Meeting, New York City: Index to Burials in Prospect Park Cemetery 1848 to 1878. (Salt Lake City: Genealogical Society of Utah), microfilm no. 17,367.

New York Monthly Meeting, New York City: Prospect Park Cemetery

1846 to 1865. (Salt Lake City: Genealogical Society of Utah), microfilm no. 17,271.

Pullis Family Burial Ground

CATEGORY: Private
YEARS OF USE: Gravestones dated 1846 to 1851
LOCATION: Beneath the intersection of 63rd Avenue and 84th Street, two blocks east of Juniper Valley Park, Middle Village, Queens.
HISTORY: A plot in the middle of Juniper Valley Park is now reserved in perpetuity as the burial ground of the Pullis family. It is surrounded by a fence and marked by a flagpole. The gravestones are gone and their whereabouts unknown.
MAILING ADDRESS: N/A
PHONE NUMBER: N/A
RECORDS: N/A
RESOURCES: Powell, Charles U., comp. and Alice H. Meigs, ed. *Description of Private and Family Cemeteries in the Borough of Queens.* City of New York, Borough of Queens, Topographical Bureau. Jamaica, N.Y.: Queens Borough Public Library, 1932. (gravestone inscriptions and map)

Quaker Cemetery
See Prospect Park Cemetery.

Quarantine Hospital Cemetery, Seguine's Point

CATEGORY: Institutional
YEARS OF USE: circa 1858 to circa 1887
LOCATION: Bayview Road at Seguine's Point, Prince's Bay, Staten Island
HISTORY: Sometime prior to 1858, Joel Wolfe sold his farm to the City of
New York for use as a Quarantine Station for newly arrived immigrants suffering from contagious disease. The city erected several hospitals on the
property and used its lawn as a graveyard. Disease promptly spread beyond
the hospital confines to the local community. Taking a cue from the residents
of Tompkinsville, who earlier objected to the Quarantine Station in their
town, the residents of Seguine's Point set the complex on fire. Temporary
hospital buildings were quickly erected, but the townspeople set them on fire
too. The government gave in and established a "floating" hospital in the
Lower Bay, opposite New Dorp, Staten Island.

The hospital's cemetery remained, but was also considered a public health
nuisance. About 1887, several newspapers took up the fight against the
cemetery and called for construction of a crematorium on Swinburne Island.
The New York State legislature subsequently mandated that the bodies be
removed and destroyed at the Swinburne Island Crematorium.
MAILING ADDRESS: N/A
PHONE NUMBER: N/A
RECORDS: N/A
RESOURCES: N/A

Quarantine Hospital Cemetery, Tompkinsville

CATEGORY: Institutional
YEARS OF USE: 1799 to 1858
LOCATION: Central Avenue, at Hyatt Street, New Brighton, Staten Island.
HISTORY: In 1799, New York City purchased thirty acres on the tip of Staten Island for use as a Quarantine Station. Over a dozen hospitals, two to three stories tall, were erected for the treatment of contagious disease. Much to the dismay of the local townspeople, yellow fever spread outside the Quarantine during the first year, and a contagious disease infected the community every year thereafter.

The problem was attributed to lax security at the site. Although the Quarantine was surrounded by a tall wall and employed security guards, employees and patients were free to come and go into the neighboring village as they pleased. Some attributed the problem to the quarantined ships that anchored in front of the hospital. The sailors were not only free to come and go into the town, but they also used the beach as a dumping ground, throwing bilge water, bedding, clothing, and containers overboard. For years, there were committees and discussions about moving the Quarantine station to a less populated area, but nothing was ever done about it.

During the summer of 1858, a group of outraged citizens gathered at the hospital, removed the patients, and burned the buildings down. When the fire department arrived to fight the fire, the firefighters were barred from the hospital, and someone cut their hose. The next night, another group of outraged citizens came back and burned the remaining structures. Although martial law was established for sometime after, and New York City erected temporary hospital buildings, the site never became fully operational again.

Central Avenue runs directly though the former site of the hospital cemetery. The bodies were removed to Silver Mount Cemetery sometime between 1858 and 1900.
MAILING ADDRESS: N/A
PHONE NUMBER: N/A
RECORDS: N/A
RESOURCES: "Are These Your Ancestors?" *The FACSI Newsletter,* vol.
15, issue 3, (Fall 1998). (list of deaths at Quarantine Marine Hospital between 1 June 1849 and 31 May 1850)

Queens County Cemetery

CATEGORY: Public
YEARS OF USE: 1737 to circa 1898
LOCATION: In the triangle formed by Hollis Avenue, Springfield Avenue, and Robard Lane, Queens Village, Queens.
HISTORY: The original towns of Queens County (Jamaica, Flushing,

Newtown, Hempstead, New Hempstead, and Oyster Bay), shared a small potter's field during the eighteenth and nineteenth centuries. Terrence Hartford, a Civil War veteran, was among those buried there.

According to one report in 1871, the cemetery had no stone gravemarkers, just wooden stakes. As soon as the stake rotted away, the person buried there "lost claim to the grave," and it was available for reuse. African-Americans were buried on one side of the cemetery and Caucasians on the other.

After Queens became part of New York City in 1898, the cemetery was converted to Wyanda Park.

MAILING ADDRESS: N/A

PHONE NUMBER: N/A

RECORDS: N/A

RESOURCES: N/A

Raffeiner Cemetery
See Most Holy Trinity Cemetery.

Randall's Island Cemetery

CATEGORY: Public
YEARS OF USE: 1843 to circa 1880
LOCATION: Randall's Island, East River, Manhattan.
HISTORY: This burial ground was used as New York City's principal public cemetery for just two years, due to its inferior soil and undesirable location. The cemetery remained in limited use after that time: *The New York Times* reported that 282 interments were made there in 1880.

Randall's Island has also been home to an Almshouse, a juvenile detention center, an insane asylum, and a cottage for sick children. It now supports the Triborough Bridge, railroad tracks, and Downing Stadium.

Randall's Island was once separated from Ward's Island by Little Hell Gate, but the two are now joined by landfill.
MAILING ADDRESS: N/A
PHONE NUMBER: N/A
RECORDS: N/A
RESOURCES: N/A

Rantus Family Burial Ground
See Troytown Cemetery.

Jacob Rapalye Family Burial Ground

CATEGORY: Private
YEARS OF USE: Gravestones date 1776 to 1830

LOCATION: Northwest corner of 21st Avenue and 21st Street, 165 feet from the corner, Astoria, Queens.

HISTORY: The Jacob Rapalye House was erected in 1749 by the only member of the Rapalye family who sympathized with the colonists during the Revolutionary War. It is located on Shore Boulevard, between 20th and 21st Avenues, Astoria. The family burial ground, set aside "forever for the descendants of Jacob Rapalye" is a short distance east of the house.

Abraham Rapalye, who died in 1798 and "sleeps on the shore of the Bowery Bay," might be among those interred here.

Consolidated Edison currently owns the house and property, preserving the graveyard as a private playground.

MAILING ADDRESS: Consolidated Edison
                              31-01 20th Avenue
                              Long Island City, New York 11105-2048

PHONE NUMBER: N/A

RECORDS: N/A

RESOURCES: Powell, Charles U., comp., and Alice H. Meigs, ed. *Description of Private and Family Cemeteries in the Borough of Queens.* City of New York, Borough of Queens, Topographical Bureau. Jamaica, N.Y.: Queens Borough Public Library, 1932. (gravestone inscriptions, maps, burial records)

Reformed Covenanted Church Cemetery
See University Place Cemetery.

Reformed Dutch Church Cemetery

CATEGORY: Reformed Dutch

YEARS OF USE: 1796 to 1851

LOCATION: South side of East Houston Street between Eldridge and Stanton Streets, Manhattan.

HISTORY: This cemetery appears to be a general burial ground for all the Reformed Dutch churches of New York City. The bodies were removed to an unspecified location about 1874.

MAILING ADDRESS: N/A

PHONE NUMBER: N/A

RECORDS: N/A

RESOURCES: N/A

Reformed Dutch Churchyard

CATEGORY: Public, Reformed Dutch

YEARS OF USE: circa 1628 to 1676

LOCATION: 27-37 Broadway, west side of the street between Exchange Place and Morris Street, Manhattan.

HISTORY: Although the church building was not erected until 1642, ecclesiastical records indicate that this burial ground was in use as early as 1628. The churchyard suffered from neglect, and by 1656, proposals were made to divide the property into lots and sell it. Those proposals came to fruition on 28 February 1677 when the city's aldermen ordered the sale of the property.

The church was originally located within the fort of New Amsterdam.

MAILING ADDRESS: N/A

PHONE NUMBER: N/A

RECORDS: On 18 February 1661, the church bell-ringer was ordered to keep a record of all who paid for burials in the cemetery, apparently to prevent price-gouging.

RESOURCES: N/A

Reformed Presbyterian Church Vault

CATEGORY: Presbyterian

YEARS OF USE: Coffins dated 1824 to 1844

LOCATION: 55 Prince Street, corner Cleveland Place, Manhattan.

HISTORY: Over three hundred bodies were removed from a vault in the rear of the Reformed Presbyterian Church in February 1877. Its church was erected in 1824 by the Society of Universalists who sold it six years later to the Union Presbyterian Church. The Union Presbyterian Church dissolved in 1838 and its property went to the Reformed Presbyterian Church.

When the property was put up for sale, the Reformed Presbyterian Church advertised for relatives to remove the bodies, but there were few responses. The congregation eventually purchased a plot in Maple Grove Cemetery where all of the remains were reinterred. Only fifteen could be identified by the nameplates on their coffins. Those that were identified were buried in individual graves, while the rest were buried in a mass grave.

MAILING ADDRESS: c/o Maple Grove Cemetery
                                83-15 Kew Gardens Road
                                Kew Gardens, New York 11415-1920

PHONE NUMBER: (718) 544-3600

RECORDS: N/A

RESOURCES: "Bodies Removed from a Church Vault." *The New York Genealogical and Biographical Record*. The New York Genealogical and Biographical Society. New York, New York. July 1877. vol. 8. page 142. (List of Identified Dead)

Reformed Protestant Dutch Cemetery of Staten Island

See Huguenot Cemetery.

Remsen Family Burial Ground

CATEGORY: Private

YEARS OF USE: Gravestones Date 1790 to 1819

LOCATION: 69-43 Trotting Course Lane, between Woodhaven Boulevard and Alderton Street, Forest Hills, Queens.

HISTORY: Colonel Jeromus Remsen, who died on 7 June 1790, established this burial ground and is the first known occupant. In its early days, the graveyard was flanked by the Remsen and Suydam houses, neither of which survive. Today, the primary focus of the plot is a WWI memorial, erected by the American Legion.

The Queens Historical Society has taken an interest in preservation of this cemetery.

MAILING ADDRESS: Remsen Family Burial Ground
c/o Queens Historical Society
Kingsland Homestead
143-35 37th Avenue
Flushing, New York 11354-5729

PHONE NUMBER: (718) 939-0647

RECORDS: N/A

RESOURCES: Brunetto, Daniel P. *Remsen Cemetery: Designation List 144 LP-1177*. New York: Landmarks Preservation Commission, 26 May 1981. (list of burials and detailed genealogy of Remsen family)

Frost, Josephine C. trans. *Long Island Cemetery Inscriptions*. vol. 1. March 1912. Brooklyn, New York. (gravestone inscriptions)

Powell, Charles U., comp., and Alice H. Meigs, ed. *Description of Private and Family Cemeteries in the Borough of Queens*. City of New York, Borough of Queens, Topographical Bureau. Jamaica, N.Y.: Queens Borough Public Library, 1932. (gravestone inscriptions and map)

Resurrection Cemetery

See Cemetery of the Resurrection.

Rezeau-Van Pelt Family Burial Ground

CATEGORY: Private

YEARS OF USE: Gravestones date 1783 to 1863

LOCATION: Center Street and Court Place, adjoining the Richmond County Courthouse, Richmondtown, Staten Island.

HISTORY: This cemetery was used by the Rezeau and Van Pelt families who occupied the Voorlezer's House, at 63 Arthur Kill Road, in eighteenth and nineteenth centuries. The largest gravestone memorializes Susannah Van Pelt, who died in 1802 at the age of ninety-nine. She is buried with her husband and members of the Johnson, Rezeau, and Wheatly families.

The Staten Island Historical Society purchased the burial ground about 1936.

MAILING ADDRESS: Staten Island Historical Society
                        441 Clarke Avenue
                        Staten Island, New York 10306-1198
PHONE NUMBER: (718) 351-1617
RECORDS: N/A
RESOURCES: Davis, William T. "Homestead Graves." *Proceedings of the Natural Science Association of Staten Island.* Staten Island, New York. Special Number 9, December 1889. (gravestone inscriptions)

Richmond County Cemetery
See New York City Farm Colony Cemetery.

Richmond Reformed Dutch Churchyard

CATEGORY: Reformed Dutch
YEARS OF USE: 1817 to 1868
LOCATION: Richmond Village, Staten Island.
HISTORY: The Reformed Dutch Church at Richmond was organized in 1808 as a branch of the Reformed Dutch Church in Port Richmond. When the congregation decided to disband and sell its property, it was required by the New York State Supreme Court to disinter all the bodies in its churchyard. The remains were taken to the Moravian Cemetery between 30 November and 7 December 1885.

Twenty-three bodies were reinterred, seven of which were not identified. Twenty-one of them were taken to Lot C, Section D. The location of the other two bodies is not yet known.

MAILING ADDRESS: c/o Gardner Sage Library
                        New Brunswick Theological Seminary
                        21 Seminary Place
                        New Brunswick, New Jersey 08901-1187
PHONE NUMBER: (908) 247-5243
RECORDS: The congregation's records were sent to the Gardner Sage Library after it disbanded.
RESOURCES: Vosburgh, Royden Woodward, trans. *Records of the Reformed Dutch Church at Richmond, Staten Island.* Staten Island, New York. October 1923. (gravestone inscriptions, 1817 to 1868; deaths and funerals, 1854 to 1870)

Ridgway Family Burial Ground

CATEGORY: Private
YEARS OF USE: Gravestones date 1771 to 1851

LOCATION: Near the northwest corner of Victory Boulevard and Travis Avenue, Chelsea, Staten Island.

HISTORY: This burial ground was leveled in February of 1988 for construction of an office tower. Friends of Abandoned Cemeteries of Staten Island notified the district attorney, who brought charges of criminal mischief against the developers.

Thirteen gravestones were recovered in good condition. The developer agreed to reconstruct the burial ground across the street, erect a monument, and contribute $2,500 toward a maintenance fund. The reconstructed burial ground was finished in 1990.

Members of the Alston, Egbert, Ridgway, Travis, and Wood families were buried there.

MAILING ADDRESS: N/A

PHONE NUMBER: N/A

RECORDS: N/A

RESOURCES: Davis, William T. "Homestead Graves." *Proceedings of the Natural Science Association of Staten Island.* Staten Island, New York. Special No. 9, December 1889. (gravestone inscriptions)

Riker-Lent Family Burial Ground

CATEGORY: Private

YEARS OF USE: Gravestones date 1721 to date

LOCATION: 78-03 19th Road, 78th Street, Astoria, Queens.

HISTORY: This family burial ground is believed to be the oldest privately owned cemetery in New York State. It is in the yard of the Abraham Riker house, built in 1654. Its current owners, Michael Smith and Marion Duckworth Smith, have restored the home and plan to be buried in the cemetery.

Dr. William J. MacNeven and Catherine Ann Tone, Irish revolutionaries to whom the Riker family extended hospitality, are interred here with over one hundred members of the Riker and Lent families.

MAILING ADDRESS: Riker-Lent Family Burial Ground
c/o Queens Historical Society
Kingsland Homestead
143-35 37th Avenue
Flushing, New York 11354-5727

PHONE NUMBER: (718) 939-0647

RECORDS: Mr. and Mrs. Smith discovered a large collection of family papers in the attic, including letters, that date back to the 18th century.

RESOURCES: Frost, Josephine C. trans. *Cemetery Inscriptions, Flatlands, Brooklyn, New York.* Brooklyn, New York. vol. 12, 1914. (gravestone inscriptions)

Powell, Charles U., comp. and Alice H. Meigs, ed. *Description of Private and Family Cemeteries in the Borough of Queens.* City of New York, Borough of Queens, Topographical Bureau. Jamaica, N.Y.: Queens Borough Public Library, 1932. (gravestone inscriptions and map)

    Riker, James Jr. *The Annals of Newtown in Queens County, New York.* D. Fanshaw, New York. 1852. Pages 299 to 319. (detailed genealogies for Riker and Lent Families)

    Skenazy, Lenore. "They've a Grave Undertaking." *New York Daily News*, 26 October 1997, p. 50, col. 1. (description of cemetery and current owners)

Romaine Family Burial Ground

See Wallabout Bay.

Rose Street Burial Ground of the Society of Friends

CATEGORY: Quaker
YEARS OF USE: circa 1775 to 1823
LOCATION: Rose Street, between Pearl Street and Duane Street, Manhattan.
HISTORY: The Society of Friends built a meeting house on Pearl Street in 1775, the second meeting house in New York City. Burials in the graveyard probably ended with the ban on interments south of Grand Street, Manhattan in 1823. The property was sold between 1850 and 1860.
MAILING ADDRESS: Friends' Historical Library
                  c/o Swarthmore College
                  500 College Avenue
                  Swarthmore, Pennsylvania 19081-1399
PHONE NUMBER: (610) 328-8000
RECORDS: Original records are now housed at the Friends' Historical Library of Swarthmore College. Tombstones were not permitted in Quaker cemeteries until 1852.
RESOURCES: *Flushing Monthly Meeting, New York: Births, Deaths, and Marriages 1640 to 1796.* (Salt Lake City: Genealogical Society of Utah), microfilm no. 17,376.

    New York Monthly Meeting, New York City: Memorials of Deceased Friends 1707 to 1820. (Salt Lake City: Genealogical Society of Utah), microfilm no. 17,353.

Rossville African Methodist Episcopal Zion Church Cemetery

CATEGORY: African, Non-Sectarian
YEARS OF USE: 1852 to date
LOCATION: South side of Crabtree Avenue, between Bloomingdale Road and

Turner Street, Woodrow, Staten Island.

HISTORY: The Rossville African Methodist Episcopal Zion Church Cemetery is in the Sandy Ground section of Staten Island, a community founded by free African-American oystermen from Maryland in the 1830s. The cemetery contains the graves of at least thirty four founding families, some of whose descendants still live in the area.

A few of those buried in the cemetery were of German and Dutch ancestry, and not all were members of the Church.

MAILING ADDRESS: Rossville AME Zion Church
                  584 Bloomingdale Road
                  Staten Island, New York 10309-2009

PHONE NUMBER: (718) 356-0200

RECORDS: N/A

RESOURCES: Blair, Jayson. "Repairs Start After Vandalism In Historic Black Cemetery." *The New York Times*, 8 July 1998, The Metropolitan Desk. (names some descendants)

Rossville Burial Ground
See Blazing Star Burial Ground.

Ryerson Family Burial Ground

CATEGORY: Private

YEARS OF USE: Gravestone dated 3 August 1798

LOCATION: Under the sidewalk of the high school at the northwest corner of 29th Street and 41st Avenue, Long Island City, Queens.

HISTORY: In 1902, workmen unearthed the tombstone of John Francis Ryerson, who died 1798 at the age of seventy-four years, three months, and twenty-two days. John Ryerson acquired the area in 1769. Afterward, his estate passed to the Debevoise family.

MAILING ADDRESS: N/A

PHONE NUMBER: N/A

RECORDS: N/A

RESOURCES: N/A

Sailor's Snug Harbor Cemetery

CATEGORY: Institutional, Seamen
YEARS OF USE: 1834 to 1976
LOCATION: Prospect Avenue and Caldera Place, Livingston, Staten Island.
HISTORY: Sailor's Snug Harbor was created in 1801 by the will of Captain Robert Richard Randall as a "home for retired, native-born sailors who served at least five years aboard a vessel flying the American flag." The Staten Island site opened in 1833 with twenty sailors. It later housed as many as 1,000 retirees at a time. In 1976, Sailor's Snug Harbor closed its Staten Island facility, sold the property to the City of New York, and reopened its doors in North Carolina. It retained ownership of the cemetery, and the older gravestones were put into storage.

The Snug Harbor Cultural Center currently occupies the remaining property. It is home to the Staten Island Botanical Garden, the Staten Island Children's Museum, and independent arts organizations.

MAILING ADDRESS: Sailor's Snug Harbor
                  Post Office Box 150
                  Sealevel, North Carolina 28577-0150
PHONE NUMBER: (252) 225-4411
RECORDS: Sailor's Snug Harbor maintains the cemetery records and will search them upon request. Researchers should also check the Staten Island RootsWeb page on the Internet to see if this cemetery has been added to their cemetery database. The address is: <http://www.rootsweb.com/~nyrichmo>.
RESOURCES: Friends of Abandoned Cemeteries of Staten Island has a blueprint of the cemetery. The graves are numbered; the blueprint shows the location of each number. FACSI can be reached at 140 Tysen Street, Staten Island, New York 10301-1120.

Lane, Doris. "By Will of a Sea Captain: Sailor's Snug Harbor Cemetery." *The FACSI Newsletter*, vol. 15, issue 3 (Fall 1998). (history of cemetery; profile of David Jeremiah Hubbard)

Saint Agnes' Cemetery
See Oceanview Cemetery.

Saint Andrew's Churchyard

CATEGORY: Protestant Episcopal
YEARS OF USE: circa 1713 to date
LOCATION: South side of Old Mill Road, between Richmond Hill Road and LaTourette Park, Richmond, Staten Island.
HISTORY: Saint Andrew's Church erected its first chapel in 1713. Queen Anne gave the congregation a chalice and paten, now on display at the Metropolitan Museum of Art in Manhattan. Queen Anne also gave the congregation a bell, and it is still in use.

Dr. Richard Bayley, father of Saint Elizabeth Ann Seton, is buried in the churchyard.
MAILING ADDRESS: Saint Andrew's Episcopal Church
                 40 Old Mill Road
                 Staten Island, New York 10306-1197
PHONE NUMBER: (718) 351-0900
RECORDS: "The church has a copy of the sexton's book in the church safe."
RESOURCES: Davis, William T., Charles W. Leng, and Royden Woodward Vosburgh. *The Church of Saint Andrew, Richmond, Staten Island: It's History, Vital Records, and Gravestone Inscriptions*. Staten Island, N.Y.: Staten Island Historical Society, 1925. (gravestone inscriptions; photos)

Vosburgh, Royden Woodward, trans. *Records of Saint Andrew's Protestant Episcopal Church*. Staten Island, New York. 1922. (Funerals 1808 to 1855; Burials 1857 to 1875)

Saint Ann-in-the-Fields Churchyard, Crypt, and Vaults

CATEGORY: Protestant Episcopal
YEARS OF USE: 1672 to 1936
LOCATION: 295 Saint Ann's Avenue, west side of the street between East 140th Street and East 141st Street, Port Morris, Bronx.
HISTORY: Gouverneur Morris II, a railroad pioneer, built Saint Ann's Church in honor of his mother, Anne Carey Randolph Morris. Erected in 1841, it is the oldest church edifice in the Bronx. Morris' mother claimed to be a descendant of Pocahontas and is buried in the church crypt. She is interred near Judge Lewis Morris, first governor of the State of New Jersey (died 1672); Lewis Morris, a signer of the Declaration of Independence (died 1798); and

Judge Robert Hunter Morris, a mayor of New York City (died 1855).

Gouverneur Morris I, who helped draft the United States Constitution in 1787, is buried in a private vault at the entrance of the church. He died in 1816.

While the burial ground is overflowing with history, its importance to the children of the Bronx is more tangible. In 1967, Saint Ann's Church told the *New York Times* that neighborhood children played amidst the gravestones because they had nowhere else to go. Said fourteen-year-old Carlos Busigo, "It's no good in the streets, so we play here. It's the only grass in the South Bronx. You forget the difference between grass where there's people buried and other grass."

Church officials added that the burial ground, which was in a state of disrepair, had not been mended or fenced off because there had never been enough money to repair the church, let alone the yard. The Morris family later donated $25,000 for restoration of the gravestones and installation of a wrought-iron fence.

MAILING ADDRESS: Saint Ann's Church
                 295 Saint Ann's Avenue
                 Bronx, New York 10454-2597
PHONE NUMBER: (718) 585-5632
RECORDS: The Rector of Saint Ann's Church is in charge of ecclesiastical and cemetery records.
RESOURCES: *Cemetery, Church, and Town Records of New York State*. vol. 118. Washington, D.C.: Daughters of the American Revolution, 1938, 56–62. (gravestone inscriptions)
    Churchyards of Trinity Parish in the City of New York: 1697 to 1947.
New York: Trinity Church Corporation, 1955. (gravestone inscriptions)

Saint Ann's Churchyard

CATEGORY: Protestant Episcopal
YEARS OF USE: Pre-1780 to 1849
LOCATION: East side of Fulton Street, opposite Clinton Street, Brooklyn.
HISTORY: Interments ceased in 1849 when the City of Brooklyn prohibited burials within the city limits. The remains were subsequently removed to Green-Wood Cemetery.
MAILING ADDRESS: Green-Wood Cemetery
                 Fifth Avenue and 25th Street
                 Brooklyn, New York 11232-1690
PHONE NUMBER: (718) 768-7300
RECORDS: Requests may be made on-site or by mail.
RESOURCES: "Old Burial Grounds. Cemeteries in Brooklyn and the County Towns." *The Brooklyn Eagle*, 29 August 1886, p. 9, col. 3. (location and history of the cemetery)

Saint Claire Pollock's Grave

See Amiable Child Monument.

Saint Clement's Church Vaults

CATEGORY: Protestant Episcopal
YEARS OF USE: circa 1834 to 1851
LOCATION: 108-110 West Third Street, between Macdougal Street and
Sullivan Street, Manhattan.
HISTORY: N/A
MAILING ADDRESS: Saint Clement's Episcopal Church
                 423 West 46th Street
                 New York, New York 10036-3592
PHONE NUMBER: (212) 246-7277
RECORDS: N/A
RESOURCES: N/A

Saint George's Churchyard of Astoria

CATEGORY: Protestant Episcopal
YEARS OF USE: circa 1827 to 1928
LOCATION: East side of 14th Street, between Astoria Boulevard and 27th
Avenue, extending to 18th Street, Astoria, Queens.
HISTORY: Saint George's Protestant Episcopal Church was established in
1827. In 1940, there were ninety nine gravestones in its churchyard, all rep-
resenting colonial families of Astoria, with members of the Blackwell family
prevailing. The remains of the Blackwell Family Burial Ground were
removed to the churchyard in October of 1900.
MAILING ADDRESS: N/A
PHONE NUMBER: N/A
RECORDS: The church registers date back to 1850.
RESOURCES: Powell, Charles U., comp., and Alice H. Meigs, ed. *Description
of Private and Family Cemeteries in the Borough of Queens.* City of New York,
Borough of Queens, Topographical Bureau. Jamaica, N.Y.: Queens Borough
Public Library, 1975 supplement. (gravestone inscriptions and maps)

Saint George's Churchyard of Flushing

CATEGORY: Protestant Episcopal
YEARS OF USE: circa 1790 to 1896
LOCATION: Main Street and 38th Avenue, Flushing, Queens.
HISTORY: Saint George's Church was organized in 1704, but the congregation
did not erect its church until 1746. Their early records are with those of Grace
Church in Jamaica. In 1782, the congregation began to keep its own records.

A visitor to the churchyard in 1912 observed that many of the grave-stones had been moved to Flushing Cemetery, while others had fallen down or had been thrown into a pile in the rear of the church. Some gravestones are still visible today.

MAILING ADDRESS: Saint George's Episcopal Church
                    135-32 38th Avenue
                    Flushing, New York 11354-4483

PHONE NUMBER: (718) 359-1171

RECORDS: N/A

RESOURCES: Frost, Josephine C. trans. *Long Island Cemetery Inscriptions.* vol. 4. Brooklyn, New York. March 1912. (Gravestone Inscriptions) Matinecock Chapter, Daughters of the American Revolution, trans. "Graveyard of Saint George's Church." *Cemetery, Church, and Town Records of New York State.* vol. 363. Washington, D.C.: Daughters of the American Revolution, 1970-1971, 86–95. (gravestone inscriptions; index)

    Scott, Kenneth, trans. "Records of Saint George's Episcopal Church, Flushing, Long Island: Burials 1790 to 1848." *The New York Genealogical and Biographical Record.* New York: The New York Genealogical and Biographical Society, 1979, 39. Continued in subsequent issues.

Saint George's Churchyard and Vaults

CATEGORY: Protestant Episcopal

YEARS OF USE: circa 1752 to 1823

LOCATION: Beekman Street, northwest corner of Cliff Street, Manhattan.

HISTORY: Saint George's Church began as a chapel of Trinity Church in 1752 and became independent in 1811. Burials in the churchyard probably came to a halt with the 1823 ban on interments south of Canal Street. When the vaults were removed, most of the bodies were taken to Trinity Church Cemetery.

MAILING ADDRESS: Saint George's Episcopal Church
                    209 East 16th Street
                    New York, New York 10003-3788

PHONE NUMBER: (212) 475-0830

RECORDS: N/A

RESOURCES: *Removal of Vaults from Saint George's Church, Beekman and Cliff Streets, New York City, 1865 to 1867.* Manuscript, from the Estate of George Ingraham Willis, at the New York Genealogical and Biographical Society. New York, New York. 1989.

Saint James' Churchyard

CATEGORY: Protestant Episcopal

YEARS OF USE: Gravestones date 1805 to 1934

LOCATION: East side of Broadway, between Saint James Avenue and Corona Avenue, Elmhurst, Queens.

HISTORY: The congregation of Saint James' Church began meeting as early as 1704, but it wasn't until 1734 that they erected their church as a Chapel of Grace Episcopal Church of Jamaica. Saint James became a separate parish in 1809.

In 1848, the congregation moved into a new church one block away. Its graveyard is situated behind this building. Nearly a century later, New York City claimed that the graveyard was a public cemetery. As such, the city asserted ownership and planned to transform the cemetery into a playground. Saint James objected, arguing that the land had always been their churchyard.

The oldest gravestone in the churchyard is that of James Hazard, Esquire, who died in 1765. It was removed from the Leverich Family Burial Ground in 1925.

MAILING ADDRESS: Saint James Episcopal Church
                  8407 Broadway
                  Flushing, New York 11373-5792

PHONE NUMBER: (718) 592-2555

RECORDS: Church records may have been destroyed by fire in the 1970s. Prior to 1809, records are probably with those of Grace Church.

RESOURCES: Frost, Josephine C. trans. *Long Island Cemetery Inscriptions*. Brooklyn, New York. Vol. 4. March 1912. (gravestone inscriptions)

Haviland, Frank. *Complete Inscriptions in the Churchyard of Saint James Episcopal Church*. Brooklyn, N.Y.: Brooklyn Historical Society, 1904, manuscript. (gravestone inscriptions)

Powell, Charles U., comp. and Alice H. Meigs, ed. *Description of Private and Family Cemeteries in the Borough of Queens*. City of New York, Borough of Queens, Topographical Bureau. Jamaica, N.Y.: Queens Borough Public Library, 1975 supplement. (gravestone inscriptions and maps)

Saint James Place Cemetery
See Chatham Square Cemetery.

Saint James' Pro-Cathedral Churchyard

CATEGORY: Roman Catholic
YEARS OF USE: 1823 to 1849
LOCATION: North side of Cathedral Place, between Flatbush Avenue and Jay Street, Brooklyn.
HISTORY: Saint James Pro-Cathedral, of the Diocese of Brooklyn, is the oldest Roman Catholic church on Long Island and the third oldest Roman Catholic church in the city of New York. In 1902, the *Brooklyn Daily Eagle* reported that nearly 1,000 people were buried in the churchyard. The first known burial was Joseph D. Grady, buried on 29 April 1823. The last two

burials were of Susannah Duffy and James McKenna, both buried on 21 May 1849.

MAILING ADDRESS: c/o Saint John's Cemetery
                     80-01 Metropolitan Avenue
                     Flushing, New York 11379-2991

PHONE NUMBER: (718) 894-4888

RECORDS: Cemetery records for the Diocese of Brooklyn are kept in the offices of Saint John's Cemetery. Requests for information must be in writing.

RESOURCES: Meehan, Thomas F. "A Village Churchyard." *Historical Records and Studies* 7 (June 1914): 183. (history)

Saint John's Cemetery, Manhattan

CATEGORY: Protestant Episcopal

YEARS OF USE: circa 1799 to 1851

LOCATION: East side of Hudson Street, between LeRoy Street, and Clarkson Street, Manhattan.

HISTORY: Approximately 10,000 people were buried in this one acre cemetery, used by the churches of Trinity Parish.

New York City, looking to create new parks, annexed the cemetery for use as Hudson Playground, now James J. Walker Park. It set 15 November 1896 as the deadline for removal of the bodies, but had to extend that deadline to the spring of 1897 when it found that only twenty-seven bodies had been disinterred. Those thousands of bodies that were not claimed by family members remain underneath the park. Trinity Church made record of all the gravestones before the city buried them several feet below the topsoil.

During construction of the park, workers uncovered a stone marked "LeRoy." This lead to romantic speculation that the grave was that of Louis Charles, the lost Dauphin of France and son of Marie Antoinette. It was probably the gravestone of parishioner Jacob LeRoy or one of his descendants.

MAILING ADDRESS: Trinity Churchyard
                     74 Trinity Place, Floor 22
                     New York, New York 10006-2003

PHONE NUMBER: (212) 285-0836

RECORDS: N/A

RESOURCES: Cox, Hope. *Records of Trinity Church and Parish, New York City.* Manuscript #NY-50 at the New York Genealogical and Biographical Society. New York, New York. vol. 6. 1933 to 1935. (Existing Gravestones in 1897) (Note: This list was printed in *The World*, 4 December 1892.)

King, Moses. "Saint John's Burying-Ground." *King's Handbook of New York City.* Boston, Mass., 1893. Reissued. New York: Benjamin Blom Inc., 1972, 512–514. (some burials)

"Saint John's Cemetery to be a Park." *The New York Genealogical and Biographical Record* 28, no. 1 (January 1897): 57.

Saint John's Cemetery, Queens

CATEGORY: Roman Catholic
YEARS OF USE: 1880 to date
LOCATION: 80-01 Metropolitan Avenue, between Woodhaven Boulevard and Cooper Avenue, Middle Village, Queens.
HISTORY: The *Brooklyn Daily Eagle* described Saint John's Cemetery in an April 1895 review of area cemeteries. It wrote, "The grounds are tastefully enclosed... surrounded with wide avenues or drives, marginal sidewalks, and handsome shade trees... When the high situation and dryness of the land and the natural beautiful contour of the grounds are taken into account, Saint John's Cemetery will be in time, as the improvements progress, one of the most suitable resting places for the dead perhaps on Long Island."

Edward Paycon Weston is buried in Saint John's Cemetery. Weston, a long distance walker, is celebrated for his 1909 trek from New York to California and for his return trip the following year. Mobsters Vito Genovese and Salvatore Charles "Lucky" Luciano are also buried here.
MAILING ADDRESS: Saint John's Cemetery
                80-01 Metropolitan Avenue
                Flushing, New York 11379-2991
PHONE NUMBER: (718) 894–4888
RECORDS: The cemetery's records are housed on-site. Requests for information must be in writing.
RESOURCES: N/A

Saint John's Churchyard

CATEGORY: Lutheran, Methodist Episcopal
YEARS OF USE: N/A
LOCATION: Jewett Avenue, west side of the avenue at Catherine Court, Port Richmond, Staten Island.
HISTORY: At one time, Trinity Methodist Episcopal Church owned, operated, and used the churchyard of the North Side Methodist Episcopal Church. The gravestones in the private plot of Robert C. Simonson are among the early Methodist gravestones. The church and its graveyard were sold to Saint John's Lutheran Church.
MAILING ADDRESS: Saint John's Lutheran Church
                9 Catherine Court
                Staten Island, New York 10302-1805
PHONE NUMBER: (718) 815-9374
RECORDS: N/A
RESOURCES: N/A

Saint Joseph's Cemetery

CATEGORY: Roman Catholic
YEARS OF USE: 1860 to 1934
LOCATION: South side of Barry Street, between Rossville Avenue and Veterans Road East, Rossville, Staten Island.
HISTORY: N/A
MAILING ADDRESS: Saints Joseph and Thomas Church
             6135 Amboy Road
             Staten Island, New York 10309-3191
PHONE NUMBER: (718) 984-4572
RECORDS: N/A
RESOURCES: N/A

Saint Luke's Cemetery

CATEGORY: Protestant Episcopal
YEARS OF USE: 1751 to 1900
LOCATION: North side of Arthur Kill Road, opposite Zebra Place, Rossville, Staten Island.
HISTORY: Saint Luke's Cemetery is the combination of four small cemeteries. The first cemetery is the Wright Family Burial Ground, located at the northeast corner of the property. Some of the bodies in the Wright Family Burial Ground may have been removed to to the second cemetery, Saint Luke's Churchyard, near Arthur Kill Road, when Saint Luke's Church was erected.

The Woglom Family Burial Ground is the third cemetery. It was sold to Saint Luke's Church in 1849 for ten dollars. The oldest known gravestone in this section is that of Sarah Woglom, wife of Abraham, who died in 1751. Another report suggests that the oldest stone dates back to 1746.

Saint Luke's Churchyard, including the Wright and Woglom Family Burial Grounds, began to run out of room about 1875. A new section was developed to the north and called Vaughn Cemetery. Saint Luke's Cemetery took title to this land on 29 December 1900. Most of the gravestones in this section were erected after 1880.

The cemetery was abandoned, but is now cared for by All Saints Episcopal Church in Willowbrook.
MAILING ADDRESS: All Saints Episcopal Church
             2329 Victory Boulevard
             Staten Island, New York 10314-6689
PHONE NUMBER: (718) 698-1338
RECORDS: Researchers should check for records on the Staten Island RootsWeb page on the Internet. The address is <http://www.rootsweb.com/~nyrichmo>.

RESOURCES: Vosburgh, Royden Woodward, trans. *Records of Saint Luke's Protestant Episcopal Church at Rossville, Staten Island.*   Staten Island, New York. September 1923. (Burial Records 1844 to 1877)

Vosburgh, Royden W., editor and transcriber, "Staten Island Gravestone Inscriptions," vol. 2, New York City, April 1925 (typed manuscript).

Saint Luke's Churchyard and Vaults

CATEGORY: Protestant Episcopal
YEARS OF USE: circa 1812 to 1851
LOCATION: 483-485 Hudson Street, at the foot of Grove Street between Christopher Street and Barrow Street, Manhattan.
HISTORY: When the congregation of Saint Luke's Church decided to move uptown, church trustees asked the descendants of those buried in the churchyard to remove the bodies to another location.

Thirty-six descendants objected and retained an attorney to prevent the removals. Members of the Aymar, Coffin, Field, Havermeyer, Ketchum, Mott, Ten Broeck, and Wilmerding families were among those who opposed the move. They agreed to drop their opposition when Saint Luke's offered to reinter the bodies at church expense.

William Waldorf Astor, concerned about untoward publicity for his family, urged the trustees to make the removals discreetly. He wrote, "It would be especially unpleasant to me were any mention of this inserted in any newspaper."

Saint Luke's Church moved to Convent Avenue and 141st Street in December of 1892. There were approximately five hundred graves in their churchyard. Most were removed to Trinity Church Cemetery.

The churchyard predates construction of Saint Luke's by about ten years. It may have served as a general burial ground for Trinity Parish during that time.
MAILING ADDRESS: Saint Luke's Episcopal Church
                            435 West 141st Street
                            New York, New York 10031-6401
PHONE NUMBER: (212) 926-2713
RECORDS: The records of the parish were transferred to the new church.
RESOURCES: Berger, Meyer. "About New York: Untenanted Century-Old Tombs Come to Light at Saint Luke's Chapel Lawn." *The New York Times*, 5 August 1995. (history and description of churchyard)

Saint Mark's African Methodist Episcopal Churchyard

CATEGORY: African, Methodist Episcopal
YEARS OF USE: 1828 to circa 1899

LOCATION: West side of Corona Avenue between 90th Street and 91st Place, extending back to 45th Avenue, Elmhurst, Queens.

HISTORY: John Coes, George Derlin, John Peterson, and John Potter purchased an old blacksmith shop in 1828 for use as Saint Mark's Church. Burials in the graveyard began shortly after the property was acquired and ended about 1899.

An elderly church member recalled that "no white people" were ever buried in the churchyard. He further stated that it was impossible to tell how many people were buried there, that no records were ever kept, and that there were never many gravestones. In 1928, the church made plans to reinter the bodies in Mount Olivet Cemetery.

MAILING ADDRESS: Saint Mark's AME Church
　　　　　　　　　 95-18 Northern Boulevard
　　　　　　　　　 Flushing, New York 11372-2036

PHONE NUMBER:　(718) 899-3306

RECORDS: The church confirmed in 1975 that it does not have any record of burials.

RESOURCES:　Powell, Charles U., comp. and Alice H. Meigs, ed. *Description of Private and Family Cemeteries in the Borough of Queens.* City of New York, Borough of Queens, Topographical Bureau. Jamaica, N.Y.: Queens Borough Public Library, 1975 supplement. (church history and map)

Saint Mark's-in-the-Bowery Churchyard and Vaults

CATEGORY: Protestant Episcopal

YEARS OF USE: 1670 to 1851

LOCATION: Stuyvesant Street, corner 10th Street, between 2nd and 3rd Avenues, Manhattan. At one point, the churchyard included the block bounded by 1st Avenue, 2nd Avenue, 11th Street and 12th Street.

HISTORY: Saint Mark's-in-the-Bowery Church was erected in 1660 on the farm of Peter Stuyvesant, Governor of New Amsterdam, where his family, his neighbors, and their slaves worshipped every Sunday. It is the oldest site of continuous worship in New York City.

By 1969, the burial ground was a garbage dump and a haven for drug addicts. That year, Reverend J. C. Michael Allen, pastor of Saint Mark's, spearheaded an effort to transform the graveyard into a playground. Allen told *The New York Times,* "A few people have complained to me about the cemetery project, but I don't think they understand. There are many ways to honor the dead, but for me and the anguished people who are my parishioners, I think the best way to honor them is not to die with them, but to live with them."

Approximately thirty teenagers were hired to help build the new playground. The yard was paved with cobblestones that were laid out in a circular design about the gravestones, crypt entrances, and trees.

MAILING ADDRESS: Saint Mark's Church
                 131 East 10th Street
                 New York, New York 10003-7590
PHONE NUMBER: (212) 674-6377
RECORDS: N/A
RESOURCES: Barber, Gertrude A., trans. *Records of Saint Mark's Church in
the Bowery*. Manuscript #NY-40 at the New York Genealogical and
Biographical Society. New York, New York. 1939. (Burials 1836 to 1841)
    King, Moses. "Saint Mark's Churchyard." *King's Handbook of New
York City*. Boston, Mass., 1893. Reissued. New York: Benjamin Blom Inc.,
1972, 511–512. (photo, some burials, Stuyvesant memorial tablet)
    "Secor Burials in Old Saint Mark's Church." *Cemetery, Church, and
Town Records of New York State*. vol. 2. Washington, D.C.: Daughters of the
American Revolution, 1927, 17.

Saint Mary of the Assumption
Church Cemetery

CATEGORY: Roman Catholic
YEARS OF USE: circa 1854 to date
LOCATION: 160 Walker Street, south side of the street between Dr. Martin
Luther King, Jr. Expressway and Trantor Place, Port Richmond, Staten Island.
HISTORY: Saint Mary of the Assumption Church was organized in 1854. The
congregation moved to a new building on Richmond Terrace in 1884, but
continued to use its old churchyard.
MAILING ADDRESS: Saint Mary of the Assumption Church
                 2230 Richmond Terrace
                 Staten Island, New York 10302-1243
PHONE NUMBER: (718) 442-6372
RECORDS: N/A
RESOURCES: N/A

Saint Mary's Cemetery
(See also Mount Saint Mary's Cemetery)

CATEGORY: Roman Catholic
YEARS OF USE: 1862 to date
LOCATION: 155 Parkinson Avenue, between Kermit Avenue and Reid Avenue,
Grasmere, Staten Island.
HISTORY: The cemetery is divided into two sections, separated by Parkinson
Avenue and Kramer Street.
MAILING ADDRESS: Saint Mary's Cemetery
                 155 Parkinson Avenue
                 Staten Island, New York 10305-2536

PHONE NUMBER: (718) 447-0598
RECORDS: The cemetery records are housed on-site.
RESOURCES: N/A

Saint Mary's Churchyard

CATEGORY: Roman Catholic
YEARS OF USE: 1837 to circa 1850
LOCATION: Corner of North 8th Street and Kent Avenue, Williamsburg, Brooklyn.
HISTORY: The congregation of Saint Mary's Church sold its property in April of 1890. The bodies in the churchyard were reinterred in Saint John's Cemetery.
MAILING ADDRESS: c/o Saint John's Cemetery
                 80-01 Metropolitan Avenue
                 Flushing, New York 11379-2991
PHONE NUMBER: (718) 894-4888
RECORDS: Saint John's records are housed on-site. Requests for information must be in writing.
RESOURCES: N/A

Saint Matthew's Cemetery, Clarkson Street

CATEGORY: Lutheran
YEARS OF USE: circa 1800 to 1851
LOCATION: Clarkson Street, opposite Varick Street, Manhattan.
HISTORY: This cemetery was probably used as a general burial ground for members of the Lutheran faith until an 1851 ban on interments below 86th Street in Manhattan forced it to close. The bodies were most likely reinterred in Lutheran Cemetery in 1869.
MAILING ADDRESS: Saint Matthew's Lutheran Church
                 200 Sherman Avenue
                 New York, New York 10034-3301
PHONE NUMBER: (212) 567-2172
RECORDS: The earliest surviving Lutheran records begin in 1704.
RESOURCES: N/A

Saint Matthew's Cemetery, East 49th Street

CATEGORY: Lutheran
YEARS OF USE: After 1843 to 1851
LOCATION: East 49th Street, near 3rd Avenue, Manhattan.
HISTORY: The East 49th Street cemetery was presumably used as a general burial ground for members of the Lutheran faith until an 1851 ban on inter-

ments below 86th Street in Manhattan forced it to close. The bodies were probably removed to Lutheran Cemetery.

MAILING ADDRESS: Saint Matthew's Lutheran Church
200 Sherman Avenue
New York, New York 10034-3301

PHONE NUMBER: (212) 567-2172

RECORDS: The earliest surviving Lutheran records begin in 1704.

RESOURCES: N/A

Saint Michael's Cemetery and Mausoleums

CATEGORY: Non-sectarian, Protestant Episcopal

YEARS OF USE: 1851 to date

LOCATION: 72-02 Astoria Boulevard, between the Brooklyn-Queens Expressway East and the Brooklyn-Queens Expressway West, Astoria, Queens.

HISTORY: Saint Michael's Cemetery was established by the Reverend T. M. Peters on the principle that poor people should be buried in graves of their own, at an affordable rate. Consequently, there are numerous plots for churches and charitable institutions in this cemetery: Leake and Watt's Orphan Home, Saint Luke's Hospital, and The Sheltering Arms of New York are among them.

Reverend Peters eventually sold the cemetery to Saint Michael's Protestant Episcopal Church, Manhattan, at a cost equal to his initial investment.

In 1895, *The Brooklyn Daily Eagle* wrote that Saint Michael's Cemetery "is laid out on the lawn system on pleasant rolling ground, backed by picturesque woods. The older portion is occupied by enclosed family plots, many of them owned by Germans, in flower time always beautiful with the glory of the flowers. In this respect Saint Michaels' challenges comparison with any cemetery hereabouts..."

American composer Scott Joplin was buried here in 1917.

MAILING ADDRESS: Saint Michael's Cemetery and Mausoleums
72-02 Astoria Boulevard
Flushing, New York 11370-1094

PHONE NUMBER: (718) 278-3240

RECORDS: The cemetery's records are housed on-site.

RESOURCES: "Our Cities of the Dead: Millions of People are at Rest in Them." *The Brooklyn Daily Eagle*, 28 April 1895, p. 28, col. 1. (lists Protestant Episcopal Churches owning plots; notable burials)

Saint Michael's Churchyard and Cemetery

CATEGORY: Protestant Episcopal

YEARS OF USE: circa 1806 to 1851

LOCATION: 99th Street and Amsterdam Avenue, Manhattan.

HISTORY: Saint Michael's Church was established in 1806. Among those buried in its churchyard are members of the Chisholm, Clarkson, Finlay, Flemming, Hazard, Livingston, de Peyster, Rockwell, Wagstaff, and Windust families. Burials probably came to an end in 1851, when Saint Michael's opened its cemetery in Astoria, Queens.

The current church building was erected in 1891, over a portion of the churchyard. Displaced graves were reinterred in a vault beneath the church and in Saint Michael's Cemetery in Astoria. The surviving portion of the churchyard exists as a garden. There are no gravestones.

Maps from 1876 and earlier indicate that Saint Michael's Church also owned a cemetery situated on the north side of 103rd Street, between Columbus Avenue and Amsterdam Avenue, Manhattan. The cemetery property is now covered by the Frederick Douglass Houses. A spokesperson for the church indicated that they are not aware of a cemetery at that location.

MAILING ADDRESS: Saint Michael's Episcopal Church
225 West 99th Street
New York, New York 10025-5014

PHONE NUMBER: (212) 222-2700

RECORDS: N/A

RESOURCES: "Tombs Under the City." *The New York Times*, 2 August 1896, p. 20, col. 1. (description of vaults; some vault owners; sketch of catacombs)

Saint Michael's Home Cemetery

CATEGORY: Roman Catholic

YEARS OF USE: N/A

LOCATION: 419 Woodrow Road, Eltingville, Staten Island.

HISTORY: This cemetery is used exclusively by the Presentation Sisters of Staten Island.

MAILING ADDRESS: Presentation Sisters
419 Woodrow Road
Staten Island, New York 10312-1396

PHONE NUMBER: (718) 356-2121

RECORDS: N/A

Resources: N/A

Saint Monica's Churchyard

CATEGORY: Roman Catholic

YEARS OF USE: circa 1901 to 1910

LOCATION: Liberty Avenue and 160th Street, Jamaica, Queens.

HISTORY: Saint Monica's Church was erected at the corner of Liberty Avenue and 160th Street in 1840, but by 1856 the congregation had outgrown the building and constructed a new church one block away. The congregation disbanded in 1973. The church is now surrounded by the campus of York College. Although York College had plans to restore and use the building, those plans were postponed when the roof collapsed during a rainstorm in May of 1998.

The churchyard remains at its original location.

MAILING ADDRESS: c/o Saint John's Cemetery
                 80-01 Metropolitan Avenue
                 Flushing, New York 11379-2991
PHONE NUMBER: (718) 894-4888
RECORDS: Cemetery records for the Diocese of Brooklyn are kept in the offices of Saint John's Cemetery. Requests for information must be in writing.
RESOURCES: N/A

Saint Patrick's Cathedral Cemetery
See Cemetery of Saints Patrick and Peter.

Saint Patrick's Cathedral Crypt

CATEGORY: Roman Catholic
YEARS OF USE: 1879 to date
LOCATION: 640 Madison Avenue, between East 51st and East 50th Street, Manhattan.
HISTORY: The Archbishops, Cardinals, and Rectors of the Archdiocese of New York are buried in a crypt beneath the main altar of Saint Patrick's Cathedral. In a description of the crypt, the *New York Times* wrote, "the way down to it is down a stone staircase, which lies under stone slabs at the back of the altar… just in front of the opening is a small altar devoted to the private service of the Archbishop, who thus performs his devotions on top of what will be his own grave." The Archbishops' honorary hats, called galeros, hang from the ceiling above their tombs.

In 1990, Pierre Toussaint was removed here from Old Saint Patrick's Cathedral. He is a candidate for sainthood and the first layperson to be buried in the crypt.

The crypt is not open to the public.

MAILING ADDRESS: Saint Patrick's Cathedral
                  640 Madison Avenue
                  New York, New York 10022-1004
PHONE NUMBER: (212) 753-2261
RECORDS: N/A
RESOURCES: "Tombs Under the City." *The New York Times*, 2 August 1896, p. 20, col. 1. (description of crypt; burials)

Saint Patrick's Cemetery

See Eleventh Street Cemetery, East.
See Old Saint Patrick's Cathedral Churchyard and Vaults.

Saint Paul's Lutheran Churchyard

CATEGORY: Lutheran
YEARS OF USE: circa 1843 to 1851
LOCATION: 6th Avenue, corner West 15th Street, Manhattan.
HISTORY: Saint Paul's Churchyard probably closed with the 1851 ban in interments south of 86th Street in Manhattan. Unable to find a new, inexpensive burial ground, the pastor of Saint Paul's Church joined with the pastor of Saint Matthew's Church to form Lutheran Cemetery, Queens, in 1852.

The churchyard remains were most likely removed to Lutheran Cemetery.
MAILING ADDRESS: Saint Paul's German Lutheran Church
315 West 22nd Street
New York, New York 10011-2601
PHONE NUMBER: (212) 929-1955
RECORDS: N/A
RESOURCES: N/A

Saint Paul's Protestant Episcopal Churchyard and Vaults

CATEGORY: Protestant Episcopal
YEARS OF USE: 1766 to 1851
LOCATION: West side of Broadway, between Vesey Street and Fulton Street, Manhattan.
HISTORY: Shakespearean actor George Frederick Cooke is said to wander around Saint Paul's Churchyard looking for his head. After his death in 1812, Cooke's head was allegedly sold to pay his doctor's bill. His body was interred in the churchyard. Some believe that his skull is used in stagings of Hamlet.

Use of Saint Paul's Churchyard probably came to an end with the 1823 ban on burials south of Grand Street, Manhattan. Interments in private vaults were tolerated for some time, but were ultimately outlawed in 1851.

Saint Paul's Chapel copied all of the legible inscriptions on its gravestones in 1897. Gravestones still surround the church.
MAILING ADDRESS: Saint Paul's Chapel
c/o Trinity Church
74 Trinity Place, Floor 22
New York, New York 10006-2003
PHONE NUMBER: (212) 285-0836
RECORDS: N/A

Resources: Betts, Reverend Beverley R. "The Heraldry of Saint Paul's Chapel, New York." *The New York Genealogical and Biographical Record* 3, no. 1 (January 1872): 21.

Cemetery, Church, and Town Records of New York State. vol. 116. Washington, D.C.: Daughters of the American Revolution, 1938, 188–192. (memorial tablet inscriptions)

Corporation of Trinity Church. *Churchyards of Trinity Parish in the City of New York: 1697 to 1947*. New York. 1948. (limited gravestone inscriptions)

Cox, Hope. *Records of Trinity Church and Parish, New York City*. Manuscript #NY-50 at the New York Genealogical and Biographical Society. New York, New York. vol. 6. 1933 to 1935. (existing gravestones in 1897; vaults as of 1897)

King, Moses. "Saint Paul's Churchyard." *King's Handbook of New York City*. Boston, Mass., 1893. Reissued. New York: Benjamin Blom Inc., 1972, 509–510. (photos; Emmett monument)

O'Brien, Michael J. *In Old New York: The Irish Dead in Trinity and Saint Paul's Churchyards*. New York: Irish Historical Society, 1928. (burial records and epitaphs)

Saint Peter's Cemetery

CATEGORY: Roman Catholic
YEARS OF USE: 1848 to date
LOCATION: 893 Clove Road, between Tyler Avenue and Bard Avenue, West New Brighton, Staten Island. The cemetery is bisected by Clove Road.
HISTORY: N/A
MAILING ADDRESS: Saint Peter's Cemetery
52 Tyler Avenue
Staten Island, New York 10310-3172
PHONE NUMBER: (718) 442-2363
RECORDS: The cemetery's records are housed on-site.
RESOURCES: N/A

Saint Peter's Churchyard, Bronx

CATEGORY: Protestant Episcopal
YEARS OF USE: Pre-1650 to date
LOCATION: 2500 Westchester Avenue, between Seabury Avenue and Saint Peter's Avenue, Westchester, Bronx.
HISTORY: Saint Peter's Parish was organized in 1693. Nine years later, the congregation erected its church on the village green in what was then the Town of Westchester. While the oldest extant gravestone is dated 1716, the burial ground may have been established before 1650.

MAILING ADDRESS: Saint Peter's Episcopal Church
2500 Westchester Avenue
Bronx, New York 10461-4588
PHONE NUMBER: (718) 931-9270 and (718) 822-8284
RECORDS: The cemetery maintains burial records, but the older records are gone, and the first interment is unknown.
RESOURCES: *Cemetery, Church, and Town Records of New York State.* vol. 118. Washington, D.C.: Daughters of the American Revolution, 1938, 1–49. (gravestone inscriptions)

Saint Peter's Protestant Episcopal Churchyard and Vaults, Manhattan

CATEGORY: Protestant Episcopal
YEARS OF USE: circa 1832 to 1851
LOCATION: 21st Street, between 8th Avenue and 9th Avenue, Manhattan.
HISTORY: Interments probably ended with the 1851 ban on burials below 86th Street in Manhattan.
MAILING ADDRESS: Saint Peter's Episcopal Church
346 West 20th Street
New York, New York 10011-3398
PHONE NUMBER: (212) 929-2390
RECORDS: N/A
RESOURCES: N/A

Saint Peter's Roman Catholic Churchyard, Manhattan

CATEGORY: Roman Catholic
YEARS OF USE: 1785 to 1836
LOCATION: 22 Barclay Street, on the southeast corner of Church Street, Manhattan.
HISTORY: Saint Peter's Church is the oldest Roman Catholic parish in New York City. When its first church building was torn down in 1836, the remains in its churchyard were removed to Old Saint Patrick's Cathedral Churchyard and Vaults. In 1883, *The New York Times* reported that "a large quantity of human remains" were discovered beneath Saint Peter's Church when an adjoining property owner began excavations for a construction project (probably in the 1850s). Those remains were reinterred in Calvary Cemetery.
MAILING ADDRESS: Saint Peter's Rectory
16 Barclay Street
New York, New York 10007-2705
PHONE NUMBER: (212) 233-8355
RECORDS: N/A
RESOURCES: "Tombs Under the City." *The New York Times.* New York,

New York. 2 August 1896. Page 20, Column One (lists some burials and vault owners in Old Saint Patrick's Cathedral Churchyard and vaults).

Saint Philip's Cemetery

CATEGORY: African, Protestant Episcopal
YEARS OF USE: 1795 to 1851
LOCATION: 195 to 197 Chrystie Street, west side of the street between Stanton Street and Rivington Street, Manhattan.
HISTORY: When the African Burial Ground closed in 1794, an organization called The African Society asked the City of New York for a new burial ground. They were granted property on Chrystie Street. In 1827, it became the burial ground of Saint Philip's Church, Centre Street.

Interments probably came to an end with the 1851 ban on burials below 86th Street in Manhattan. The bodies were removed to Cypress Hills Cemetery in 1863.
MAILING ADDRESS: Saint Philip's Church
               208 West 134th Street
               New York, New York 10030-3002
PHONE NUMBER: (212) 862-4940
RECORDS: N/A
RESOURCES: *Cypress Hills Cemetery*. Brooklyn, N.Y.: Cypress Hills Cemetery, 1880. (extensive list of plot owners and location of plot, maps, rules, and history of cemetery)

Saint Raymond's Churchyard

CATEGORY: Roman Catholic
YEARS OF USE: circa 1845 to 1875
LOCATION: 1759 Castle Hill Avenue, corner of East Tremont Avenue, Schuylerville, Bronx.
HISTORY: Saint Raymond's Church was organized in 1842 and erected its church in 1845. Before the expansion of its cemetery in 1953, its churchyard was called Old Saint Raymond's Cemetery.
MAILING ADDRESS: Saint Raymond's Church
               1759 Castle Hill Avenue
               Bronx, New York 10462-4297
PHONE NUMBER: (718) 792-4044
RECORDS: N/A
RESOURCES: N/A

Saint Raymond's New Cemetery

CATEGORY: Roman Catholic
YEARS OF USE: 1953 to date

LOCATION: East 177th Street and Lafayette Avenue, Schuylerville, Bronx.
HISTORY: Singer Billie Holiday is among those buried here.
MAILING ADDRESS: Saint Raymond's New Cemetery
                              East 177th Street and Lafayette Avenue
                              Bronx, New York 10465-1134
Phone Numbers: (718) 792-1133
RECORDS: Cemetery records are housed on-site. Written requests for information are preferred.
RESOURCES: N/A

Saint Raymond's Old Cemetery

CATEGORY: Roman Catholic
YEARS OF USE: circa 1875 to 1963
LOCATION: Whittemore Avenue, corner East Tremont Avenue, Schuylerville, Bronx.
HISTORY: Prior to the cemetery's expansion in 1953, this section was known as New Saint Raymond's Cemetery, and the Churchyard was known as Old Saint Raymond's. After the expansion, this section was called Old Saint Raymond's Cemetery.

The main gate, at Whittemore Street, is where John F. "Jafsie" Condon paid Bruno Richard Hauptmann a ransom of fifty thousand dollars for the promised return of Charles A. Lindbergh's missing son in 1932.
MAILING ADDRESS: Saint Raymond's Old Cemetery
                              1201 Balcom Avenue
                              Bronx, New York 10465-1801
PHONE NUMBER: (718) 792-2080
RECORDS: Cemetery records are housed on-site. Written requests for information are preferred.
RESOURCES: N/A

Saint Stephen's Church
Cemetery and Vaults

CATEGORY: Protestant Episcopal
YEARS OF USE: circa 1805 to 1851
LOCATION: Church located at the southeast corner of Chrystie Street and Broome Street, Manhattan.
HISTORY: Saint Stephen's congregation first came together on 12 March 1805 and erected a church on the corner of Chrystie and Broome Streets soon after. The congregation held its last service in the church on 1 July 1866.

In an interview with *The New York Times*, Saint Stephen's announced that it would remove the remains in its burial grounds to Cypress Hills Cemetery, excepting those removed privately. Henry B. Price, son of the rector, handled the arrangements. Bodies were apparently taken from the church vaults and from the church cemetery, on First Street between First and Second Avenues, Manhattan. Approximately 2,500 bodies were reinterred.

The exact location of the cemetery is unclear; it does not appear on maps, nor does it appear in city directories.

MAILING ADDRESS: c/o Cypress Hills Cemetery
833 Jamaica Avenue
Brooklyn, New York 11208-1593
PHONE NUMBER: (718) 277-2900
RECORDS: Cypress Hills' records are housed on-site. Write for searches.
RESOURCES: *Cypress Hills Cemetery*. Brooklyn, N.Y.: Cypress Hills Cemetery, 1880. (extensive list of plot owners and location of plot, maps, rules, and history of cemetery)

Salem Fields Cemetery

CATEGORY: Jewish
YEARS OF USE: 1852 to date
LOCATION: 775 Jamaica Avenue, north side of the avenue between Cypress Hills Street and National Cemetery, East New York, Brooklyn.
HISTORY: This cemetery is owned by Temple Emanu-El in Manhattan.
MAILING ADDRESS: Salem Fields Cemetery
775 Jamaica Avenue
Brooklyn, New York 11208-1413
PHONE NUMBER: (718) 277-3898
RECORDS: The cemetery's records are housed on-site.
RESOURCES: Stern, Myer. *The Rise and Progress of Reform Judaism: Embracing a History Made From the Official Records of Temple Emanu-El of New York, with a Description of Salem Field Cemetery, its City of the Dead, with Illustrations of its Vaults, Monuments, and Landscape Effects; in Connection With the Celebration of the Fiftieth Anniversary of the Founding of the Congregation, April 1895.* M. Stern. New York. 1895.

Sands Street Churchyard

CATEGORY: Methodist Episcopal
YEARS OF USE: 1796 to 1837
LOCATION: South side of Sands Street, at the entrance to the Brooklyn Bridge, Brooklyn.
HISTORY: The Sands Street Methodist Episcopal Church was established in 1794. Its churchyard was used by all Methodists until 1806, when the church trustees adopted a measure to prohibit burial of anyone but active church members in the churchyard. They further prohibited the burial of

anyone who committed suicide.

The Sands Street Church was sold to developers in 1888. That spring, the *New York Times* reported "some 300 of the early members of the society were buried in the little churchyard between 1796 and 1837. Their tombs have gone to decay, and all that remain to tell the story of their lives are a few defaced and crumbling slabs of granite... The sexton, Mr. Allen, has been advertising for friends to come and claim the remains, but very few have responded, and those unclaimed will be placed in boxes and buried in a single excavation at the Cemetery of the Evergreens." The remains were reinterred in May 1888.

The *New York Times* also observed that most of the early gravestones were destroyed by fire in 1847. Some stones were replaced by relatives, but the replacement stones were not always positioned above the correct grave.

MAILING ADDRESS: Cemetery of the Evergreens
                 1629 Bushwick Avenue
                 Brooklyn, New York 11207-1849
PHONE NUMBER: (718) 455-5300
RECORDS: Cemetery of the Evergreens will verify interment over the phone, but you must make requests for copies of the burial record in writing. The cemetery's records may contain the decedent's name, age, date of death, place of death, and date of burial.
RESOURCES: E., F. J. "Old Burial Grounds. Cemeteries in Brooklyn and the County Towns." *The Brooklyn Eagle*, 29 August 1886 p. 9, col. 3. (gravestone inscription of Rev. John Summerfield)

"Moving Day for the Dead: Work in the Sands Street Churchyard, Brooklyn. A Surprising Discovery - A Possibility that an Eminent Preacher's Bones are not Where they are Supposed to Be." *The New York Times*, 19 May 1888, p. 8, col. 3. (description of cemetery; Summerfield graves)

"None to Claim Their Bodies: Relics of an Old Brooklyn Graveyard." *The New York Times*, 21 April 1888, p. 3, col.2. (lists some burials)

Warriner, Edwin. *The Old Sands Street Methodist Episcopal Church of Brooklyn, New York*. Clinton, Connecticut. 1885. (sketch of churchyard, some burials)

Sandy Ground Cemetery
See Rossville African Methodist Episcopal Zion Church Cemetery.

Saviour's Church Cemetery
See Saint Stephen's Church Cemetery and Vaults.

Schenck-Wyckoff Family Burial Ground

CATEGORY: Private
YEARS OF USE: circa 1724 to 1858

LOCATION: 1325 Flushing Avenue, near the Brooklyn-Queens border.

HISTORY: Peter Schenck established this burial ground in 1724. It was located behind his house and appeared on maps well into the 1900s. The house was demolished in 1970 for construction of a factory. The factory's storage yard is situated in the area where the graveyard used to be.

The remains may have been taken to Green-Wood Cemetery, and some of the gravestones may be in the possession of the Museum of the City of New York.

MAILING ADDRESS: N/A

PHONE NUMBER: N/A

RECORDS: N/A

RESOURCES: Armbruster, Eugene L. "Schenck Family Burial Ground on the Wyckoff Farm, copied 1860." *The Eastern District of Brooklyn*. New York. 1912. Page 156. (gravestone inscriptions 1729 to 1858)

Frost, Josephine C. trans. *Long Island Cemetery Inscriptions*. Brooklyn, New York. Vol. 1, March 1912. (gravestone inscriptions)

Hutter, Walter J. *Our Community, It's History and People: Ridgewood, Glendale, Maspeth, Middle Village, Liberty Park*. Ridgewood, N.Y.: Greater Ridgewood Historical Society, 1976, 204. (description of burial ground and gravestone inscription)

Inscriptions from the Schenck Burying Ground, Kings County. Brooklyn, N.Y.: Brooklyn Historical Society, manuscript. (BHS closed indefinitely)

Schermerhorn Family Burial Ground

CATEGORY: Private

YEARS OF USE: Gravestones date 1803 to 1822

LOCATION: On the grounds of Rockefeller University, at East 66th Street near the East River, Manhattan.

HISTORY: The Schermerhorn family reserved the right to be interred in the family burial ground when their summer estate was sold. The family never exercised this right.

The surviving gravestones name members of the Adams, Bass, Carr, Hardenbrook, and Thompson families.

MAILING ADDRESS: N/A

PHONE NUMBER: N/A

RECORDS: N/A

RESOURCES: "Ancient New York Tombstones." *The New York Genealogical and Biographical Record* 17, no. 1 (January 1886): 39. (gravestone inscriptions)

"Notes and Queries." *The New York Genealogical and Biographical Record* 25, no. 3 (July 1894): 143–144. (gravestone inscriptions)

Scotch Presbyterian Church Cemetery, West Eleventh Street

CATEGORY: Presbyterian
YEARS OF USE: circa 1823 to 1851
LOCATION: West 11th Street, Manhattan.
HISTORY: Scotch Presbyterian Church, on Grand Street, owned this cemetery when it was damaged by the opening of West 11th Street in 1830. The congregation is now known as the Second Presbyterian Church.
MAILING ADDRESS: N/A
PHONE NUMBER: N/A
RECORDS: The Second Presbyterian Church does not have records dating back to the nineteenth century. A spokesperson for the church stated that if anyone kept burial or death registers, Second Presbyterian Church does not know where they are located today.
RESOURCES: N/A

Scotch Presbyterian Church Cemetery, West Twenty-Eighth Street

CATEGORY: Presbyterian
YEARS OF USE: circa 1827 to 1851
LOCATION: South Side of West 28th Street, between 9th and 10th Avenues, Manhattan.
HISTORY: The Scotch Presbyterian Church may have sold its cemetery property on West 28th Street in 1855. Some, if not all, of the bodies were reinterred in Covenantor Cemetery in the Bronx. The congregation is now known as the Second Presbyterian Church.
MAILING ADDRESS: N/A
PHONE NUMBER: N/A
RECORDS: The Second Presbyterian Church does not have records dating back to the nineteenth century. A spokesperson for the church stated that if anyone kept burial or death registers, Second Presbyterian Church does not know where they are located today.
RESOURCES: N/A

Scotch Presbyterian Churchyard

CATEGORY: Presbyterian
YEARS OF USE: circa 1756 to 1823
LOCATION: South side of Cedar Street, between Broadway and Nassau Street, Manhattan.
HISTORY: Scotch Presbyterian Church was established in 1756 by a group that seceded from the First Presbyterian Church on Wall Street. It is said that

the chief cause of the split was a "difference of opinion regarding the use of musical instruments in the church." The congregation erected its first church on Cedar Street. Burials in the churchyard probably came to an end with the 1823 ban on interments south of Grand Street, Manhattan. The bodies were removed to an unspecified location when the congregation sold its property in 1833.

This church was also known as Associate Presbyterian Church, Seceders' Church, and Second Presbyterian Church of New York.

MAILING ADDRESS: N/A

PHONE NUMBER: N/A

RECORDS: The Second Presbyterian Church does not have records dating back to the eighteenth and nineteenth centuries. A spokesperson for the church stated that if anyone kept burial or death registers, Second Presbyterian Church does not know where they are located today.

RESOURCES: N/A

Seamen's Retreat Cemetery

CATEGORY: Institutional, Seamen

YEARS OF USE: circa 1831 to 1920

LOCATION: Warren Street, Staten Island.

HISTORY: The Seamen's Retreat was established in 1831 by the State of New York for the care of sick and disabled seamen. It later opened its doors to members of the Coast Guard and select government employees.

The Retreat was run by New York State until 1883, when it was taken over by the United States Public Health Service to replace the hospital it lost on Bedloe's (Liberty) Island due to construction of the Statue of Liberty. In 1981, it became Bayley-Seton Hospital.

Bayley-Seton Hospital is located at the northwest intersection of Bay Street and Vanderbilt Avenue. The Seamen's Retreat Cemetery appears to have been located a short distance to the west, on Warren Street. Friends of Abandoned Cemeteries of Staten Island reports that it is no longer there.

MAILING ADDRESS: Seaman's Retreat Cemetery
                  c/o Friends of Abandoned Cemeteries of Staten Island
                  140 Tysen Street
                  Staten Island, New York 10301-1120

PHONE NUMBER: N/A

RECORDS: Friends of Abandoned Cemeteries of Staten Island maintains a database of records from this cemetery, created from the Seamen's Retreat Burial Records (1840-1876) in the National Archives and death records in the New York City Municipal Archives. An interment list has been posted on the Richmond County RootsWeb project Web site. The address is:
<http://www.rootsweb.com/~nyrichmo>

RESOURCES: N/A

Seceders' Presbyterian Church Cemetery
See Scotch Presbyterian Church Cemetery.

Second Asbury African
Methodist Episcopal Church Cemetery
See Cherry Lane Second African Methodist Episcopal Cemetery.

Second Calvary Cemetery
See Calvary Cemetery.

Second Congregational Churchyard
See Bethel Baptist Churchyard and Burial Vaults.

Second Methodist Episcopal Churchyard
See Forsyth Street Methodist Episcopal Churchyard.

Second Reformed Presbyterian Church Cemetery

CATEGORY: Reformed Presbyterian
YEARS OF USE: Pre-1837 to 1851
LOCATION: South side of West 41st Street, between 9th and 10th Avenues, Manhattan.
HISTORY: The Second Reformed Presbyterian Church, located at the corner of Waverly Place and Grove Street, sold its property in February 1858.
MAILING ADDRESS: N/A
PHONE NUMBER: N/A
RECORDS: N/A
RESOURCES: N/A

Seguine Burial Ground
See Blazing Star Burial Ground.

Seventh Street Methodist Episcopal Churchyard

CATEGORY: Methodist Episcopal
YEARS OF USE: circa 1820 to 1851
LOCATION: 24 East 7th Street, north side of the street between 2nd Avenue and 3rd Avenue, Manhattan.
HISTORY: Although the 7th Street Church was established in 1786, the congregation did not erect its first house of worship until the 1820s.

   After an 1851 ban on burials below 86th Street in Manhattan, the trustees of the Seventh Street Church decided to move their dead to a plot in Cypress Hills Cemetery. The removals began in 1854 and lasted for two years. The *Brooklyn Daily Eagle* interviewed a watchman who stated that the bones and coffins were buried in trenches, while the best headstones were "put up to look good."

The congregation disbanded in 1911.

MAILING ADDRESS: c/o Cypress Hills Cemetery
                            833 Jamaica Avenue
                            Brooklyn, New York 11208-1593
PHONE NUMBER: (718) 277-2900
RECORDS: Cypress Hills Cemetery prefers written requests for searches.
RESOURCES: *Cypress Hills Cemetery*. Brooklyn, N.Y.: Cypress Hills
Cemetery, 1880. (extensive list of plot owners and location of plot, maps, rules, and history of cemetery)

"The Forgotten Dead: Many Neglected Graves in Cypress Hills Cemetery." *The Brooklyn Daily Eagle*, 13 August 1893, p. 8, col. 7. (description of the Methodist plot)

Seventy-First Street Cemetery

CATEGORY: Jewish
YEARS OF USE: 1828 to 1864
LOCATION: East side of Park Avenue, between 71st Street and 72nd Street, Manhattan.
HISTORY: The Seventy-First Street Cemetery was purchased by Congregation Shearith Israel in 1828. It was never used. The Congregation was already complaining about the expense of getting to the Twenty-First Street Cemetery. Of the Twenty-First Street Cemetery, one member wrote, "Owing to the distance of the [cemetery] from the populous parts of the city, recourse is frequently had to carriages to convey those who attend (as well as the mourners) at a heavy expense, which in many cases falls heavily upon the survivors of the deceased whose circumstances do not justify same."

The cemetery committee began to search for a new burial ground immediately after the Seventy-First Street site was purchased. The grounds were sold in January 1864.

MAILING ADDRESS: N/A
PHONE NUMBER: N/A
RECORDS: N/A
RESOURCES: de Sola Pool, Rev. Dr. David. *Portraits Etched in Stone: Early Jewish Settlers 1682 to 1831*. New York: Columbia University Press, 1952, 130–133. (history)

Shearith Israel Cemetery

See Beth-Olom Fields Cemetery, Chatham Square Cemetery, East Bank Cemetery, Milligan Street Cemetery, Seventy-First Street Cemetery or Twenty-First Street Cemetery.

Silver Lake Cemetery

CATEGORY: Jewish
YEARS OF USE: 1892 to 1909
LOCATION: 926 Victory Boulevard, south side of the Boulevard between Silver Mount Cemetery and Woodland Cemetery, Grymes Hill, Staten Island.
HISTORY: Founded in 1889 by the Hebrew Free Burial Association, Silver Lake Cemetery was used to "bury those Jews who could not afford the cost of funerals or plots." When this cemetery was filled, the Hebrew Free Burial Association founded Mount Richmond Cemetery, which is still in use today.

Sandra Wiesel, Administrator of the Hebrew Free Burial Association, writes that most of those buried here "were immigrants who lived in New York's Jewish ghettos... workers who toiled unglamorously in sweatshops... who never were able to master English and were left behind."
MAILING ADDRESS: Silver Lake Cemetery
                          926 Victory Boulevard
                          Staten Island, New York 10301-3703
PHONE NUMBER: N/A
RECORDS: N/A
RESOURCES: Crane, Fred. "The Hebrew Free Burial Association: Silver Lake and Mount Richmond Cemeteries." *The FACSI Newsletter*, vol. 14, issue 2/3 (Summer/Fall 1997). (vignette)

Silver Mount Cemetery

CATEGORY: Non-sectarian
YEARS OF USE: circa 1875 to date
LOCATION: 918 Victory Boulevard, south side of the boulevard adjacent to Silver Lake Cemetery and Arlo Road, Grymes Hill, Staten Island.
HISTORY: Silver Mount Cemetery is a not-for-profit burial ground. Although there have been complaints about the condition of the grounds, the cemetery manager told the *New York Times*, "If I know it's a really overgrown area... we'll open it up for you and we'll clear it out for you."

Silver Mount Cemetery is also known as Cooper's Cemetery.
MAILING ADDRESS: Silver Mount Cemetery Association
                          918 Victory Boulevard
                          Staten Island, New York 10301-3703
PHONE NUMBER: (718) 727-7020
RECORDS: The cemetery's records are housed on-site. Written requests for information are preferred. Records prior to 1900 are gone.
RESOURCES: N/A

Silvie's Cemetery
See Lake Cemetery.

Simonson Family Burial Ground

CATEGORY: Private
YEARS OF USE: Gravestones dated 1807 and 1874
LOCATION: East of Richmond Avenue, New Springville, Staten Island.
HISTORY: The exact location of this burial ground is not clear. It was
described as being "a few stones... back on a lane leading easterly from
Richmond Avenue in New Springville... to the Simonson Farm... and a long
way back from the little stone house in the front."

   Several people were buried here, but in 1889 there was only a marble
slab to the memory of Barnett and Abigail Simonson who both died in 1807,
and their daughter, Johannah H. Simonson, who died in 1874. Friends of
Abandoned Cemeteries of Staten Island reports that the cemetery is no longer
there.
MAILING ADDRESS: N/A
PHONE NUMBER: N/A
RECORDS: N/A
RESOURCES: Davis, William T. "Homestead Graves." *Proceedings of the
Natural Science Association of Staten Island.* New York. Special No. 9,
December 1889. (gravestone inscriptions)

Simonson Family Vault

CATEGORY: Private
YEARS OF USE: Prior to 1852
LOCATION: Castleton Corners, Staten Island.
HISTORY: On 17 January 1852, a story was told that "Mr. Simonson" and
two children were buried in a vault "just below the Four Corners." When his
widow sold the property, she reserved the family's right to be buried in the
vault, along with an acre of land, but "the La Forges... ploughed it up."
MAILING ADDRESS: N/A
PHONE NUMBER: N/A
RECORDS: N/A
RESOURCES: N/A

Sixteenth Street Baptist Church Vaults

CATEGORY: Baptist
YEARS OF USE: circa 1843 to 1851
LOCATION: 255-259 West 16th Street, between 7th Avenue and 8th Avenue,
Manhattan.
HISTORY: Burials were in vaults beneath the church. Use of this vault proba-
bly ended with the 1851 ban on interments south of 86th Street in
Manhattan.

MAILING ADDRESS: N/A
PHONE NUMBER: N/A
RECORDS: N/A
RESOURCES: N/A

Sleight-Winant Family Burial Ground
See Blazing Star Burial Ground.

Snug Harbor Cemetery
See Sailor's Snug Harbor Cemetery.

Society for Ethical Culture Cemetery
See Citizen's Union-Mount Pleasant Cemetery.

Society of Universalists Church Vault
See Reformed Presbyterian Church Vault.

South Dutch Churchyard

CATEGORY: Reformed Dutch
YEARS OF USE: 1701 to 1766
LOCATION: North side of Garden Street (now Exchange Place), between
Broad Street and William Street, Manhattan.
HISTORY: The South Reformed Dutch Church was erected in 1693. Eight years
later, the congregation petitioned the City of New York for permission to establish its churchyard. While the city's permission does not appear in any records,
it was apparently granted. The congregation claimed that their churchyard was
full and petitioned the city for a new burial ground on 31 January 1766.

The church building and graveyard were destroyed by fire in 1835. The
graves were dug up and the bodies were removed to Vaults 191 and 192 in
the New York Marble Cemetery, excepting those removed by family.
MAILING ADDRESS: c/o Gardner Sage Library
                 New Brunswick Theological Seminary
                 21 Seminary Place
                 New Brunswick, New Jersey 08901-1187
PHONE NUMBER: (908) 247-5243
RECORDS: The congregation disbanded in 1914 and its records were deposited with the Gardner Sage Library. Records prior to 1812 are part of the
Collegiate Church Register (or common register).
RESOURCES: "Burials in the Dutch Church of New York City, 1804 to
1813." *The New York Genealogical and Biographical Record*, vol. 75 (July
1944). Continued in subsequent issues.

Records of the Collegiate Churches, Burials 1727 to 1804. Manuscript
#NY-53 at the New York Genealogical and Biographical Society. New York,

New York. (dates of death and burial)

Records of the Collegiate Churches, Burials 1814 to 1820. Manuscript at
The New York Genealogical and Biographical Society. New York, New York.
File "New York City-Churches-Dutch."

Year Book of the Holland Society of New York. New York, New York.
1899. Pages 139 to 211. (alphabetized list of deaths 1727 to 1803)

Southside Cemetery

CATEGORY: Private
YEARS OF USE: circa 1687 to 1919
LOCATION: The north side of Redding Street, corner of Albert Road, Ozone
Park, Queens.
HISTORY: The Van Wicklen family donated land for the Southside Cemetery
when it settled in this section of the Town of Jamaica in 1687. Each house-
hold was given a plot at that time. Among them were the Durlands,
Fredericks, Ryders, and Stoothoffs.

The last burial in the graveyard was that of Mr. Harry L. Van Wicklen,
who died in 1919.

The Fairchild Cemetery Manual of 1910 states that the plots have been
"buried over and over again" and notes that descendants of "the old settlers
[have] taken no interest in the grounds." Street construction, vandalism, and
neglect contributed to its decline. By 1932, there were only seventy-nine
headstones left in a cemetery with over 1,900 interments. By 1935, there
were only ten gravestones.

This cemetery is also known as Aqueduct Cemetery, Homestead
Cemetery, Old Farmers' Cemetery, and Van Wicklen Cemetery. The Queens
Historical Society has taken an interest in preservation of this cemetery.
MAILING ADDRESS: Southside Cemetery
                 c/o Queens Historical Society
                 Kingsland Homestead
                 143-35 37th Avenue
                 Flushing, New York 11354-5729
PHONE NUMBER: (718) 939-0647
RECORDS: N/A
RESOURCES: Frost, Josephine C. trans. Long Island Cemetery Inscriptions.
Brooklyn, New York. vols. 1 and 8. March 1912. (gravestone inscriptions)

McCowan, Dorthea Elizabeth and June Ann McCowan. Southside Burial
Ground, Ozone Park, New York. For the Woodhaven Cultural and Historical
Society. New York. 1994. (gravestone inscriptions, genealogical data, map)

Powell, Charles U., comp., and Alice H. Meigs, ed. Description of Private
and Family Cemeteries in the Borough of Queens. City of New York,
Borough of Queens, Topographical Bureau. Jamaica, N.Y.: Queens Borough
Public Library, 1932. (gravestone inscriptions and map)

Springfield Cemetery

CATEGORY: Private
YEARS OF USE: circa 1670 to 1934
LOCATION: Springfield Boulevard, within Montefiore Cemetery between 198 Street and 199 Street, Springfield Gardens, Queens.
HISTORY: Springfield Cemetery, one of the oldest in Queens, contains the burial ground used by the area's earliest settlers. Each household was given its own plot. The original owners were the families of Amberman, Bayles, Bennet, Boerum, Covert, Fosdick, Golden, Hendrickson, Higbie, Lamberson, Losee, Mills, Nostrand, Remsen, Skidmore, Rider, Smith, and Van Ausdoll. Ownership has passed down from one generation to the next.
     This cemetery is also known as Old Springfield Cemetery.
MAILING ADDRESS: Springfield Cemetery Society
               121-83 Springfield Boulevard
               Jamaica, New York 11413-1158
PHONE NUMBER: (718) 528-1700
RECORDS: N/A
RESOURCES: Eardeley, William Applebie. *Springfield, Jamaica, Queens County, Long Island, New York Cemetery*. Brooklyn, N.Y., November 1912. (gravestone inscriptions)
     MacCormack, Elizabeth Janet. *Burials in Old Springfield Cemetery*. New York: New York Genealogical and Biographical Society, 1946, manuscript.

Spring's Churchyard, Doctor
See Brick Presbyterian Churchyard and Vaults.

Springville Cemetery
See Asbury Methodist Episcopal Churchyard and Cemetery.

Stapleton Union African Methodist Episcopal Churchyard

CATEGORY: African, Methodist Episcopal
YEARS OF USE: N/A
LOCATION: 49 Tompkins Avenue, Stapleton, Staten Island. Possibly between Bromwell and Quinn Streets.
HISTORY: "The oldest black-owned church on Staten Island, which has a cemetery on its grounds."
MAILING ADDRESS: Stapleton Union AME Church
               49 Tompkins Avenue
               Staten Island, New York 10304-2628
PHONE NUMBER: (718) 273-2857
RECORDS: N/A
RESOURCES: N/A

Staten Island Cemetery

CATEGORY: African, Non-sectarian

YEARS OF USE: Pre-1846 to 1934

LOCATION: 1636 Richmond Terrace, on the south side of the terrace between Taylor Street and Alaska Street, West New Brighton, Staten Island.

HISTORY: Joseph Ryerss, a former slave, purchased land for this cemetery in 1811. When Ryerss sold the cemetery in 1846, it became known as Staten Island Cemetery.

Together with Trinity Chapel Burial Ground, this cemetery is known as Factoryville Cemetery. It is under the care of Friends of Abandoned Cemeteries of Staten Island.

MAILING ADDRESS: Staten Island Cemetery
c/o Friends of Abandoned Cemeteries of Staten Island
140 Tysen Street
Staten Island, New York 10301-1120

PHONE NUMBER: N/A

RECORDS: Friends of Abandoned Cemeteries of Staten Island maintains a database of records from this cemetery. An interment list has been posted on the Richmond County RootsWeb project Web site. The address is: <http://www.rootsweb.com/~nyrichmo>.

RESOURCES: "Are These Your Ancestors?" *The FACSI Newsletter*, vol. 15, issue 1/2 (Spring/Summer 1998). (cemetery records of Britton, Malloy, Smith, and Wright Families)

"Are These Your Ancestors?" *The FACSI Newsletter*, vol. 14, issue 2/3 (Summer/Fall 1997). (cemetery records of Stephen D. Barnes and Gertrude DeHart)

"Are These Your Ancestors?" *The FACSI Newsletter*, vol. 14, issue 1 (Spring 1997). (facsimile cemetery records of Benjamin VanBuskirk and William VanName)

"Some Civil War Burials at Staten Island Cemetery." *The FACSI Newsletter*, vol. 15, issue 3 (Winter 1998-1999). (burials of Civil War vets)

"Descendants of the DeHart Family." *The FACSI Newsletter*, vol. 1, issue 6 (November/December 1984). (DeHart family plot)

"From the Record Books: Staten Island Cemetery Association, West New Brighton." *The FACSI Newsletter*, vol. 14, issue 2/3 (Summer/Fall 1997). (history of cemetery; names some lot owners)

"From the Record Books: Staten Island Cemetery Association, West New Brighton." *The FACSI Newsletter*, vol. 14, issue 4 (Winter 1997). (history of cemetery; names some lot owners)

"Original Lot Owners of Staten Island Cemetery." *The FACSI Newsletter*, vol. 15, issue 3 (Winter 1998-1999). (names owner and lot number)

Staten Island Cemetery Association. *Report, Rules, and By-Laws of the Staten Island Cemetery Association.* West New Brighton, Staten Island, New

York. 1893. (register of original lot owners)

Vosburgh, Royden W., editor and transcriber, *Staten Island Gravestone Inscriptions*, vol. 1, New York City, March 1924 (typed manuscript). An interment list has been posted on the Richmond County RootsWeb project Web site. The address is: <http://www.rootsweb.com/~nyrichmo>

Staten Island Reformed Dutch Churchyard
See Port Richmond Reformed Dutch Churchyard.

Stillwell's Church Cemetery
See Methodist Cemetery, Manhattan.

Stoothoff Family Burial Ground
See Southside Cemetery.

Sullivan Street Church Vaults

CATEGORY: Methodist Episcopal, Methodist Protestant
YEARS OF USE: 1837 and 1849
LOCATION: 214 Sullivan Street, between West 3rd Street and Bleeker Street, Manhattan.
HISTORY: The Sullivan Street Methodist Episcopal Church was organized in 1833 as a Methodist Protestant church. It became Methodist Episcopal in 1842.

When the congregation put its church up for sale in the 1860s, another Methodist Episcopal congregation offered to buy the property on condition that the burial vaults be emptied. The Sullivan Street congregation agreed and made plans to remove the bodies to the New York Bay-Bay View Cemetery.

On 19 January 1863, the *New York Times* made a shocking allegation. "For the sake of having the work done cheaply," it wrote, "the trustees, instead of removing each body by itself, and preserving as far as possible its identity, commenced the job by smashing up the coffins, and emptying their contents indiscriminately into large rough boxes capable of holding from ten to fifteen bodies each. The plates are rudely torn from the coffins and thrown to one side in a heap, and in numerous instances where the coffins were found to be perfectly sound, they have been chopped in pieces, with an axe and their contents thrown into the large box, to save the expense of removing each coffin by itself."

Mr. Miller, *The New York Times* informant, "states that he beheld one case where the body taken from the coffin was too long for the large box, and workmen twisted the head off to make it fit. In another case the feet were chopped off at the ankles, and in almost every instance, the large box would be filled so full that the lid would not shut tight without being pressed, which was done by several brawny workmen getting upon the box and jumping up and down. In this way some five hundred or six hundred bodies have been packed in these boxes during the last two weeks, but none of them have yet been removed..."

The Sullivan Street Church's trustees were called into the City Inspector's office to answer to Mr. Miller's charges. During that meeting, Miller also claimed that "the workmen tore out the linings of the coffins... these together with the plates were to be given to the workmen as perquisites."

After Mr. Miller's testimony, the City Inspector said that the rest of the removal would be done under the direction of his office.

MAILING ADDRESS: c/o Washington Square United Methodist Church
                 133 West Fourth Street
                 New York, New York 10012-1095
PHONE NUMBER: (212) 777-2528
RECORDS: *The New York Times* also announced that "Mr. Charles S. Hallock, undertaker, of 266 Eighth Avenue, was the sexton of the church during the whole time that burials were being made there, and has in his possession a record of the name, age, date of burial, &c. of each person deposited in the vaults. The record is of great value to those wishing to identify their friends, and may enable them to rescue their remains from the fate ordained them by the money-saving survivors, the trustees of the church." The location of this record is currently unknown.
RESOURCES: N/A

Suydam Family Burial Ground

CATEGORY: Private
YEARS OF USE: N/A
LOCATION: Corner of Woodbine Street and Evergreen Avenue, Bedford-Stuyvesant, Brooklyn.
HISTORY: Some of the bodies were transferred to Cypress Hills Cemetery.
MAILING ADDRESS: Cypress Hills Cemetery
                 833 Jamaica Avenue
                 Brooklyn, New York 11208-1593
PHONE NUMBER: (718) 277-2900
RECORDS: Records are housed on site. Write for searches.
RESOURCES: *Cypress Hills Cemetery*. Brooklyn, N.Y.: Cypress Hills Cemetery, 1880. (extensive list of plot owners and location of plot, maps, rules, and history of cemetery)

Swamp Church Graveyard
See Christ Lutheran Churchyard.

Swinburne Island Crematorium

CATEGORY: Public

YEARS OF USE: circa 1878 to 1928

LOCATION: In Lower New York Bay, three and one-half miles below the Narrows, half-way between Staten and Coney Islands.

HISTORY: Swinburne Island served as an immigration quarantine station for the Port of New York from 1870 to 1928. Immigrants who suffered from infectious disease were housed here before they were allowed to proceed to the receiving center at Castle Clinton (Castle Garden) or Ellis Island. Those who died on Swinburne Island were buried at Seguine's Point, Staten Island. In 1887, Staten Islanders who opposed the burial of the victims of disease on their island successfully lobbied for the construction of a crematorium on Swinburne Island. The bodies in the Seguine's Point Cemetery were removed and cremated. Swinburne Island Crematorium closed in 1928.

Following its closure, vandals immediately visited the empty island, using urns like the one for a five-year-old Austrian girl, Anne Kowrah, for target practice. Most of the buildings were destroyed in a 1934 fire.

MAILING ADDRESS: N/A

PHONE NUMBER: N/A

RECORDS: N/A

RESOURCES: N/A

Sylvan Cemetery

See Sylvan Grove Cemetery.

Sylvan Grove Cemetery

CATEGORY: Private

YEARS OF USE: Gravestones date 1781 to 1840

LOCATION: Victory Boulevard, north side of the boulevard between Melvin Avenue and Glen Street, Travis, Staten Island.

HISTORY: Sylvan Grove Cemetery may have originated as the private burial ground of the James Wood family. Several generations of the Decker family are also buried here.

Friends of Abandoned Cemeteries of Staten Island reports that the grounds are abandoned. The group has endorsed the proposal of a local businessman, John Pabone, who plans to develop property adjacent to the cemetery. Pabone has offered to "construct a fence around Sylvan Cemetery and provide all the necessary landscaping works to maintain the property and its facilities... and provide a three-foot sidewalk around the property." The plans also calls for adequate lighting to discourage vandalism.

MAILING ADDRESS: N/A

PHONE NUMBER: N/A

RECORDS: Researchers should check the Staten Island RootsWeb page, on the Internet, to see if this cemetery has been added to their cemetery database. The address is <http://www.rootsweb.com/~nyrichmo>.

RESOURCES: Vosburgh, Royden W., editor and transcriber, *Staten Island Gravestone Inscriptions*, vol. 1, New York City, March 1924 (typed manuscript). An interment list has been posted on the Richmond County RootsWeb project Web site. The address is:
<http://www.rootsweb.com/~nyrichmo>

Third Baptist Churchyard
See Amity Street Churchyard.

Third Calvary Cemetery
See Calvary Cemetery.

Thirteenth Street Cemetery
See East Bank Cemetery.

Thoburn's Garden Cemetery
See Little Green Street Burial Ground of the Society of Friends.

Tompkinsville Reformed Dutch Churchyard

CATEGORY: Reformed Dutch
YEARS OF USE: circa 1820 to 1864
LOCATION: Van Duzer Street, corner Victory Boulevard and Bay Street, Tompkinsville, Staten Island.
HISTORY: The Reformed Dutch Church at Tompkinsville was organized in 1823. The congregation erected its first church at the intersection of Victory Boulevard and Bay Street and remained there until 1864. When the congregation outgrew its original building, it moved to Brighton Heights. The gravestones were transferred to Silver Mount Cemetery.
MAILING ADDRESS: Brighton Heights Reformed Church
320 Saint Mark's Place
Staten Island, New York 10301-2409
PHONE NUMBER: (718) 448-0165
RECORDS: N/A
RESOURCES: N/A

Trinity Chapel Burial Ground

CATEGORY: Protestant Episcopal
YEARS OF USE: 1802 to 1914, 1963
LOCATION: Richmond Terrace, at the southwest corner of Tompkins Court,
West New Brighton, Staten Island.
HISTORY: Trinity Chapel was erected in 1802 as an extension of Saint
Andrew's Parish. It was set off as Church of the Ascension in May of 1869.
The church burned down in 1952. Its graveyard was abandoned, but Friends
of Abandoned Cemeteries of Staten Island has taken an interest in the
grounds.
      Trinity Chapel Cemetery is also known as "Church of the Ascension
Burying Ground" and "North Shore Protestant Episcopal Church Cemetery."
Trinity Chapel Burial Ground and Staten Island Cemetery, together, are
known as "Factoryville Cemetery."
MAILING ADDRESS: Trinity Chapel Cemetery
                  c/o Friends of Abandoned Cemeteries of Staten Island
                  140 Tysen Street
                  Staten Island, New York 10301-1120
PHONE NUMBER: N/A
RECORDS: Friends of Abandoned Cemeteries of Staten Island maintains a
database of records from this cemetery. An interment list has been posted on
the Richmond County RootsWeb project Web site. The address is:
<http://www.rootsweb.com/~nyrichmo>.
RESOURCES: Vosburgh, Royden W., editor and transcriber, *Staten Island
Gravestone Inscriptions*, vol. 1, New York City, March 1924 (typed manu-
script). An interment list has been posted on the Richmond County
RootsWeb project Web site. The address is:
<http://www.rootsweb.com/~nyrichmo>

Trinity Church Cemetery and Vaults

CATEGORY: Non-sectarian, Protestant Episcopal
YEARS OF USE: May 1, 1843 to date
LOCATION: West 153rd Street to West 155th Street, between Riverside Drive
and Amsterdam Avenue, Manhattan.
HISTORY: This peaceful and scenic cemetery is situated on the Upper West
Side of Manhattan on a sloping hill that extends from Amsterdam Avenue
toward the Hudson River.
      John Jacob Astor, John James Audubon, and Clement Clarke Moore are
among the 75,000 people buried here. Moore has been honored every
Christmas since 1911 with a reading of his poem "A Visit From Saint
Nicholas" and a candle-lit procession to adorn his grave with a Christmas
wreath.

In December 1993, Trinity Church Cemetery announced that it was running out of space and expected to sell its last available graves by the following spring. It is the last active cemetery in Manhattan.

MAILING ADDRESS: Trinity Cemetery
770 Riverside Drive
New York, New York 10032-7535

PHONE NUMBER: (212) 368-1600

RECORDS: N/A

RESOURCES: Corporation of Trinity Church. *Churchyards of Trinity Parish in the City of New York: 1697 to 1947*. New York. 1948. (some gravestone inscriptions)

Cox, Hope. *Records of Trinity Church and Parish, New York City*. Manuscript #NY-50 at the New York Genealogical and Biographical Society. New York, New York. vol. 6. 1933 to 1935. (burials 1843 to 1871)

Jacobs, Andrew. "Desperately Seeking Solitude: Ravens' Cawing Buries the Roar of Broadway." *The New York Times*, 21 June 1998, The City Weekly Desk. (description of cemetery)

King, Moses. "Trinity Church Cemetery." *King's Handbook of New York City*. Boston, Mass., 1893. Reissued. New York: Benjamin Blom Inc., 1972, 514–15. (notable burials and family plots; photos)

Trinity Churchyard, Manhattan

CATEGORY: Protestant Episcopal, Public

YEARS OF USE: circa 1681 to 1822

LOCATION: Broadway, opposite Wall Street, Manhattan.

HISTORY: The congregation of Trinity Church organized in 1664. Their church was erected on Broadway in 1697 and has been at that location ever since. It is said that Trinity Church was built upon a burial ground which held the remains of seventy-five Algonquin Indians who perished in a battle with the Dutch in 1643.

Trinity Church bordered New Amsterdam's public burial ground. In February of 1703, the congregation took control of that cemetery, on condition that the city be allowed to continue using the cemetery. This kind of arrangement was not new to Trinity. It purchased cemetery property from the Lutheran Church in 1697 on condition that the Lutherans be allowed to bury their dead in Trinity Churchyard.

Although its burial policy was essentially non-sectarian, the congregation did not welcome everyone into the graveyard. In October of 1697, Trinity ordered that "no Negroes be buried within the bounds and limits of the Churchyard of Trinity Church, that is to say, in the rear of the present burying place and that no person or Negro whatsoever, do presume… to break up any ground for the burying of his Negro, as they will answer to it at their peril." This policy was reinforced in 1790 when the church made a similar decree against the burial of Africans in the churchyard.

In May of 1784, Trinity decided to prohibit all burials in the graveyard, except for those families who already owned a burial vault. The church noted that due to the great number of interments during the Revolutionary War, it had become difficult to dig a new grave without unearthing another body. Many bodies were interred less than three feet under. On 18 August 1822, the New York City Common Council passed a law prohibiting burials in Trinity Churchyard. There was a raging yellow fever epidemic that year, and health officials believed that the shallow graves were contributing to the problem.

About 1840, one historian estimated that 160,000 people had been interred in the graveyard, a number equal to the population of New York that year. No doubt, there are tens of thousands buried in the yard. Among them is Alexander Hamilton, who died in 1804, a statesman and first Secretary of the Treasury.

MAILING ADDRESS: Trinity Churchyard
74 Trinity Place, Floor 22
New York, New York 10006-2003

PHONE NUMBER: (212) 285-0836

RECORDS: Fires in 1750 and 1776 destroyed parish records. There are no burial records between 1777 and 1800. Over one thousand gravestones are legible. Researchers should remember that the clergymen of other parishes sometimes officiated at funerals in the graveyard, without reporting the funeral to Trinity.

RESOURCES: *Cemetery, Church, and Town Records of New York State.* vol. 116. Washington, D.C.: Daughters of the American Revolution, 1938, 205–209. (some gravestone inscriptions)

Corporation of Trinity Church. *Churchyards of Trinity Parish in the City of New York: 1697 to 1947.* New York. 1948. (some gravestone inscriptions)

Cox, Hope. *Records of Trinity Church and Parish, New York City.* Manuscript #NY-50 at the New York Genealogical and Biographical Society. New York, New York. vol. 6. 1933 to 1935. (existing gravestones in 1897; vault records up to 1930s)

Cox, Hope. *Records of Trinity Church and Parish, New York City.* Manuscript #NY-50 at the New York Genealogical and Biographical Society. New York, New York. vol. 7. 1933 to 1935. (burials 1777 to 1783)

King, Moses. "Trinity Churchyard." *King's Handbook of New York City.* Boston, Mass., 1893. Reissued. New York: Benjamin Blom Inc., 1972, 506–509. (photos, notable burials, gravestone inscriptions)

Mines, John Flavel. *Walks in our Churchyards: Old New York Trinity Parish.* New York: G.G. Peck, 1896.

O'Brien, Michael J. *In Old New York: The Irish Dead in Trinity and Saint Paul's Churchyards.* New York: Irish Historical Society, 1928. (some burial records, epitaphs)

Trinity Churchyard, Queens

CATEGORY: Methodist Episcopal
YEARS OF USE: circa 1842 to 1886
LOCATION: South side of Main Street, at Astoria Boulevard, Astoria, Queens.
HISTORY: Trinity Church was organized in 1840 as the First Methodist Episcopal Church of Astoria and erected its first house of worship on Main Street. The congregation moved to Crescent Street and 30th Road in 1886. At that time, descendants of the dead were asked to remove their relatives from the old churchyard. Construction workers unearthed the unclaimed remains in 1961. Those bodies were taken to Hart Island Cemetery.
MAILING ADDRESS: N/A
PHONE NUMBER: N/A
RECORDS: N/A
RESOURCES: N/A

Trinity Lutheran Churchyard

CATEGORY: Lutheran
Years of use: circa 1676 to 1805
LOCATION: Southwest corner of Broadway and Rector Street, Manhattan.
HISTORY: Trinity Lutheran Church, the predecessor of Saint Matthew's Church, was organized in 1664. The congregation erected its first church on Rector Street in 1676. About one hundred thirty years later, Saint Matthew's sold the property to Trinity [Protestant Episcopal] Corporation. One unsubstantiated story alleged that corpses from the churchyard were "hauled off in open box carts" and dumped into the Hudson River circa 1805.
MAILING ADDRESS: Saint Matthew's Lutheran Church
200 Sherman Avenue
New York, New York 10034-3301
PHONE NUMBER: (212) 567-2172
RECORDS: The earliest surviving Lutheran records begin with 1704.
RESOURCES: *First Record Book of Trinity Lutheran Church*. Manuscript on Microfilm #32.1 at the New York Genealogical and Biographical Society. New York, New York. Reel Number 6. (burials 1704 to 1775)

Stryker-Rodda, Kenn, transcriber. "Lutheran Church Burials, 1763 to 1775." *The New York Genealogical and Biographical Record*, vol. 105, no. 3 (July 1973).

"Trinity Church Burials." *Church Records*. vol. 87. New York: Holland Society of New York. (burials to 1772)

Troytown Cemetery

CATEGORY: African, Private

YEARS OF USE: circa 1853 to 1903

LOCATION: Southwest corner of 149th Street and Gravett Road, near Queens College, Flushing, Queens.

HISTORY: Troy Rantus established this cemetery about 1853. Fifty years later, the burial ground was used exclusively by the Rantus family and no plots or graves were for sale. The last known interment was that of James Rantus, who died in 1903.

The heirs of Troy Rantus sold the cemetery in 1915. When a developer decided to deed the ground to the City of New York in 1952, the bodies were removed to Cemetery of the Evergreens. There were only two gravestones.

MAILING ADDRESS: c/o Cemetery of the Evergreens
                  1629 Bushwick Avenue
                  Brooklyn, New York 11207-1849

PHONE NUMBER: (718) 455-5300

RECORDS: Cemetery of the Evergreens will verify interment over the phone, but you must make requests for copies of the burial record in writing. The records contain the decedent's name, age, date of death, place of death, and date of burial. Note: the records may only contain the names of those persons identified at the time of removal.

RESOURCES: Powell, Charles U., comp., and Alice H. Meigs, ed. *Description of Private and Family Cemeteries in the Borough of Queens.* City of New York, Borough of Queens, Topographical Bureau. Jamaica. N.Y.: Queens Borough Public Library, 1932. (gravestone inscriptions and maps)

Twenty-First Street Cemetery

CATEGORY: Jewish

YEARS OF USE: 5 November 1829 to 25 April 1851

LOCATION: 98-110 West 21st Street, between 6th Avenue and 7th Avenue, Manhattan.

HISTORY: Congregation Shearith Israel's third cemetery opened on 5 November 1829. It remained in use for the next twenty-two years, until an 1851 ban on interments south of 86th Street in Manhattan forced the cemetery to close.

In 1856, the Chatham Square Cemetery lost a portion of its property due to an extension of the Bowery. Two hundred and fifty-three bodies were subsequently reinterred in the Twenty-First Street Cemetery.

MAILING ADDRESS: c/o Congregation Shearith Israel
                  8 West 70th Street
                  New York, New York 10023-4601

PHONE NUMBER: (212) 873-0300
RECORDS: Records are maintained by the Congregation.
RESOURCES: de Sola Pool, Rev. Dr. David. *Portraits Etched in Stone: Early Jewish Settlers 1682 to 1831*. New York: Columbia University Press, 1952, 133–141, 440. (list of burials, map)

Tysen-Decker Family Burial Ground

CATEGORY: Private
YEARS OF USE: Gravestones date 1805 to 1839
LOCATION: "Between Richmond and New Springville in the woods near the cleared land about 1.5 miles from the Kill." Staten Island.
HISTORY: There were three gravestones standing when historian William T. Davis visited the cemetery in 1889: those of James Decker, John Tysen, and Tysen's wife, Cornelia.
MAILING ADDRESS: N/A
PHONE NUMBER: N/A
RECORDS: N/A
RESOURCES: Davis, William T. "Homestead Graves." *Proceedings of the Natural Science Association of Staten Island*. New York. Special No. 9, December 1889. (gravestone inscriptions)

Underhill Family Burial Ground

CATEGORY: Private
YEARS OF USE: circa 1775 to 1806
LOCATION: Vicinity Adee Avenue and Colden Avenue, Williamsbridge, Bronx.
HISTORY: New York City purchased this burial ground about 1900 to make way for a street extension. The remains were removed to Saint Paul's Church "in Eastchester," now Mount Vernon, New York. Saint Paul's Church disbanded in 1940. Its church and cemetery are operated by the National Parks Service as a National Historic Site.
MAILING ADDRESS: Saint Paul's Church National Historic Site
c/o 26 Wall Street
New York, New York 10005-1996
PHONE NUMBER: (212) 260-1616
RECORDS: Burial records are housed in the New York City office.
RESOURCES: Frost, Josephine C. trans. *Underhill Genealogy: Descendants of Captain John Underhill*. vol. 2. New York: Myron C. Taylor for The Underhill Society of America, 1932, 119–20, and under individual names. (gravestone inscriptions, photos)

Union Baptist Church Cemetery
See Hillside Cemetery.

Union Cemetery

CATEGORY: Methodist Protestant
YEARS OF USE: 1851 to 1893
LOCATION: The cemetery was bounded by Putnam Avenue, Palmetto Street,

Knickerbocker Avenue, and Irving Avenue, Bedford-Stuyvesant, Brooklyn.
HISTORY: Union Cemetery was established in 1851 by the Associated
Methodist Protestant Church of New York and the Methodist Protestant
Church of Williamsburg.

Approximately 30,000 people were buried in this cemetery between 1851
and its closure in 1893. The bodies were removed to a ten-acre plot in
Cedar Grove Cemetery. Removals began on Monday, 12 December 1897
and lasted for about two months. The *New York Tribune* noted that one cas-
ket had been reserved for each body, even if there was little left to move, and
that the gravestones would be set up on the new graves.

According to the *Newtown Register*, Union Cemetery's records were
given to Cedar Grove Cemetery.

The property was sold for residential development. A playground covers
a large portion of the former cemetery today.
MAILING ADDRESS: Cedar Grove Cemetery
13416 Horace Harding Expressway
Flushing, New York 11367-1099
PHONE NUMBER: (718) 939-2041
RECORDS: Inquire by mail. It is asked that you include the deceased's name
and date of death.
RESOURCES: N/A

Union Field Cemetery

CATEGORY: Jewish
YEARS OF USE: 1868 to date
LOCATION: 8211 Cypress Avenue, at 80th Road, Ridgewood, Queens.
HISTORY: Businessmen Henry Rothschild and Levi Strauss are among those
buried at Union Field.
MAILING ADDRESS: Union Field Cemetery
82-11 Cypress Avenue
Flushing, New York 11385-6716
PHONE NUMBER: (718) 366-3748
RECORDS: The cemetery records are housed on-site.
RESOURCES: N/A

Union Presbyterian Church Vault
See Reformed Presbyterian Church Vault.

United Brethren Cemetery
See Moravian Cemetery.

United German Lutheran Churchyard
See Christ Lutheran Churchyard.

United Hebrew Cemetery

CATEGORY: Jewish
YEARS OF USE: 1908 to date
LOCATION: 122 Arthur Kill Road, south side of the road near Clarke Avenue,
Richmond, between Mount Richmond Cemetery and Oceanview Cemetery,
Staten Island.
HISTORY: N/A
MAILING ADDRESS: United Hebrew Cemetery
                              Post Office Box 6
                              Staten Island, New York   10306-0001
PHONE NUMBER: (718) 351-0230
RECORDS: The cemetery's records are housed on-site.
RESOURCES: N/A

United States Cremation Company, Ltd.
See Fresh Pond Crematory.

United States Merchant Marine Hospital Cemetery

CATEGORY: Institutional, Seamen
YEARS OF USE: 1901 to 1935, 1937
LOCATION Within the northern section of Oceanview Cemetery, Richmond,
Staten Island.
HISTORY: This cemetery is the final resting place of seamen who died in the
United States Marine Hospital, now Bayley-Seton Hospital.
     The graves of eight hundred twenty one men were marked with tradition-
al gravestones, the most recent dated 8 May 1929. The remaining men were
memorialized with metal markers. Each marker held a typewritten card,
with the name of the deceased, under a glass slide. These markers were
obliterated by the elements.
     Those who died in 1921 and 1922 are buried in a mass grave.
     Patients who died in 1936 are buried in Hillside Cemetery, and those
who died between 1938 and 1941 are buried in Silver Mount Cemetery.
Thereafter, the dead were buried at Rose Hill Cemetery in Linden, New
Jersey.
     The United States Merchant Marine Cemetery was in a severe state of
neglect by 1946. Friends of Abandoned Cemeteries of Staten Island reports
that the cemetery is abandoned.
MAILING ADDRESS: N/A
PHONE NUMBER: N/A
RECORDS: N/A
RESOURCES: The *Staten Island Advance* wrote on 13 January 1964 that the
gravestone inscriptions had been copied, but the location of that list is unclear.

United States Naval Hospital Cemetery

CATEGORY: Institutional, Military

YEARS OF USE: 1834 to 1910

LOCATION: Kent Avenue at Hewes Street, United States Naval Station, Williamsburg, Brooklyn.

HISTORY: The United States Naval Hospital was established in 1828, as part of a larger Naval complex, the Brooklyn Navy Yard. The Hospital maintained its own graveyard for sailors who died at the hospital or aboard ship. Officers and sailors from foreign navies were also interred here. Among them were Japanese, Spanish, and Russian nationals.

In 1897, the *New York Times* noted that the cemetery was "little larger than an ordinary city block, and is enclosed on the hospital side with a high brick wall, and on the other three sides with a tall iron fence, which is badly in need of a coat of paint." Some of the dead were memorialized with gravestones, but most of the graves were marked by simple cast-iron headpieces that disintegrated with time.

The cemetery closed in 1910, and the bodies were removed to Cypress Hills National Cemetery about 1926. The site was subsequently home to tennis courts, a baseball field, and underground fuel tanks.

When the Brooklyn Navy Yard was decommissioned in 1993, Navy personnel reviewed burial records to make sure that all of the bodies had been reinterred in 1926. They found that of the 1,381 recorded burials, only 926 had been removed.

In 1997, the *New York Post* reported that Navy workers uncarthed "human remains, bits of bone, and what may have been pieces of a complete burial" during an exploratory dig in the former burial ground. Hearings were scheduled to decide what should be done with the site.

According to the Navy, ten percent of those buried in the cemetery were of African-American heritage. Mrs. Williamina Wallace, who worked in the Naval Hospital during the Civil War, is the only known female burial.

MAILING ADDRESS: Cypress Hills National Cemetery
                         c/o Long Island National Cemetery
                         2040 Wellwood Avenue
                         Farmingdale, New York 11735-1211

PHONE NUMBER: (516) 454-4949

RECORDS: Information is available through the Long Island National Cemetery. Availability of in-depth searches will be determined on a case-by-case basis. The *New York Times* claimed that "the office records tell little or nothing of the history of these men."

RESOURCES: "Jack Tar's Burial Ground." *The New York Times*, 19 December 1897, p. 23, col. 1.   (description of cemetery, some burials)

University Place Cemetery

CATEGORY: Presbyterian

YEARS OF USE: circa 1816 to 1851

LOCATION: University Place, in the middle of the block bounded by 12th Street, 13th Street, and 5th Avenue, Manhattan.

HISTORY: Land records indicate that this cemetery was jointly owned and used by the Associate Presbyterian Church, the Associate Reformed Presbyterian Church, and the Reformed Covenanted Church. Interments probably came to an end with the 1851 ban on burials below 86th Street in Manhattan. The property was sold two years later.

MAILING ADDRESS: N/A

PHONE NUMBER: N/A

RECORDS: N/A

RESOURCES: N/A

Valentine-Varian Family Cemetery

CATEGORY: Private
YEARS OF USE: Gravestones from the 1700s
LOCATION: 277 Van Cortlandt Avenue East, corner Bainbridge Avenue, Bronx.
HISTORY: In 1775, Isaac Valentine built his house on land purchased from the Reformed Dutch Church. Sixteen years later, Isaac Varian bought the house and its adjoining property. The estate remained in the Varian family until 1964, when the family finally sold it. Fortunately, a provision in the will of one owner stipulated that the house had to be preserved. In 1965, it was moved across the street.
MAILING ADDRESS: Museum of Bronx County History
3266 Bainbridge Avenue
Bronx, New York 10467-3004
PHONE NUMBER: (212) 881-8900
RECORDS: N/A
RESOURCES: N/A

Valhalla Burial Park
See Oceanview Cemetery.

Van Alst Family Burial Ground

CATEGORY: Private
YEARS OF USE: Pre-1887
LOCATION: One block south of Queens Plaza, between Jackson Avenue and the Long Island Rail Road tracks, Long Island City, Queens.
HISTORY: Members of the Hunter, Parsell and Van Alst families were memo-

rialized on six gravestones in the Van Alst Family Burial Ground. The remaining graves were marked by crude fieldstones inscribed with initials.

A Van Alst descendant reported that the bodies were removed to Cypress Hills Cemetery. The grounds were sold, and the Romaine Canning Factory stood on the site until 1925, when the property was redeveloped.

MAILING ADDRESS: c/o Cypress Hills Cemetery
                 833 Jamaica Avenue
                 Brooklyn, New York 11208-1593
PHONE NUMBER: (718) 277-2900
RECORDS: Cypress Hills Cemetery prefers written requests for searches.
RESOURCES: *Cypress Hills Cemetery*. Brooklyn, N.Y.: Cypress Hills
    Cemetery, 1880. (extensive list of plot owners and location of plot, maps, rules, and history of cemetery)

Van Cortlandt Family Burial Ground and Vault

CATEGORY: Private
YEARS OF USE: circa 1748 to 1884
LOCATION: The burial vault is in the Parade Field, off Broadway, a half mile north of the Van Cortlandt Mansion in Van Cortlandt Park, Bronx. The burial ground is near the mansion. The mansion stands in the south part of the park, near Broadway and 242nd Street.
HISTORY: The Van Cortlandt Family Vault, located about a half mile north of the family mansion, is probably best known for its role during the Revolutionary War. In 1781, General George Washington ordered his soldiers to burn campfires on "Vault Hill" to deceive the British while he withdrew his troops for the decisive Yorktown thrust. Augustus Van Cortlandt, Tory Clerk of the Common Council of New York, hid a strongbox filled with municipal records inside the vault. Augustus is currently in the vault: the strongbox is in the mansion.

The property was owned by the Van Cortlandt family from 1691 until its sale to New York City in 1889. Caretakers believe that burials in the vault began after the mansion was constructed in 1748, and ended in 1884. The family now uses ground in Woodlawn Cemetery.

Vandalism has taken its toll on the vault and burial ground—several gravestones have been removed to the mansion for safekeeping, and the vault itself has been sealed. The precise location of the vault is now undisclosed, for security purposes.

MAILING ADDRESS: c/o Van Cortlandt Mansion
                 Broadway at West 246th Street
                 Bronx, New York 10471
PHONE NUMBER: (718) 543-3344
RECORDS: The Van Cortlandt family has not released its private family records to the public or to the staff at the mansion.
RESOURCES: N/A

Van Der Vanter Burial Vault

CATEGORY: Private
YEARS OF USE: circa 1785
LOCATION: On the grounds of Fort Wadsworth Naval Station near the
Verrazano Narrows Bridge, Staten Island.
HISTORY: This vault is mentioned in the will of Cornelius Van Der Vanter,
1785, who asked that the vault on his land always to be preserved for the use
of his descendants.

Christian Jacobson was Van Der Vanter's brother-in-law. He was interred
in the vault along with the rest of his family. A descendant, Peter Jacobson,
removed the bodies to Moravian Cemetery.
MAILING ADDRESS: c/o Moravian Cemetery
                           2205 Richmond Road
                           Staten Island, New York 10306-2557
PHONE NUMBER: (718) 351-0136
RECORDS: Moravian Cemetery's records are housed on-site. They are also
available on microfilm at the Staten Island Institute of Arts and Sciences.
RESOURCES: N/A

Van Street Burial Plot
See Fountain Cemetery.

Van Wicklen Cemetery
See Southside Cemetery.

Vaughn Cemetery
See Saint Luke's Cemetery.

Vault Hill
See Van Cortlandt Family Burial Ground and Vault.

Visitation Sisters Monastery Burial Ground

CATEGORY: Roman Catholic
YEARS OF USE: N/A
LOCATION: 5655 Arlington Avenue, Bronx.
HISTORY: The bodies in this cemetery were removed to an undisclosed loca-
tion when the Monastery became the Saint John Neuman Residence of the
Catholic Archdiocese of New York.
MAILING ADDRESS: N/A
PHONE NUMBER: N/A
RECORDS: N/A
RESOURCES: N/A

Wallabout Bay

CATEGORY: Military
YEARS OF USE: 1776 to 1783
LOCATION: Brooklyn Navy Yard, east side of Wallabout Bay, Brooklyn.
HISTORY: During the American Revolution, tens of thousands of Continental Soldiers were imprisoned aboard British ships moored in Wallabout Bay. Conditions were so bad that an estimated eleven thousand soldiers died from starvation, disease, fire, flogging, and other forms of violence. The dead were buried by their compatriots in shallow, sandy graves along the shore of the bay.

Captain Thomas Dring, a prisoner aboard the ship *Jersey*, remembered that the burial ground was near the house of a miller: "We had been told that a tide-mill, which he attended, was in its immediate vicinity, as a landing place for which the wharf where we stood had been erected." This was also known as Remsen's Mill.

Walt Whitman, writing for *The Brooklyn Standard* in 1862, noted that "all the terra firma of the present Navy Yard, and much of the land adjoining it also, has since been reclaimed from the dominion of old Neptune—that is, it has been filled in. Of course, the whole face of the scene has been completely changed from what it was in the times of the Revolutionary War when the ships lay here. At that period, the spot that is now just west of the wall along Flushing Avenue was a low-stretching sand hill, and it was in and adjacent to this spot that the thousands of the American martyrs were mostly buried."

In 1791, John Jackson acquired the Remsen property. As the tide eroded the beach, and bones were exposed, Jackson collected the remains. In 1808, they were placed in thirteen coffins, representing the thirteen colonies, and laid to rest in a vault on Jackson's farm outside the Navy Yard wall, at the corner of Hudson Avenue and York Street.

Benjamin Romaine, a former prisoner of the British, purchased Jackson's farm in 1839 and erected an antechamber over the vault, caring for it at his own expense. He was buried there in 1844, having adopted the spot as his own family burial ground.

The Martyrs' Monument Association formed in 1855. They selected a site in Fort Greene Park where, in 1873, a brick vault was constructed for the soldiers' remains. A monument was erected over the vault. Designed by Stanford White, and dedicated in 1908, the 148-foot granite shaft supports a large bronze urn that was intended to house an eternal flame. A stone staircase, one hundred feet wide, leads from the street to the column.

In 1993, construction of a garbage incinerator at the Brooklyn Navy Yard was halted until the historical significance of the site was considered.

MAILING ADDRESS: N/A

PHONE NUMBER: N/A

RECORDS: There is no known record of prisoners, excepting an undated list of about eight thousand soldiers who were imprisoned aboard the British ship *Jersey*. The list was found among the papers of the British War Department.

RESOURCES: Greene, Albert G. *Recollections of the Jersey Prison-Ship; Taken and Prepared for Publication from the Original Manuscript of the Late Captain Thomas Dring of Providence, Rhode Island, One of the Prisoners*. ch. 9. Providence, R.I.: H. H. Brown, 1829, 57–63. (interment of the dead)

"Revolution/Prisoners of War Burials, Brooklyn." *Iowa City Genealogical Society Newsletter*, vol. 20, issue 2 (February 1993).

Wallabout Cemetery

CATEGORY: Public

YEARS OF USE: 1825 to 1857

LOCATION: North Portland Avenue, between Auburn Place and Park Avenue, Williamsburg, Brooklyn.

HISTORY: Situated on land purchased from the Leffert family in 1824, Wallabout Cemetery was used as a public burial ground by the Town of Brooklyn and its churches. The denominations assigned plots in the graveyard were Baptist, Dutch Reformed, Methodist Episcopal, Presbyterian, Roman Catholic, Society of Friends, and Society of Universalists.

The Baptists and Universalists exchanged plots in 1836, after it was revealed that the Baptists made an error when locating their plot in the first place. Soon after, the Society of Universalists disbanded. Their plot reverted back to Brooklyn in 1844.

In 1857, the New York State Legislature gave Brooklyn permission to remove the bodies and gravestones in the cemetery. The state mandated that the City of Brooklyn remove the bodies to a cemetery whose grounds were "in or adjacent to the city of Brooklyn, to which they shall... carefully remove all the remains, relics, monuments and headstones there left in or upon that part of the present burial plat marked 'common' on the map herein mentioned, and shall replace them in the land so purchased, as nearly in the same manner as may be, as they at present are in the burial plot so sold." Each denomination was given the option to remove the bodies in their plots to the burial ground of their choice. The Roman Catholic section was removed to Holy Cross Cemetery, while the Dutch Reformed section was removed to Green-Wood Cemetery. The Methodist section may have been removed to a plot in Cypress Hills Cemetery, jointly held by the Methodist churches of New York City and Williamsburg.

Brooklyn removed all the remains in plots abandoned by an ecclesiastical group to plots in an unspecified cemetery, purchased in the name of each denomination.

MAILING ADDRESS: N/A

PHONE NUMBER: N/A

RECORDS: N/A

RESOURCES: "An Act to Sell the Burial Ground at the Wallabout in the City of Brooklyn, and to Provide Places of Burial in Relation to Sales of Places so Provided." *New York State Session Laws of 1857.* chapter 20, p. 31. (procedure for removal of burial ground)

Cypress Hills Cemetery. Brooklyn, N.Y.: Cypress Hills Cemetery, 1880. (extensive list of plot owners and location of plot, maps, rules, and history of cemetery)

E., F. J. "Old Burial Grounds. Cemeteries in Brooklyn and the County Towns." *The Brooklyn Eagle*, 29 August 1886, p. 9, col. 3. (three gravestone inscriptions from monument in Green-Wood Cemetery)

Ward's Island Cemetery

CATEGORY: Public

YEARS OF USE: June 1852 to circa 1880

LOCATION: Ward's Island, East River, Manhattan.

HISTORY: New York City purchased approximately seventy-five acres on Ward's Island for use as a public cemetery. One hundred thousand bodies from the Fiftieth Street Cemetery in Manhattan were reinterred here in 1858. Ward's Island Cemetery apparently declined with the opening of Hart Island Cemetery in 1869, but *The New York Times* reported that Ward's Island Cemetery was still in use as late as 1880. There were 243 burials that year.

Ward's Island was once separated from Randall's Island by Little Hell Gate, but the two are now joined by landfill.

MAILING ADDRESS: N/A

PHONE NUMBER: N/A
RECORDS: N/A
RESOURCES: N/A

Washington Cemetery

CATEGORY: Jewish
YEARS OF USE: circa 1850 to date
LOCATION: 5400 Bay Parkway, Midwood, Brooklyn. Generally bounded by
18th Avenue, 54th Street, Bay Parkway, and 58th Street.
HISTORY: A cemetery manual from the early 1900s noted that although the
cemetery is Jewish, there are many Christians buried within its grounds.
Most, if not all, of the plots in Washington Cemetery are held by societies,
lodges, and congregations.

    This cemetery is also known as Meretz Cemetery.
MAILING ADDRESS: Washington Cemetery
               5400 Bay Parkway
               Brooklyn, New York 11230-3346
PHONE NUMBER: (718) 377-8690
RECORDS: One visitor to the cemetery observed a ledger that list births in
chronological order, giving the decedent's name, address, cause of death, and
other information.
RESOURCES: N/A

Washington Square Cemetery

CATEGORY: Public
YEARS OF USE: 1797 to April 30, 1825
LOCATION: Present-day Washington Square, outlined by Washington Square
North, South, East and West, Manhattan.
HISTORY: When the New York City Council opened its public cemetery in a
fashionable neighborhood, residents objected loudly. Homeowner Alexander
Hamilton and fifty-six of his neighbors formed a committee that inundated
the City Council with complaints and counterproposals. In one letter, the
group lamented that they would have to "abandon their seats or submit to
the disagreeable sensations arising from an unavoidable view of and close situation to a burial place of this description destined for the victims of conta-
gion." They offered to buy another site for the city's use, but their plan was
rejected.

    Concerns about public health and the placement of cemeteries in densely
populated areas of Manhattan forced the Council to abandon the burial
ground in 1825. Within fifteen years, all traces of the cemetery were gone.
The grounds became a popular public park surrounded by the stately marble
and brick homes of the Brevoorts, Delanos and Roosevelts.

An estimated ten thousand people were buried in the Washington Square
Cemetery. The bodies were not removed.
MAILING ADDRESS: N/A
PHONE NUMBER: N/A
RECORDS: N/A
RESOURCES: N/A

Waters Cemetery

CATEGORY: Native American, Private
YEARS OF USE: Gravestones date 1859 to 1904
LOCATION: West side of Northern Boulevard, opposite Browvale Lane, Little
Neck, Queens.
HISTORY: James E. Waters, also known as Chief Wild Pigeon, wrote that
Silvia Hicks purchased nine acres for use as a cemetery after their tribe was
forced to abandon its burial ground in Douglass Manor. He did not give his
relationship to Silvia Hicks or report when the purchase was made.

Of the thirteen gravestones standing in 1932, only six were inscribed.
Five were dedicated to members of the Waters family, while the sixth was to
a member of the Smith family.

The bodies were moved to the Douglaston Zion Episcopal Churchyard
between 1930 and 1938.
MAILING ADDRESS: c/o Douglaston Zion Episcopal Church
                 243-01 Northern Boulevard
                 Flushing, New York 11362-1161
PHONE NUMBER: (718) 225-0466
RECORDS: N/A
RESOURCES: "Judge Overrides Objections to Moving Indian Bodies: Grants
Application for Reburial in Zion Cemetery." *Long Island Press*, 30 August
1938. (names descendants of those buried in cemetery)

Powell, Charles U., comp., and Alice H. Meigs, ed. *Description of Private
and Family Cemeteries in the Borough of Queens*. City of New York,
Borough of Queens, Topographical Bureau. Jamaica, N.Y.: Queens Borough
Public Library, 1932. (gravestone inscriptions and map)

Way Family Burial Ground

CATEGORY: Private
YEARS OF USE: One confirmed burial in 1839
LOCATION: Way Farm, Maspeth, Queens.
HISTORY: Henry Mott was buried on the Way Farm, at Maspeth, after his
death in New York City on 17 December 1839. His son was also buried "at
Maspeth" in 1827.

MAILING ADDRESS: N/A
PHONE NUMBER: N/A
RECORDS: N/A
RESOURCES: Harris, Edward Doubleday, comp. "The Descendants of William and Elizabeth Mott of Great Neck, Long Island." *The New York Genealogical and Biographical Record*, 36 (October 1905): 281.

Wesley Chapel Burial Ground
See John Street Methodist Episcopal Churchyard.

West Baptist Church Cemetery

CATEGORY: Baptist
YEARS OF USE: circa 1847 to 1980s
LOCATION: 4125 Arthur Kill Road, west side of the road, north of Sharrotts Road, Port Mobil, Staten Island.
HISTORY: The West Baptist Church, erected 1847, was home to three successive congregations that held services in English, German, and Hungarian. Although the building was demolished in the 1970s, burials in its churchyard continued into the 1980s. Approximately one hundred people are buried here. Gravestones name members of the Androvette, Ellis, Huttar, Kellmeyer, Nielsen and Storer families. Today, the churchyard is considered abandoned, and the Charleston Civic Association is working with students and community service volunteers to restore the grounds.
MAILING ADDRESS: c/o Friends of Abandoned Cemeteries of Staten Island
                            140 Tysen Street
                            Staten Island, New York 10301-1120
PHONE NUMBER: N/A
RECORDS: Researchers should check for records on the Staten Island RootsWeb page, on the internet. The address is
<http://www.rootsweb.com/~nyrichmo>.
RESOURCES: Vosburgh, Royden W., editor and transcriber. *Staten Island Gravestone Inscriptions*. vol. 2, New York City, April 1925 (typed manuscript).

Westchester Methodist Episcopal Churchyard

CATEGORY: Methodist Episcopal
YEARS OF USE: circa 1825 to 1940
LOCATION: 2547 East Tremont Avenue, at Overing Street, Westchester, Bronx.
HISTORY: The Westchester Methodist Episcopal Church was organized in 1808 and erected its chapel in 1825. The church was destroyed by fire in 1910.
    This graveyard contained members of the Fowler family, as well as church

members and townsmen. In 1940, the bodies were removed to an unspecified cemetery in Jamaica, Queens.

MAILING ADDRESS: Westchester United Methodist Church
                  2547 East Tremont Avenue
                  Bronx, New York 10461-2812
PHONE NUMBER: (718) 931-8760
RECORDS: Vital records date back to 1861.
RESOURCES: N/A

West Farms Presbyterian Churchyard

CATEGORY: Military, Presbyterian
YEARS OF USE: circa 1815 to Post-WWI
LOCATION: 980 East 180th Street, at Bryant Avenue, Bronx.
HISTORY: Beck Memorial Presbyterian Church was organized in 1814 as the First Presbyterian Church in the Village of West Farms. It remained at its original location until 1895, when the congregation moved into a new church building across the street. At the time, Rev. Charles N. Mallery told the *New York Times* that "the congregation was sorry to abandon the ancient sanctuary and its surrounding cemetery, but the old church must give way to a new structure, which will be erected and maintained by the fund... bequeathed by the late Charles Bathgate Beck."

Veterans of the War of 1812, the Civil War, the Spanish-American War, and World War I are buried in the old churchyard, which fell into a state of neglect during the early 1900s. The American Legion lobbied for its upkeep: the grounds were subsequently purchased by the City of New York.

MAILING ADDRESS: Beck Memorial Presbyterian Church
                  980 East 180th Street
                  Bronx, New York 10460-2230
PHONE NUMBER: (718) 991-5757
RECORDS: Vital records date back to 1814.
RESOURCES: N/A

West Farms Reformed Dutch Church Cemetery

CATEGORY: Reformed Dutch
YEARS OF USE: circa 1840 to Pre-1927
LOCATION: Boone Avenue and 172nd Street, Bronx.
HISTORY: The West Farms Reformed Dutch Church was organized in 1839 by former members of the West Farms Presbyterian Church. The group erected its first church on East 179th Street and Boston Road in 1840, where it remained until 1906. Its cemetery was a short distance away.

In 1927, there were only three gravestones left in the graveyard. They

named members of the Cortelyou, Edwards, and Kelly families. The rest of
the bodies had been removed to Woodlawn Cemetery.

MAILING ADDRESS: Woodlawn Cemetery
                             233rd Street and Webster Avenue
                             Bronx, New York 10471

PHONE NUMBER: (718) 920-0500

RECORDS: The cemetery's records are housed on-site. The church's vital
records date back to 1843.

RESOURCES: Bergman, Edward F. *Woodlawn Remembers: Cemetery of
American History*. Utica, N.Y.: North Country Books, 1988.

    Cemetery, Church, and Town Records of New York State. vol. 9.
Washington, D.C.: Daughters of the American Revolution, 1927, 236.
(gravestone inscriptions)

West Farms Soldiers' Cemetery
See West Farms Presbyterian Churchyard.

West Presbyterian Churchyard and Vaults

CATEGORY: Presbyterian

YEARS OF USE: circa 1832 to 1851

LOCATION: Varick Street, between Carmine Street and Leroy Street,
Manhattan.

HISTORY: West Presbyterian Church opened in 1832. Burials in its churchyard and vaults probably came to an end with the 1851 ban on interments
south of 86th Street in Manhattan.

    Approximately 3,500 bodies were removed from this churchyard to a
plot in Cypress Hills Cemetery.

MAILING ADDRESS: West Park Presbyterian Church
                             165 West 86th Street
                             New York, New York 10024-3496

PHONE NUMBER: (212) 362-4890

RECORDS: N/A

RESOURCES: *Cypress Hills Cemetery*. Brooklyn, N.Y.: Cypress Hills
    Cemetery, 1880. (extensive list of plot owners and location of plot,
maps, rules, and history of cemetery)

    West Presbyterian Church, Sexton Records 1835 to 1838. Manuscript
#NYC-Churches-Presbyterian, at the New York Genealogical and
Biographical Society. New York, New York.

White Church on the Hill Cemetery
See Douglaston Zion Churchyard.

Willett Family Burial Ground

CATEGORY: Private
YEARS OF USE: Gravestones date 1722 to 1797
LOCATION: South Flushing, Queens. Where Cedar Grove Cemetery now lies.
The graveyard was on the northern line on Northern Boulevard.
HISTORY: In 1766, Thomas Willett sold his farm to Lieutenant Governor
Coldwallader Colden, reserving the right of the Willett family to be buried in
the graveyard and giving Colden permission to be buried with the Willetts.
Colden's estate was confiscated and sold after the Revolution. The property
was eventually purchased by Harrison Durkee, of Manhattan. In 1894, the
Brooklyn Daily Eagle reported that the Durkee farm had been sold for use as
Cedar Grove Cemetery.

A few years later, Cedar Grove's brochure described the Willett Family
Burial Ground: "At the right, as you drive through the entrance, in one corner of the cemetery, surrounded by stately trees, is an old burying place used
in ante-revolutionary days by several Long Island families."

Cedar Grove adopted Coldwallader Colden's house as its office, but has
since demolished it. The land about the house was graded, and the graveyard
is entirely gone.

Although Governor Colden is probably buried here, the only stones stand-
ing in the late 1800s were to the memory of the Willett and Whiting families.
MAILING ADDRESS: c/o Cedar Grove Cemetery
                 13416 Horace Harding Expressway
                 Flushing, New York 11367-1099
PHONE NUMBER: (718) 939-2041
RECORDS: Cedar Grove Cemetery does not have any independent record of
the burials in the Willett Family Burial Ground.
RESOURCES: Pelletreau, William S. "Abstracts of Wills on File in the
Surrogate's Office, City of New York, vol. 5, 1754 to 1760 with Letters of
Administration Granted 1753 to 1760." *Collections of the New York
Historical Society for the Year 1896.* New York, New York. Pages 416 to
417. (gravestone inscriptions and description of burial ground)

Powell, Charles U., comp., and Alice H. Meigs, ed. *Description of Private
and Family Cemeteries in the Borough of Queens.* City of New York,
Borough of Queens, Topographical Bureau. Jamaica, N.Y.: Queens Borough
Public Library, 1932. (gravestone inscriptions and maps)

Purple, Edwin R. "Notes, Biographical and Genealogical, of the Colden
Family, and some of its Collateral Branches in America." *The New York
Genealogical and Biographical Record* 4 (October 1873): 161–181. (grave-
stone inscriptions; detailed Colden genealogy, some Willett genealogy)

Willett's Point Cemetery
See Fort Totten Cemetery.

Willett Street Methodist Episcopal Churchyard

CATEGORY: Methodist Episcopal
YEARS OF USE: circa 1826 to 1851
LOCATION: 7-13 Bialystoker Place, west side of Willett Street between Grand Street and Broome Street, Manhattan.
HISTORY: The Willett Street Methodist Episcopal Church was erected in 1826. After an 1851 ban on burials below 86th Street in Manhattan, the trustees of the Willett Street Church decided to move their dead to a plot in Cypress Hills Cemetery. The removals began in 1854 and lasted for two years. The *Brooklyn Daily Eagle* interviewed a watchman who stated that the bones and coffins were buried in trenches, while the best headstones were "put up to look good."

The Willett Street Methodist Episcopal Church disbanded in 1905. The Bialystoker Synagogue purchased their church that year.
MAILING ADDRESS: c/o Cypress Hills Cemetery
                  833 Jamaica Avenue
                  Brooklyn, New York 11208-1593
PHONE NUMBER: (718) 277-2900
RECORDS: Cypress Hills Cemetery prefers written requests for searches.
RESOURCES: *Cypress Hills Cemetery*. Brooklyn, N.Y.: Cypress Hills Cemetery, 1880. (extensive list of plot owners and location of plot, maps, rules, and history of cemetery)

"The Forgotten Dead: Many Neglected Graves in Cypress Hills Cemetery." *The Brooklyn Daily Eagle*, 13 August 1893, p. 8, col. 7. (description of the Methodist plot)

Winant Family Burial Ground

CATEGORY: Private
YEARS OF USE: Gravestones date 1783 to 1847
LOCATION: Winant Place, Port Mobil, Staten Island.
HISTORY: The Winant Family Burial Ground had six known graves. The first three graves belonged to members of the DuBois, Mersereau, and Winant families, were dated 1783 to 1812, and were moved to Saint Andrew's Churchyard about 1930. The last three belonged to members of the Morgan and Winant families, were dated 1804 to 1847, and were moved to Bethel United Methodist Church Cemetery.
MAILING ADDRESS: N/A
PHONE NUMBER: N/A
RECORDS: N/A
RESOURCES: Davis, William T. "Homestead Graves." Proceedings of the Natural Science Association of Staten Island. Staten Island, New York. Special Number 9, December 1889. (gravestone inscriptions)

Woglom Family Burial Ground
See Saint Luke's Cemetery.

Wood Family Cemetery
See Sylvan Grove Cemetery.

Woodland Cemetery

CATEGORY: Non-sectarian
YEARS OF USE: circa 1850 to date
LOCATION: 982 Victory Boulevard, east side of the boulevard between
Highland Avenue and Silver Lake Cemetery, Grymes Hill, Staten Island.
HISTORY: N/A
MAILING ADDRESS: Woodland Cemetery
                 982 Victory Boulevard
                 Staten Island, New York 10301-3703
PHONE NUMBER: (718) 727-0222
RECORDS: The cemetery's records are housed on-site.
RESOURCES: N/A

Woodlawn Cemetery

CATEGORY: Non-sectarian
YEARS OF USE: 14 January 1865 to date
LOCATION: 233rd Street and Webster Avenue, Bronx. Bounded by East 233rd
Street, Webster Avenue, East 211th Street, Bainbridge, and Jerome Avenue.
HISTORY: Woodlawn Cemetery became the burial ground of "Robber Barons
and Millionaires" when railroad tycoon Jay Gould erected its first mausoleum about 1883. His primary business competitor, Collis P. Huntington,
literally took their rivalry to the grave. Huntington's mausoleum was under
construction by 1893 and had a budget of $300,000.

Gould and Huntington were joined by the likes of Oliver Belmont, Gail
Borden, R.H. Macy, J.C. Penny, Joseph Pulitzer, Charles Scribner, Cornelius
Vanderbilt, George Westinghouse, and F.W. Woolworth. The cemetery is not
without its notable politicians, entertainers, and writers. The list includes
actress Diana Barrymore, journalist Elizabeth "Nellie Bly" Cochran, musician
Duke Ellington, New York City Mayor Fiorello LaGuardia, and novelist
Herman Melville.

Of course, the greater part of the cemetery is filled with every-day folk
and include thousands of bodies removed from graveyards in Manhattan.
Who knows how many of these were on track to become a "Robber Baron"
or "Millionaire" when their lives were cut short? One nominee might be
George Spenser, who died at the age of fifteen in 1909. His epitaph? "Lost
life by stab in falling on ink eraser, evading six young women trying to give

him birthday kisses in office of Metropolitan Life Building."
MAILING ADDRESS: Woodlawn Cemetery
                 233rd Street and Webster Avenue
                 Bronx, New York 10471
PHONE NUMBER: (718) 920-0500
RECORDS: The cemetery's records are housed on-site. A list of forty people
buried in the plot of Harlem Lodge #457 Free and Accepted Masons has
been posted on the Internet at
    <http://www.nycgenweb.com/woodlawn.htm>.
RESOURCES: Bergman, Edward F. *Woodlawn Remembers: Cemetery of
American History*. Utica, N.Y.: North Country Books, 1988.

     King, Moses. "Woodlawn Cemetery." *King's Handbook of New York
City*. Boston, Mass., 1893. Reissued. New York: Benjamin Blom Inc., 1972,
515–519. (photos, notable burials and gravestone inscriptions)

     Streeter, Edward. *The Story of Woodlawn Cemetery*. *Woodlawn
Cemetery*. Bronx, New York. 1972.

Woodrow United Methodist Churchyard

CATEGORY: Methodist Episcopal
YEARS OF USE: circa 1787 to 1934
LOCATION: 1075 Woodrow Road, north of Huguenot Avenue, Woodrow,
Staten Island.
HISTORY: Woodrow United Methodist Church was established in 1787.
When the Reverend Joseph Totten died in 1875 at the age of one hundred,
the "first white [marble] gravestone" was erected to his memory. People
came from all over to look at it.

     Two gravestones memorializing members of the Winant family, who died
in 1809 and 1824, are located across the street from the church.
MAILING ADDRESS: Woodrow United Methodist Church
                 1075 Woodrow Road
                 Staten Island, New York 10312-1109
PHONE NUMBER: (718) 984-0148
RECORDS: The church's vital records end in 1841. From 1842 to 1850, vital
statistics were recorded in the Bethel United Methodist Church books.
Writer Royden Vosburgh reported in 1922 that the vital records between
1842 and 1859 were missing.
RESOURCES: Davis, William T. "Homestead Graves." *Proceedings of the
Natural Science Association of Staten Island*. New York. Special Number 9,
December 1889. (gravestone inscriptions)

     Vosburgh, Royden Woodward, trans. *Records of the Woodrow United
Methodist Church*. Staten Island, New York. June 1922. (gravestone
inscriptions)

Wright Family Burial Ground
See Saint Luke's Cemetery.

Wyckoff-Snedicker Cemetery

CATEGORY: Private
YEARS OF USE: Gravestones date 1793 to 1892
LOCATION: In the triangle formed by Jamaica Avenue, 96th Street, and 98th Street, Richmond Hill, Queens.
HISTORY: The Wyckoff and Snedicker families gave equal portions of their farms for use as a burial ground. Members of the Bennet, Eldert, Ditmars, Hendrickson, Lott, Snedicker, Suydam, Van Dine, and Wyckoff families are buried here.

The Queens Historical Society has taken an interest in preservation of the cemetery. It is also known as the Lott Family Burial Ground.
MAILING ADDRESS: Wyckoff-Snedicker Cemetery
c/o Queens Historical Society
Kingsland Homestead
143-35 37th Avenue
Flushing, New York 11354-5729
PHONE NUMBER: (718) 939-0647
RECORDS: N/A
RESOURCES: Eardeley, William A. *Cemeteries in Kings and Queens Counties, Long Island, New York: 1793 to 1902.* Brooklyn, New York. vol. 2, March 1916. (gravestone inscriptions and genealogical data on the Ditmars, Eldert, Hendrickson, Lott, Suydam, Van Duyn, and Wyckoff families)

Frost, Josephine C. trans. *Long Island Cemetery Inscriptions.* Brooklyn, New York. vol. 9. 1914. (gravestone inscriptions)

Goddard, Herbert V. "In Woodhaven, A Cemetery." *The Leader Observer*, 31 October 1975. (list of Elderts buried in cemetery; Eldert family genealogy)

Powell, Charles U., comp., and Alice H. Meigs, ed. *Description of Private and Family Cemeteries in the Borough of Queens.* City of New York, Borough of Queens, Topographical Bureau. Jamaica, N.Y.: Queens Borough Public Library, 1932. (gravestone inscriptions and maps)

Zion Methodist Episcopal Churchyard
See Cherry Lane Second Asbury African Methodist Episcopal Cemetery.

Zion Protestant Episcopal Churchyard
See Douglaston Zion Churchyard.

APPENDIXES

New York City Metropolitan Area Cemeteries

─── ❦ ───

New York State Cemeteries

Airmont Lutheran Cemetery
South Airmont Road
Suffern, NY 10901
(914) 357-3344

Ascension Cemetery
650 Saddle River Road
Monsey, NY 10952
(914) 352-7220

Beechwoods Cemetery
179 Beechwood Avenue
New Rochelle, NY 10801
(914) 632-2350

Cemetery of The Gate of Heaven
Stevens Avenue
Hawthorne, NY 10532
(914) 769-3672

Cortlandt Cemetery
1033 Oregon Road
Peekskill, NY 10566
(914) 737-2929

Dale Cemetery
104 Havell Street
Ossining, NY 10562
(914) 941-1155

Fair Ridge Cemetery
476 Quaker Road
Chappaqua, NY 10514
(914) 238-4507

Ferncliff Cemetery
281 Secor Road
Hartsdale, NY 10530
(914) 693-4700

Greenwood-Union Cemetery
North Street
Rye, NY 10580
(914) 967-0095

Hillside Cemetery
1033 Oregon Road
Peekskill, NY 10566
(914) 737-2929

Holy Mount Cemetery
53 Winter Hill Road
Tuckahoe, NY 10707
(914) 961-9396

Holy Sepulchre Cemetery
15 Beauchamp Place
New Rochelle, NY 10801
(914) 636-6343

Kensico Cemetery
273 Lakeview Avenue
Valhalla, NY 10595
(914) 949-0347

Middle Patent Rural Cemetery, The
6 Bedford Banksville Road
Bedford, NY 10506
(914) 234-9300

Mount Calvary Cemetery
575 Hillside Avenue
White Plains, NY 10603
(914) 949-0671

Mount Eden Jewish Cemetery
20 Commerce Street
Hawthorne, NY 10532
(914) 769-0603

Mount Hope Cemetery
Saw Mill River Road
Hastings-On-Hudson, NY 10706
(914) 478-1855

Mount Pleasant Cemetery
80 Commerce Street
Hawthorne, NY 10532
(914) 769-0397

Mount Repose Cemetery
Routes 202 and 9W
Haverstraw, NY 10927
(914) 429-8383

Oak Hill Cemetery
140 North Highland Avenue
Nyack, NY 10960
(914) 358-0012

Oakland Cemetery
2 Saw Mill River Road
Yonkers, NY 10701
(914) 963-1077

Rockland Cemetery
Kings Highway
Sparkill, NY 10976
(914) 359-0172

Saint Augustine Cemetery
Hawkes Avenue
Ossining, NY 10562
(914) 941-6711

Saint Francis Of Assisi Cemetery
2 Green Street
Mount Kisco, NY 10549
(914) 666-9390

Saint Joseph's Cemetery
Truman Avenue
Yonkers, NY 10703
(914) 963-0780

Saint Mary's Cemetery
Sprain Road
Yonkers, NY 10701
(914) 965-4890

Saint Patrick's Cemetery
Broadway
Buchanan, NY 10511
(914) 739-2722

Saint Paul's Church, Eastchester
National Historic Site
c/o 26 Wall Street
New York, NY 10005
(212) 260-1616

Sleepy Hollow Cemetery
540 North Broadway
North Tarrytown, NY 10591
(914) 631-0081

Temple Israel Cemetery
  Mount Hope
  Hastings-On-Hudson, NY 10706
  (914) 478-1343

White Plains Rural Cemetery
  167 North Broadway
  White Plains, NY 10603
  (914) 949-0072

Wise Free Synagogue Cemetery
  400 SW Mill River Road
  Hastings-On-Hudson, NY 10706
  (914) 478-1767

Long Island Cemeteries

Beth David Cemetery
  300 Elmont Road
  Elmont, NY 11003
  (516) 328-1300

Beth Moses Cemetery
  Wellwood Avenue
  Huntington, NY 11743
  (516) 249-2290

Brookville Cemetery
  1057 Jericho Oyster Bay Road
  East Norwich, NY 11732
  (516) 759-1053

Brookville Cemetery
  25 Walnut Street
  Glen Head, NY 11545
  (516) 759-1053

Cedar Hill Cemetery
  354 Smith Road
  Lake Ronkonkoma, NY 11779
  (516) 467-4834

Cemetery Of The Holy Rood
  Old Country Road
  Westbury, NY 11590
  (516) 334-7990

Commack Cemetery
  6 Campden Lane
  Commack, NY 11725
  (516) 499-3921

East Hillside Cemetery
  43 Kirkwood Drive
  Glen Cove, NY 11542
  (516) 671-9220

Genola Rural Cemetery
  140 Laurel Road
  East Northport, NY 11731
  (516) 757-5968

Greenfield Cemetery
  650 Nassau Road
  Uniondale, NY 11553
  (516) 483-6500

Hicksville Community Mausoleum
  279 West Old Country Road
  Hicksville, NY 11801
  (516) 938-0155

Huntington Rural Cemetery
  555 New York Avenue
  Huntington, NY 11743
  (516) 427-1272

John P. Halpin
  84 Carleton Avenue
  Central Islip, NY 11722
  (516) 234-7474

Locust Valley Cemetery
  Ryefield Road
  Locust Valley, NY 11560
  (516) 676-5290

Long Island National Cemetery
2040 Wellwood Avenue
Farmingdale, NY 11735
(516) 454-4949

Maimonides Cemetery
90 Elmont Avenue
Elmont, NY 11003
(516) 775-6222

Mount Ararat Cemetery
Southern State Parkway
Farmingdale, NY 11735
(516) 957-2277

Nassau Knolls Cemetery
500 Port Washington Boulevard
Port Washington, NY 11050
(516) 944-8530

New Montefiore Cemetery
Wellwood Avenue
Huntington, NY 11743
(516) 249-7000

Northport Rural Cemetery
45 Tompkins Street,
East Northport, NY 11731
(516) 261-7268

Oakwood Cemetery
Moffitt Boulevard and
Brentwood Road
Bay Shore, NY 11706
(516) 665-0638

Pinelawn Memorial Park
Pinelawn Road
Farmingdale, NY 11735
(516) 249-6100

Queen Of All Saints Cemetery
Wheeler Road
Central Islip, NY 11722
(516) 234-8297

Rockville Cemetery
348 Merrick Road
Lynbrook, NY 11563
(516) 599-0411

Roslyn Cemetery
12 Preston Street
Port Washington, NY 11050
(516) 944-6730

Southampton Cemetery
North Sea Road
Southampton, NY 11968
(516) 283-3212

Saint Charles' Cemetery
c/o Saint John's Cemetery
80-01 Metropolitan Avenue
Flushing, NY 11379
(718) 894-4888

Saint John's Memorial Cemetery
Route 25A
Syossett, NY 11791
(516) 692-6748

Saint Margaret's Cemetery
1000 Washington Avenue
Plainview, NY 11803
(516) 692-5267

Saint Mary Star of the Sea Cemetery
Rockaway Turnpike
Lawrence, NY 11559
(516) 239-8296

Trinity Roman Catholic Cemetery
c/o Saint John's Cemetery
80-01 Metropolitan Avenue
Flushing, NY 11379
(718) 894-4888

Wellwood Cemetery
Wellwood Avenue
Huntington, NY 11743
(516) 249-2300

New Jersey Cemeteries

Archdiocese Of Newark Cemeteries
340 Ridge Road
North Arlington, NJ 07031
(201) 991-7404

Arlington Cemetery
748 Schuyler Avenue
Kearny, NJ 07032
(201) 991-1611

Arlington Jewish Cemetery
308 Grove Street
Newark, NJ 07103
(201) 373-0144

Bay View-New York Bay Cemetery
321 Garfield Avenue
Jersey City, NJ 07305
(202) 433-2400

Beth-El Cemetery
Forest Avenue
Paramus, NJ 07652
(201) 261-7878

Bloomfield Cemetery
383 Belleville Avenue
Bloomfield, NJ 07003
(201) 748-0131

Calvary Cemetery
58 McLean Boulevard
Paterson, NJ 07513
(201) 279-2900

Cedar Lawn Cemetery & Crematory
McLean Boulevard and
Crooks Avenue
Paterson, NJ 07504
(201) 279-1161

Cedar Park Cemetery
Forest Avenue
Paramus, NJ 07652
(201) 262-1100

Christ King Cemetery
980 Huron Road
Franklin Lakes, NJ 07417
(201) 891-9191

Clinton Cemetery
195 Union Avenue
Irvington, NJ 07111
(201) 373-3137

Crest Haven Memorial Park
Passaic Avenue
Clifton, NJ 07014
(201) 473-3270

East Ridgelawn Cemetery
255 Main Avenue
Clifton, NJ 07014
(201) 777-1920

Epstein Sanford Cemetery
308 Grove Street
Newark, NJ 07103
(201) 373-0144

Evergreen Cemetery
65 Martin Luther King Avenue
Morristown, NJ 07960
(201) 538-2111

Fair Lawn Memorial Cemetery
Maple Avenue
Fair Lawn, NJ 07410
(201) 796-1485

Fair Mount Cemetery
233 Hills Avenue
Chatham, NJ 07928
(201) 635-2393

Fairmount Cemetery
620 Central Avenue
Newark, NJ 07107
(201) 623-0695

Fairview Cemetery
500 Fairview Avenue
Fairview, NJ 07022
(201) 943-6161

Fidelity Cemetery
Forest Avenue
Paramus, NJ 07652
(201) 261-7878

Flower Hill Cemetery
5433 Kennedy Boulevard
North Bergen, NJ 07047
(201) 867-0013

Garden Of Memories
Pascack Road
Washington Township, NJ 07675
(201) 262-2722

Gate of Heaven Catholic Cemetery
225 Ridgedale Avenue
East Hanover, NJ 07936
(201) 887-0286

George Washington Cemetery
234 Paramus Road
Paramus, NJ 07652
(201) 652-4300

Glendale Cemetery
28 Hoover Avenue
Bloomfield, NJ 07003
(201) 748-1253

Glenwood Cemetery
926 County Highway 517
Vernon, NJ 07462
(201) 764-3584

Grove Reformed Church
1132 46th Street
North Bergen, NJ 07047
(201) 863-0432

Hackensack Cemetery
289 Hackensack Avenue
Hackensack, NJ 07601
(201) 342-1475

Heavenly Rest Memorial Park
268 Ridgedale Avenue
East Hanover, NJ 07936
(201) 887-0386

Hillside Cemetery
Rutherford Avenue
Rutherford, NJ 07070
(201) 438-1612

Hilltop Cemetery
4 Hillcrest Avenue
Mendham, NJ 07945
(201) 543-4386

Holy Cross Cemetery
340 Ridge Road
North Arlington, NJ 07031
(201) 997-1900

Holy Cross Chapel Mausoleum
340 Ridge Road
North Arlington, NJ 07031
(201) 997-8500

Holy Name Cemetery
823 West Side Avenue
Jersey City, NJ 07306
(201) 433-0342

Holy Rood Roman Catholic
Cemetery
  91 Maple Avenue
  Morristown, NJ 07960
  (201) 539-7501

Holy Sepulchre Cemetery
  52 Totowa Road
  Totowa, NJ 07512
  (201) 942-3368

Holy Sepulchre Cemetery
  125 Central Avenue
  East Orange, NJ 07018
  (201) 678-3757

Immaculate Conception Cemetery
  Mount Hebron Road
  Montclair, NJ 07043
  (201) 744-5939

Jersey City Cemetery
  435 Newark Avenue
  Jersey City, NJ 07302
  (201) 653-1360

Laurel Grove Cemetery
  295 Totowa Road
  Totowa, NJ 07512
  (201) 956-0711

Locust Hill Cemetery
  168 North Sussex Street
  Dover, NJ 07801
  (201) 366-0038

Lodi Cemetery Company
  Passaic Avenue & Terrace Avenue
  Lodi, NJ 07644
  (201) 777-7559

Machpelah Cemetery
  5810 Tonnelle Avenue
  North Bergen, NJ 07047
  (201) 867-7130

Madonna Church
  2070 Hoefleys Lane
  Fort Lee, NJ 07024
  (201) 944-7723

Maple Grove Park Cemetery
  535 Hudson Street
  Hackensack, NJ 07601
  (201) 440-1607

Mount Carmel Cemetery
  10 Serpentine Road
  Tenafly, NJ 07670
  (201) 569-8727

Mount Holiness Memorial Park
  58 Brown Avenue
  Butler, NJ 07405
  (201) 838-1199

Mount Moriah Jewish Cemetery
  685 Fairview Avenue
  Fairview, NJ 07022
  (201) 943-6163

Mount Olivet Cemetery
  23 Cottage Place
  Bloomfield, NJ 07003
  (201) 748-8384

Mount Olivet Catholic Cemetery
  220 Mount Olivet Avenue
  Newark, NJ 07114
  (201) 621-2220

Mount Pleasant Cemetery
  375 Broadway
  Newark, NJ 07104
  (201) 483-0288

Newark Jewish Cemeteries
  616 South Orange Avenue
  Newark, NJ 07106
  (201) 375-0717

Newton Cemetery
Longwood Avenue
Newton, NJ 07860
(201) 383-4680

New York Bay—Bay View Cemetery
321 Garfield Avenue
Jersey City, NJ 07305
(202) 433-2400

North Arlington Cemetery
340 Ridge Road
North Arlington, NJ 07031
(201) 997-1900

North Hardyston Cemetery
North Church Road
Hamburg, NJ 07419
(201) 827-9375

Parsippany Presbyterian Cemetery
1774 US Highway 46
Parsippany, NJ 07054
(201) 334-0992

Prospect Hill Cemetery
Bloomfield Avenue and
Roseland Avenue
Caldwell, NJ 07006
(201) 228-4410

Restland Memorial Park
77 Deforest Avenue
East Hanover, NJ 07936
(201) 887-2050

Ridgefield Cemetery
1040 Edgewater Avenue
Ridgefield, NJ 07657
(201) 943-5628

Rosedale Cemetery & Crematory
367 Washington Street
Orange, NJ 07050
(201) 673-0127

Rosemount Cemetery & Mausoleum
US Highway One and McClellan
Newark, NJ 07114
(201) 824-6871

Sanctuary Of Abraham And Sarah
Forest Avenue
Paramus, NJ 07652
(201) 262-1128

Solomon King Memorial Park
Dwasline Road and Allwood Road
Clifton, NJ 07012
(201) 473-5646

Sparta Presbyterian Methodist
Cemetery
48 Skyline Drive
Sparta, NJ 07871
(201) 827-0017

Saint Joseph Cemetery
179 Hackensack Avenue
Hackensack, NJ 07601
(201) 342-2096

Saint Mary's Cemetery
Outwater Lane
Rochelle Park, NJ 07662
(201) 843-7179

Saint Nicholas Cemetery
2 Terrace Avenue
Lodi, NJ 07644
(201) 779-7272

Stanhope Union Cemetery
Waterloo Road
Stanhope, NJ 07874
(201) 347-2584

Valleau Cemetery
660 East Glen Avenue
Ridgewood, NJ 07450
(201) 444-3230

Weehawken Cemetery
  4000 Bergen Turnpike
  North Bergen, NJ 07047
  (201) 867-0151

Westwood Cemetery
  Kinderkamack Road
  Westwood, NJ 07675
  (201) 664-7161

Bibliography

───── ✿ ─────

Hundreds of sources were consulted for *The Graveyard Shift*—most appear as "resources" under pertinent cemetery entries. This selected bibliography contains various items that were especially helpful during my research.

Allen, Francis D. *Documents and Facts, Showing the Fatal Effects of Interments in Populous Cities.* New York: F.D. Allen, 1822, pamphlet.

Asbury, Edith Evans. "Lower East Side Diggers Find Graves on a Construction Site." *The New York Times.* 18 December 1964, p. 39, col. 3.

Bailey, Rosalie Fellows. *Guide to Genealogical and Biographical Sources for New York City (Manhattan) 1783 to 1898.* New York: the author, 1954.

Basile, Dominick S. "Cemetery Becoming a Dump." *The New York Times.* 3 February 1974, p. 87, col. 1.

Bayles, Richard M., ed. *History of Richmond County, New York.* New York: L.E. Preston & Co., 1887.

Biederman, Marcia. "Neighborhood Report: Prospect Park, Park Slope; He's Here for Eternity, but Don't Ask Where." *The New York Times.* 27 September 1998, The City Weekly Desk.

Bell, Charles W. "Poor Dead Not Forgotten: Project Emerges as Passover Nears." *The Daily News*. 20 April 1997, p. 8, col. 1.

Beretta, Walter, comp. Catalogue of Public Works of Art, Borough of the Bronx. New York: The Division of Monuments, Department of Parks, circa 1940.

Brown, Anne W. "A Brief History of the Marble Cemetery." http://www.chesapeake.net/~stovy/nymc/nymchist.htm (1998).

Brown, Elicia. "Beneath a Playground, a Burial Ground for 1,000." *The New York Times*. 9 June 1996, p. 12, col. 4.

"Burial Ground for Journalists." *The New York Times*. 17 May 1874, p. 2, col. 7.

Burr, David H., cart. *City of New York*. New York: J.H. Colton & Company, 1834, map.

Butler, Janet, and Gary Hermalyn, comps. *Genealogy in the Bronx: An Annotated Resource Guide to Sources of Information. Bronx County Historical Society*. Bronx, N.Y.: Bronx County Historical Society, 1977.

"The Cathedral Cemetery Case." *The New York Times*. 5 June 1883, p. 3, col. 2.

"Catholic Cemetery on Staten Island is Approved." *The New York Times*. 29 November 1977, p. 22, col. 1.

"Cellar Strewn with Skeletons: Conselyea, Whose Armed Ancestors Watched Nights to Prevent Grave Robbings, Will Sue the Church." *The New York Times*. 30 April 1895, p. 10, col. 2.

"Cemeteries Crowded Out: Old Burying Grounds Cut Up for Building Lots in Greater New York." *The New York Times*. 12 December 1897, illustrated supplement, p. 1, col. 1.

"The Cemeteries of New York." *The New York Times*. 30 March 1866, p. 2, col. 3.

"Cemetery Not to be Closed. Gravesend Burial Place, One of the Oldest on the Island, Still to be Used." *The Brooklyn Daily Eagle*. 3 March 1900, p. 18, col. 2.

"Chapter 137. An Act to Authorize the Board of Education of the City of New York to Remove and Reinter the Human Remains Buried in the Old Burying-Ground, Between First and Second Streets and First and Second Avenues in Said City..." *Laws of the State of New York Passed at the 114th Legislature.* Albany, N.Y.: Banks & Brothers, 1891.

"Chapter 196. An Act Relating to the Union Cemetery, in the Town of Bushwick, County of Kings." *Laws of the State of New York Passed at the 76th Session of the Legislature.* Albany, N.Y.: J. Munsell, 1853.

"Chapter 232. An Act to Amend an Act Entitled 'An Act to Sell the Burial Ground at the Wallabout, in the City of Brooklyn, and to Provide Places of Burial,' Passed February Seventh, Eighteen Hundred and Fifty-Seven." *Laws of the State of New York Passed at the 81st Session of the Legislature.* Albany, N.Y.: J. Munsell, 1858.

"Chapter 352. An Act to Authorize the Trustees of the Methodist Protestant Church of the Village of Williamsburg to Sell Their Land Embracing Union Cemetery and to Remove the Remains Therefrom." *Laws of the State of New York Passed at the 116th Session of the Legislature.* Albany, N.Y.: James B. Lyon, Printer, 1893.

"Chapter 423. An Act in Relation to the Cemetery Grounds of the Congregation Shearith Israel." *Laws of the State of New York Passed at the 76th Session of the Legislature.* Albany, N.Y.: J. Munsell, 1853.

"Church Against Church: The Armed Conselyea Stands 'Twixt the Two Bushwicks." *The New York Times.* 4 April 1895, p. 9, col. 5.

Churchyards of Trinity Parish in the City of New York, 1697 to 1947. New York: Corporation of Trinity Church, 1948.

Cirri, John. "A Cemetery is Born Again." *The Daily News.* 23 April 1980, p. 65.

Cleaton, Stephannia. "Black Burial Grounds a Window to the Past." *The Staten Island Advance.* 28 February 1993, p. A21.

Cleaton, Stephannia. "History Alive at 2 Black Cemeteries on Island." *The Staten Island Advance.* 1 March 1993, p. A13, col. 1.

Cohen, Mark Francis. "Settler Burial Ground Falls Victim to Neglect." *The New York Times.* 24 September 1995, p. CY9, col. 3.

Cornell Cemetery. (Cornell Cemetery Corporation, P.O. Box 97, Rockaway Beach, New York 11693), pamphlet.

Culbertson, Judi and Tom Randall. *Permanent New Yorkers: A Biographical Guide to the Cemeteries of New York.* Chelsea, Vt.: Chelsea Green Publishing Company, 1987.

Cunningham, Eugene. *Long Island's Cemeteries: Past and Present.* Flushing, N.Y.: Long Island Division: The Central Library, April 1974, manuscript.

Davis, William T. "Homestead Graves." *Proceedings of the Natural Science Association of Staten Island.* Staten Island, N.Y.: The Natural Science Association of Staten Island, 1889, 1890, 1902.

"The Descendants Protest: Objections Which Stand in the Way of a Church Sale." *The New York Times.* 16 October 1889. p. 9, col. 4.

"Desecration of the Dead of Sullivan Street Church." *The New York Times.* 20 January 1863, p. 2, col. 5.

"Deserting Old Cemeteries: Bodies are Being Removed from Downtown Burying-Ground." *The New York Times.* 10 March 1895, p. 17, col. 5.

de Sola Pool, Rev. Dr. David. *Portraits Etched in Stone: Early Jewish Settlers 1682 to 1831.* New York: Columbia University Press, 1952.

"Destroying Old Memories: Removing the Bodies from St. Luke's Church Cemetery." *The New York Times.* 18 December 1888, p. 3, col. 2.

"A Dilemma of a Cemetery-Park. Bronx Church Land Abused by Youths Who Play There." *The New York Times.* 23 August 1957, p. 47, col. 1.

Doggett's New York City Directory. New York: John Doggett, Jr., 1843-44, 1846-47, 1850-51.

Dolkart, Andrew S. *Guide to New York City Landmarks.* Washington, D.C.: The Preservation Press, National Trust for Historic Preservation, special [Democratic] convention edition, 1992.

Donohue, Pete and Sharline Chiang. "What's a Body to Do? City Running Out of Room for Graves." *The Daily News.* 8 February 1995, p. 6, col. 1.

Dripps, Matthew, cartographer. *Map of the City of New York Extending Northward to 50th Street.* New York: Matthew Dripps, 1851.

Dripps, Matthew, cart. *Plan of New York City*. New York: Matthew Dripps, 1867.

E., F. J. "Old Burial Grounds. Cemeteries in Brooklyn and the County Towns." *The Brooklyn Daily Eagle*. 29 August 1886, p. 9, col. 3.

English, Merle. "Cemetery is No 'Playground': Activist Battles City Over Recreational Site." *New York Newsday*. 22 October 1996, p. A5.

English, Merle. "Grounds for Debate: Council's Tour Stirs Playground Dispute." *New York Newsday*. 27 February 1997, p. A8, col. 1.

"Excited Roman Catholics: The Proposed Removal of Dead Bodies from a Cemetery." *The New York Times*. 4 January 1883, p. 8, col. 1.

Fairchild Cemetery Manual. Brooklyn, N.Y.: Fairchild Sons, 1910. Fernow, Berthold, ed. *The Records of New Amsterdam: From 1653 to 1674*. vol. 2. Baltimore, Md.: Genealogical Publishing Company, 1976.

Fodor, Joe. "The Grave's a Fine and Private Place: Controversial Cemetery Holds a Treasure Trove of Obscure Borough History." *Brooklyn Bridge Magazine*. vol. 3. no. 10. Brooklyn, N.Y.: (October 1998): 26–27.

Fosburgh, Lacey. "Saint Mark's Building a Playground in its Cemetery, the City's Oldest." *The New York Times*. 2 February 1970, p. 1, col. 1.

French, John H. *Historical and Statistical Gazetteer of New York State: Embracing a Comprehensive View of the Geography, Geology, and General History of the State, and a Complete History and Description of Every County, City, Town, Village, and Locality, With Full Tables of Statistics*. Syracuse, N.Y.: R. P. Smith, 1860.

Fried, Joseph P. "Descendants of the Entombed Revive Decaying Graveyard." *The New York Times*. 19 December 1981, p. B1.

Fried, Joseph P. "Weeds Hide a Precious Patch of Past." *The New York Times*. 14 October 1991 p. B3, col. 1.

"From Cemetery to Park: The Site Selected for the New Ninth Ward Pleasure Ground." *The New York Times*. 24 July 1892, p. 8, col. 5.

Goodrich, Andrew T., cart. *A Map of the City of New York*. New York: A.T. Goodrich, 1827.

"Graveyard for a Park: Proposition to Remove Remains Interred in Pro-Cathedral Cemetery in Jay Street." *The Brooklyn Daily Eagle*. 18 April 1902, p. 20, col. 4.

"A Graveyard Within a Graveyard." *The Brooklyn Daily Eagle*. 1 July 1894, p. 22, col. 3.

Greenwood, John. "Public Burial Ground." *The Brooklyn Daily Eagle*. 25 January 1844, p. 2, col. 4.

Gross, Don. "Cemetery Records Stored for Institute Researchers: Moravian Cemetery Files Copied Permanently on Microfilm." *The Staten Island Advance*. 22 January 1994, p. A7.

Guide to Trinity Church. (Trinity Church, 74 Trinity Place, New York, New York 10006), pamphlet.

Guzik, Estelle M., ed. *Genealogical Resources in the New York Metropolitan Area*. New York: Jewish Genealogical Society New York, 1989.

Hardt, Robert Jr. "Brooklyn Ball Field May be Built on Bones of Dead Marines." *The New York Post*. 24 July 1997, p. 7.

"Harlem's Old Dutch Church. It Goes Back Almost as Far as New York City Itself." *The New York Times*. 28 January 1894, p. 20, col. 4.

"The Haunted Church: The Pastor of the Reformed Bushwick Tells Its History." *The New York Times*. 6 May 1895, p. 2, col. 7.

Hernandez, Raymond. "Grave Site May be Under Proposed Incinerator." *The New York Times*. 27 December 1992, Metro Section, p. 32, col. 1.

"Historic Church to Go. Old Bedford Street Methodists will Merge with Metropolitan Temple." *The New York Times*. 3 October 1913, p. 7, col. 6.

Hooker, William, cart. *Hooker's New Pocket Plan of the City of New York*. New York: William Hooker, 1833.

Hope and Henderson's Consolidated Brooklyn City Directory. Brooklyn, N.Y.: Hope and Henderson, 1856-57.

Hurd, H.R., comp. *New York Charities Directory: An Authoritative, Classified and Descriptive Directory to the Philanthropic, Educational and Religious Resources of the City of New York, Including the Borough of*

Manhattan, The Bronx, Brooklyn, Queens, Richmond. New York: Charity Organization Society, 1909.

"Interments in the Cemeteries." *The New York Times.* 5 January 1880, p.8, col. 1.

Jackson, Kenneth T., ed. *The Encyclopedia of New York City.* New Haven, Conn.: Yale University Press, 1995.

Jacobs, Andrew. "Lonely Are the Dead: For Poor Jews, a Prayer or Two at the End of the Road." *The New York Times.* 24 March 1996, City Section, p. 3, col. 1.

Jones, H.A., cart. *Map of that Part of the City and County of New York North of 50th Street.* New York: Matthew Dripps, 1851.

Joyce, Patrick. "Island Cemeteries Reflect Our 'Tender Mercies.'" *The Staten Island Advance.* 28 April 1990, p. A21, col. 1.

"Joy in Old Churches. Three City Congregations Celebrate Their Birthdays." *The New York Times.* 14 November 1895, p. 8, col. 3.

Judson, Selden C. *The Cemeteries of New York and How to Reach Them.* New York: G.H. Burton Book and Job Printer, 1881.

Kim, Rose. "Cemetery Vandals Burn Remains." *New York Newsday.* 9 June 1997, p. A3.

Knowles, Clayton. "City May End Hart Island Ferry." *The New York Times.* 31 January 1967, p. 45, col. 5.

Koykka, Arthur S. *Project Remember: A National Index of Gravesites of Notable Americans.* Algonac, Mich.: Reference Publications, Inc., 1986.

Lain's Brooklyn Directory. New York: J. Lain and Company, 1859-60.

"Last Chance... No Kidding." *The New York Times.* 19 December 1993, sec. 13CY, p. 8, col. 1.

LeDuff, Charlie. "Colonial-Era Human Remains are Unearthed Near City Hall." *The New York Times.* 25 October 1998, Metropolitan Desk. Leng, Charles W., and William T. Davis. *Staten Island and Its People.* New York: Lewis Historical Publishing Co., Inc., 1930.

Leonard, John Henry. *The Leonard Manual of the Cemeteries of New York and Vicinity.* New York: J. H. Leonard, 1895, 1901.

Lockwood, Charles. "Where a Plainer Past Endures." *The New York Times.* 10 December 1978, part 8, p. 1, col. 1.

"Long Forgotten Dead. Many Neglected Graves in Cypress Hills Cemetery." *The Brooklyn Daily Eagle.* 13 August 1893, p. 8, col. 7.

Longworth's New York City Directory. New York: Thomas Longworth, 1839-40.

Macmillan, William W. "The Old Dutch Cemetery. Correspondent Suggests that it be Made Into a Playground for the Children." Letter to the Editor. *The Brooklyn Daily Eagle.* 13 August 1900, p. 4, col. 1.

Macy, Harry Jr. "Dutch Reformed Records of New York City in the NYG&BS Library." *The NYG&B Newsletter.* The New York Genealogical and Biographical Society, vol. 5 no. 1. (Spring 1994.): 4–5.

Macy, Harry Jr. "Episcopal Church Records of New York City in the NYG&BS Library." *The NYG&B Newsletter.* The New York Genealogical and Biographical Society, vol. 6 no. 1 (Spring 1995): 4–5, 7.

Macy, Harry Jr. "Kings County's Colonial Church Records." *The NYG&B Newsletter.* The New York Genealogical and Biographical Society, vol. 8 no. 4. (Winter 1997): 3–4.

Macy, Harry Jr. "Lutheran Records of New York City in the NYG&BS Library." *The NYG&B Newsletter.* The New York Genealogical and Biographical Society, vol. 5 no. 4. (Winter 1994): 27–28.

Macy, Harry Jr. "Methodist Records of New York City in the NYG&BS Library." *The NYG&B Newsletter.* The New York Genealogical and Biographical Society, vol. 4 no. 4 (Winter 1993): 27–28.

Macy, Harry Jr. "Presbyterian Records of New York City in the NYG&BS Library." *The NYG&B Newsletter.* The New York Genealogical and Biographical Society, vol. 6 no. 3, (Fall 1995): 20–21.

Maerschalck, Francis, cart. *A Plan of the City of New York From an Actual Survey.* New York: Gerardus Duyckinck, 1754.

Marmor, Florence. "About Cemetery Recording Project: Mokom Sholom, Bayside and Acacia Cemeteries, Ozone Park, New York." http://www.jewishgen.org/infofiles/mokom.cem.txt (March 1999)

McMillen, Loring. "The Abandoned Cemeteries of Staten Island." *Chronicles of Staten Island* 1, no. 9 (Fall 1987): 79–82.

McMillen, Loring. "Family Burial Grounds Give Way Before Vandals and Weather." *The Staten Island Advance*. Staten Island, New York. September 22, 1941.

McMillen, Loring. "Homestead Graves." *Chronicles of Staten Island*. Staten Island, New York. vol. 1, no. 12. Summer 1988. p. 100 to 104.

McMillen, Loring. "I Remember Old Staten Island." *The Staten Island Advance*. Staten Island, New York. September 5, 1965.

McNamara, John. "The Bronx in History: Old Bensonia Cemetery Now Site of PS 38." *The Bronx Press Review*. Bronx, New York. December 24, 1959.

McVetty, Suzanne. "Records of the Society of Friends (Quakers), New York Yearly Meeting." *The NYG&B Newsletter*. The New York Genealogical and Biographical Society. New York, New York. Fall 1997. p. 27 to 30.

"Memories of Old Saint John's. Many Persons of Past Renown Buried in the Cemetery." *The New York Times*. New York, New York. February 26, 1894. p. 2. Column 5.

Meyers, Stephen Lee. "On Going Private: Mayor Wants to Sell Canarsie Cemetery." *The New York Times*. New York, New York. March 8, 1995. p. B3, Column 1.

Meyers, Stephen Lee. "Unearthing Early Cemeteries, New York Turns Up Politics." *The New York Times*. New York, New York. May 23, 1993. p. 1, Column 5.

Munsell, W.W. *History of Queens County, New York*. W.W. Munsell & Co., New York. 1882.

Murphy, Walter G. "Indian Cemetery Isn't—But It's Also No Dump." *New York World-Telegram and Sun*. New York, New York. January 27, 1964.

Napolitano, Jo. "Colonial-Era Cemetery Eyed As a Landmark." *New York Newsday*. New York, New York. January 14, 1997. p. A33.

"New Cemetery Planned." *The New York Times*. New York, New York. November 16, 1977. p. 44. Column 1.

New York As It Is. T.B. Tanner, Publisher. New York, New York. 1840.
New York City 5 Borough Pocket Atlas. Hangstrom Map Company, Inc., Maspeth, New York. 1992.

"None to Claim Their Bones. Relics of an Old Brooklyn Graveyard." *The New York Times*. New York, New York. April 21, 1888. p. 3, Column 2.

"Notice: The Brick Presbyterian Church." *The New York Times*. New York, New York. May 27, 1856. p. 5, Column 1.

"The North Dutch Church. Concerning the Removal of the Ancient Landmark: History of the Edifice." *The New York Times*. New York, New York. January 21, 1866. p. 8. Column 3.

"North Side News." *The Brooklyn Daily Eagle*. Brooklyn, New York. March 1, 1894. p. 6, Column 6.

O'Connell, Margaret F. "Potter's Field Has Found a Resting Place at Last." *The New York Times*. New York, New York. August 31, 1975. Section 8, p. 1, Column 1.

"Old Church to Go. Members of Bedford Street Methodist Together for Last Services." *The New York Times*. New York, New York. November 17, 1913. p. 9, Column 5.

"The Oldest Tombstone in the Cemetery." *The Brooklyn Daily Eagle*. Brooklyn, New York. August 14, 1900. p. 14. Column 3.

"100-Year-Old Burial Plot Dug Up in 18th St.: Bone-Filled Vault Found by Excavators on Site of Old Methodist Church." *The New York Herald-Tribune*. New York, New York. March 25, 1950.

Onishi, Norimitsu. "Preserving His 'Realm,' His Pocket of Bayside, Cause by Cause." *The New York Times*. New York, New York. September 4, 1994. Section 13CY, p. 8, Column 1.

"Our Cities of the Dead. Millions of People are at Rest in Them." *The Brooklyn Daily Eagle*. Brooklyn, New York. April 28, 1895. p. 28. Column 1.

Patrick, Reginald. "Brooklyn Incinerator Sited Near Burial Grounds: Anti-Incinerator Activists Seize on Colonial Graves' Proximity." *The Staten Island Advance*. Staten Island, New York. September 2, 1992. p. A7, Column 1.

Powell, Charles U., compiler and Alice H. Meigs, editor. *Description of Private and Family Cemeteries in the Borough of Queens.* City of New York, Borough of Queens, Topographical Bureau. Published by the Queens Borough Public Library. Jamaica, New York. 1932, and 1975 Supplement.

Power, John. *Law as to Cemeteries, Undertakers, Embalmers and Burials in the State of New York with Statutory Amendments Down To and Including the Session of 1901.* W.C. Little & Company. Albany, New York. 1901.

"Practicing Digging Up the Past, Class Finds Artifacts of the 30's." *The New York Times.* New York, New York. July 6, 1978. p. B18, Column 1.

"Queens Cemetery to be Restored After a Long Search for Owner." *The New York Times.* New York, New York. October 1, 1963. p. 31. Column 3.

Quindlen, Anna. "Bury Them Not in the Potter's Field." *The New York Times.* New York, New York. October 24, 1981. p. 27, Column 1.

Randall, Sidwell S. "Parks of Disused Cemeteries." *The New York Times.* New York, New York. December 27, 1903. p. 9, Column 4.

Reiser, Howard. "Who Owns the Moore Cemetery?" *Long Island Daily Press.* Jamaica, New York. June 15, 1966.

Rode's New York City Directory. New York, New York. 1850-1.

Sachs, Arline. "American Jewish Genealogical Society Cemetery Project: New York City, Brooklyn and Manhattan." International Association of Jewish Genealogical Societies. Published on the Internet at <http://www.jewishgen.org/cemetery/usnycbkl.htm> 1998.

Sachs, Arline. "American Jewish Genealogical Society Cemetery Project: New York City, Queens." International Association of Jewish Genealogical Societies. Published on the Internet at <http://www.jewishgen.org/cemetery/usnycqee.htm> 1998.

"The Sands Street Church Sold." *The New York Times.* New York, New York. March 23, 1888. p. 8, Column 2.

"A Scene in a Cemetery. Sexton Dixon Surrounded by Indignant Lot Owners." *The Brooklyn Daily Eagle.* Brooklyn, New York. August 28, 1893. p. 10, Column 2.

Schuster, Karla. "Razed Family Cemetery to be Restored by Builder." *The Staten Island Advance*. Staten Island, New York. July 14, 1989. p. A3, Column 1.

Secor, David Pell. "Where the Pells Lie." Letter to the Editor. *The New York Daily Tribune*. New York, New York. December 27, 1903. p. 9, Column 3.

Seitz, Sharon and Stuart Miller. *The Other Islands of New York City*. The Countryman Press, Woodstock, Vermont. 1996.

Seversmith, Herbert F. and Kenn Stryker-Rodda. *Long Island Genealogical Source Material*. National Genealogical Society. Washington, DC. 1962.

"Shameful Desecration of the Dead. Vultures in a Church Vault." *The New York Times*. New York, New York. January 19, 1863. p. 5. Column 3.

Smith's Brooklyn City Directory. Brooklyn, New York. 1855-56.

Staples, Brent. "Manhattan's African Dead: Colonial New York, From the Grave." Editorial. *The New York Times*. New York, New York. May 22, 1995. p. A14.

"Staten Island Cemeteries." Friends of Abandoned Cemeteries of Staten Island, Inc. Staten Island, New York. January, 1993.

Stokes, I.N. Phelps. *The Iconography of Manhattan Island, 1498 to 1909, Compiled from Original Sources and Illustrated by Photo-Intaglio Reproductions of Important Maps, Plans, Views, and Documents in Public and Private Collections*. Robert H. Dodd. New York. 1915 to 1928.

"Tombs Under the City. Catacombs for the Dead Beneath Several Churches." *The New York Times*. New York, New York. August 2, 1896. p. 20, Column 1.

"Trinity Church Graveyard." Letter to the Editor. *The New York Times*. New York, New York. July 27, 1890. p. 13, Column 4.

Trow's New York City Directory. R.L. Polk & Company, Publishers. New York, New York. 1891, 1900-1, 1904-5, 1913-14, 1915, 1933-34.

"Unearth a Potter's Field. Laborers Find Human Remains of 1800s in Washington Square." *The New York Times*. New York, New York. March 13, 1941. p. 23. Column 8.

"Volunteers Restore Old Cemetery." *The New York Times*. New York, New York. April 16, 1972. p. 60. Column 3.

Weir, Richard. "Neighborhood Report: Flushing; Ground for Burial or Play?" *The New York Times*. New York, New York. September 13, 1998. The City Weekly Desk.

Welch, Richard F. *The Gravestones of Early Long Island, 1680 to 1810*. Friends for Long Island's Heritage. Syosset, New York. 1983.

"Where the Pells Lie." *The New York Daily Tribune*. New York, New York. December 6, 1903. p. 14, Column 6.

Wilson's Business Directory of New York City. New York, New York. 1851.

Wright, Carol von Pressentin. *Blue Guide New York*. W.W., Norton & Company, Inc. New York. 1991.

The WPA Guide to New York City: The Federal Writers Project Guide to 1930s New York, With an Introduction by William H. Whyte. Reprint by The New Press. New York, New York. 1995.

Yellin, Deena. "Cemetery Finds a Measure of Peace: Increased Upkeep May Cut Vandalism." *New York Newsday*. October 16, 1997. p. A39.

Cemeteries and Churchyards
for Future Editions

———————— ❧ ————————

The following cemeteries were not included in this edition of *The Graveyard Shift*. In some cases, they were omitted for lack of available information; in others, for lack of evidence that they even existed. Every attempt will be made to include them in future editions of this book.

Congregational Church, Broadway and Worth Street, Manhattan

Ebenezer Baptist Church, Worth Street, Manhattan

Edsall Family Burial Ground, Queens

Elizabeth Street Presbyterian Church, Elizabeth Street and Hester Street, Manhattan

Fair Street Baptist Church, East of Broadway on Fulton Street, Manhattan

First Congregational Church, Warren Street, Manhattan

First Reformed Dutch Church of Jamaica, Queens

Folk Family Burial Ground, Trains Meadow Road, Queens

Friends Cemetery, Newtown, Queens (Some remains were removed to Flushing Cemetery after 1852)

Horn Family Cemetery, Bloomingdale Road, Manhattan

Hunt Family Burial Ground, Van Nest Avenue, Victor Street and Unionport Road, Bronx

Hyatt Family Burial Ground, Queens

Jewish Cemetery at East 89th Street and Madison Avenue, Manhattan

Jewish Cemetery at East 88th Street and Madison Avenue, Manhattan

Jewish Cemetery at East 94th Street, Manhattan

Jewish Cemetery at East 105th Street, Manhattan

Jewish Cemetery at West 45th Street and Sixth Avenue, Manhattan

Jewish Cemetery at West 89th Street and Sixth Avenue, Manhattan

Jewish Cemetery at 32nd Street, between Bloomingdale Road and
    Third Avenue, Manhattan

Jewish Cemetery at 86th Street, between Bloomingdale Road and
    Third Avenue, Manhattan

Kings County Farm Cemetery, Brooklyn

Lincoln Cemetery, Brooklyn

Marine Society Cemetery, Vanderbilt Avenue, Staten Island

Market Street Reformed Dutch Church Vaults, Northeast corner of
    Market Street and Henry Street, Manhattan

Mersereau Family Vault, Morningstar Road, Staten Island

Moravian Cemetery, Orchard Street, Manhattan

Moravian Cemetery, Pell Street and Mott Street, Manhattan

North Baptist Church, Van Dam Street and Varick Street, Manhattan

Oliver Street Baptist Church, Manhattan

Roman Catholic Cemetery on the west side of Seventh Avenue,
    between West 123rd Street and West 124th Street, Manhattan

Saint Charles' Roman Catholic Church, Brooklyn

Saint James Protestant Episcopal Church, East 69th Street and
    Lexington Avenue, Manhattan

Saint John's Lutheran Church, New Utrecht, Brooklyn

Slave Cemetery, Liberty Avenue and 80th Street, Queens

Spring Street Presbyterian Church, Spring Street and Varick Street,
    Manhattan

Universalist Baptist Church, Rose Street and Pearl Street, Manhattan

Vechte Family Burial Ground, Fifth Avenue and Third Street, Brooklyn

Welsh Baptist Church, Mott Street, Manhattan

Wooster Street Presbyterian Cemetery, Waverly Place and Washington
    Square East, Manhattan

Wright Family Burial Ground, Locust Point, Bronx

Zoar Baptist Church, Rose Street and Pearl Street, Manhattan

Additions

———— ✿ ————

Do you have comments, suggestions, questions or corrections for future editions of this book? Do you know of a cemetery that's been left out? Is there a particular cemetery experience or story that you'd like to share with other researchers? I'd love to hear your ideas. Please send correspondence to:

Carolee R. Inskeep
c/o Ancestry® Publications
P.O. Box 990
Orem, UT 84059

Index

About the Author

©Fiedler Images

C arolee Inskeep was born and reared in upstate New York. She lived, worked and studied in New York City for eight years, before moving to her current home in Washington, D.C. While working on her master's degree at New York University, she volunteered to do genealogical research for Orphan Train Riders who sought to find their New York City roots from afar. Their inability to find useful genealogical resources in their home states inspired her to write *The New York Foundling Hospital: An Index to its Federal, State and Local Census Records (1870-1925); The Children's Aid Society: An Index to the Federal, State and Local Census Records of its Lodging Houses (1855-1925)*; and, ultimately, *The Graveyard Shift.*